CROWN, GOVERNMENT AND PEOPLE IN THE FIFTEENTH CENTURY

CROWN, GOVERNMENT AND PEOPLE IN THE FIFTEENTH CENTURY

EDITED BY
ROWENA E. ARCHER

ST. MARTIN'S PRESS · NEW YORK

St. Martin's Press, Scholarly and Reference Division, 175 Fifth Avenue, New York, N.Y. 10010

Printed in Great Britain

ISBN 0-312-12591-7

Library of Congress Cataloging-in-Publication Data

Crown, government and people in the fifteenth century edited by
   Rowena E. Archer. — 1st ed.
      p. cm.
   Contains essays first given at a conference at Manchester College
Oxford in 1992.
   Includes bibliographical references and index.
   ISBN 0-312-12591-7
   1. Great Britain—History—Lancaster and York, 1399–1485–
–Congresses. 2. Great Britain—Politics and government—1399–1485–
–Congresses. 3. Great Britain—Social life and customs—1066–1485–
–Congresses. 4. Great Britain—Church history—1066–1485–
–Congresses. I. Archer, Rowena E.
DA245.P65 1995
942.04—dc20
                                                              95–16664
                                                                    CIP

First Edition 1995

ACKNOWLEDGEMENT

The editor and publisher gratefully acknowledge the generosity of Dr Edward Johnson of ISISE (Institute of Scholars in International Studies – Europe), whose funding helped to cover the costs of publication.

CONTENTS

CONTRIBUTORS

Philip Morgan is Lecturer in Local History, Keele University

Maureen Jurkowski is a Research Assistant in the Public Record Office, London

Helen Castor is Fellow and Director of Studies in History, Sidney Sussex College, Cambridge

James A. Doig is an Officer in the Federal Department of Communications and the Arts, Canberra, Australia

Diana Dunn is Senior Lecturer in History, Chester College

Dominic Luckett is a Master at Harrow School

Matthew Davies is a Research Officer at the History of Parliament

Jane Laughton has a Research Fellowship at Birmingham University

Margaret Wade Labarge is an Adjunct Professor at Carleton University

Joel T. Rosenthal is Professor of History at the State University of New York, Stoney Brook

ABBREVIATIONS

Unless otherwise stated, the place of publication of cited works is London.

BIHR	*Bulletin of the Institute of Historical Research*
BJRL	*Bulletin of the John Rylands Library*
BL	British Library
CChR	*Calendar of Charter Rolls*
CCR	*Calendar of the Close Rolls*
CFR	*Calendar of the Fine Rolls*
CIPM	*Calendar of Inquisitions Post-Mortem*
CPL	*Calendar of Papal Registers, Papal Letters*
CPR	*Calendar of the Patent Rolls*
EETS	Early English Text Society
EcHR	*Economic History Review*
EHR	*English Historical Review*
Foedera	*Foedera, Conventiones, Literae . . .* ed. T. Rymer (20 vols. 1727–35)
GEC	G.E. Cokayne, *The Complete Peerage*, ed. V.H. Gibbs *et al.* (13 vols. 1910–59)
JMH	*Journal of Medieval History*
MS(S)	Manuscript(s)
Paston L&P	*Paston Letters and Papers*, ed. N. Davis (2 vols. Oxford, 1971–6)
PPC	*Proceedings and Ordinances of the Privy Council of England*, ed. N.H. Nicolas (7 vols. 1834–7)
PRO	Public Record Office
RO	Record Office
RP	*Rotuli Parliamentorum*, ed. J. Strachey *et al.* (6 vols. 1767–77)
RS	Rolls Series
SR	*Statutes of the Realm* (11 vols. Record Commission, 1810–28)
TRHS	*Transactions of the Royal Historical Society*
VCH	*Victoria County History*

INTRODUCTION

T hese papers – with one exception – were first given at the conference on Recent Research in Fifteenth-Century History which was hosted at Manchester College, Oxford, from 11 to 13 September 1992. This was the thirteenth conference in the series which began at Cardiff in 1970 and the seventh designed to afford an opportunity for younger postgraduates to present the earliest fruits of their labours. In view of Oxford's failure on a previous occasion to organize the conference, this was a particularly satisfying meeting and for Manchester College, which had just seen its first mature students complete their Oxford degrees, it seemed especially appropriate to be able to welcome this academic community and to have two mature postgraduates numbered among the contributors.

It is a matter of some regret that three of the papers given at the conference could not be gathered here with the others, but it is a pleasure to be able to include Diana Dunn's reassessment of Margaret of Anjou. Nearly sixty people – including the contributors – attended the meeting which was marked, as in the past, by the warmth and good nature of a professional body which has always managed to combine scholarship and friendship. The spirit of co-operation is surely one of the main reasons for the enduring vitality of the fifteenth century as we approach the third millennium.

A novelty at this gathering was the abandonment of the former practice of circulating written communications in advance in favour of rather shorter papers, all of which were delivered by their authors. This seems to be especially important for the research students, all of whom impressed the conference with their performances, not least by adhering strictly to their allotted time. The papers here published are, for the most part, in an expanded form. Employment prospects for younger scholars remain gloomy, but it is encouraging to report that Matthew Davies, Helen Castor and Dominic Luckett have secured permanent academic posts.

It is now traditional that no theme is set for this 'junior' conference and it would be difficult, not to say misleading, to argue that these papers aim to cover any one aspect of life in the fifteenth century. In their very diversity, however, they bear witness to the richness of the period and remind us that there is yet good work to be done. Some lies in under-used archives, such as the records of the Merchant Tailors of London which have been so profitably mined by Matthew Davies. Through them, Dr Davies has been able to study 'the operation of the principles of community and mutual support' by an organized and committed craft guild which could boast the earliest construction of an almshouse by a London livery company. The archives of the city of Chester have enabled Jane Laughton to bring together an account of brewing from the supplying of barley, wheat and oats to its consumption in 'rowdy establishments where men gathered to drink and ultimately came to blows'. That much can still be done with the Public Records in London is well demonstrated by Maureen Jurkowski's veritable detective work which has uncovered the quite remarkable story of Thomas Tykhill. There is too the important work of re-assessing the history of the fifteenth century, improving our perspectives and challenging our assumptions, as both Helen Castor and Diana Dunn are doing here, with two central but very diverse subjects.

Although disparate, these papers do, nevertheless, touch upon recurring themes, so that taken together they add substantially to an understanding of certain aspects of the fifteenth-century world view. In different guises a number of authors raise questions about what ordinary people thought, reminding us that history is as much, if not more, a matter of what people believed as it is what our intractable, inadequate, biassed evidence may allow us to present as fact. What stories, Joel Rosenthal asks, were 'drawn from the memory-bank of reminiscence' by those grandfathers and grandmothers, 'transmitters of family lore and tradition', and passed on to their heirs? How widespread was the view of Thomas Hunt who allegedly remarked that he would be glad to see Margaret of Anjou drowned because no good had come of her arrival in England, or of a Canterbury man who, we are told, delivered himself of the opinion in 1448 that Margaret was 'none abyle to be quene of Inglond . . . because that sche bereth no child'? There are great difficulties in defining popular opinion, more in determining its origins. Gossip was at the heart of rumour. That among the Chester alewives or in the unsalubrious semi-subterranean undercrofts of the city – such as 'Helle' in Bridge Street – may be hidden from us but, as Mavis Mate has recently pointed out, it was at the alehouse that people came to drink and socialize and among the artisans that there was the opportunity to think and converse about the state of the world.[1] It was reputedly in the alehouse, in 1448, that John and William Merfold had called Henry VI 'a natural fool'.[2]

That wild rumour had to be taken seriously; that its spread was fast and furious, not easily controlled; and that men and women were capable of remarkable levels of credulity and volatility is amply seen in Philip Morgan's description of the survival of Richard II whose death and burial did not terminate his lordship and whose 'vicarious existence' over many years left the new dynasty 'embattled and imperilled'. If there were indeed 10,000 people in England in 1404 who believed that Richard II was alive this was not an issue which his supplanter could ignore, especially given the ease with which such folk could become rebels. As K.B. McFarlane pointed out over thirty years ago, the commons 'were disposed to regard whoever was in power as responsible for the evils they suffered',[3] and Dr Morgan argues that opposition could be marshalled around the powerful image of a 'lost and just king under the unjust rule of his usurper', and yet without necessarily being a supporter of such a man.

Propaganda was thus a necessity for fifteenth-century governments as a response to seditious rumour in an effort to regain the initiative. Yorkist skills in the use of propaganda were investigated by Professor Charles Ross in a paper given to the Swansea conference in 1979.[4] Diana Dunn begins by showing how that propaganda has long clouded judgements about Margaret of Anjou, while Philip Morgan and James Doig examine how the crown sought to sway public opinion earlier in the century. Henry IV's regime, while endeavouring to take action against prophecies which foretold that Richard II would rise again, engaged in prophecy in an effort to boost the new dynasty's standing. James

---

[1] Mavis Mate, 'The Economic and Social Roots of Medieval Popular Rebellion: Sussex in 1450–1451', *EcHR*, XLV (1992), pp. 668–70.

[2] *English Historical Documents, IV, 1327–1485*, ed. A.R. Myers (1969), p. 264.

[3] K.B. McFarlane, 'The Wars of the Roses', *Proceedings of the British Academy*, L (1964), p. 113.

[4] Charles Ross, 'Rumour, Propaganda and Popular Opinion During the Wars of the Roses', in *Patronage, the Crown and the Provinces in Later Medieval England* (Gloucester, 1981), pp. 15–32.

Doig shows how the crown used every means – proclamations, sermons, processions, parliaments, sponsored verse – to fortify the resolve of its subjects to fight on in France, by vilifying the false duke of Burgundy following the Congress of Arras, and did so with considerable success. He concludes that the methods which raised support for the siege of Calais a year after Arras 'placed the national agenda before the mass of the population frequently and effectively'.

Charles Ross pointed out in 1979 that the spread of literacy was a precondition of political propaganda[5] and this issue is developed by James Doig. Here too are critical problems for which solutions are still sought. Increasing literacy is a useful banner for the fifteenth-century historian, but precisely how far we may run with it is not clear.[6] In drawing conclusions from Thomas Tykhill's forgery of Queen Joan of Navarre's title documents, Maureen Jurkowski points out that he would not have contemplated such an action 'without the confidence and arrogance acquired with his ability to read and write'. Tykhill's literacy skills had always been 'his most effective tools in advancing himself' and they were, moreover, blended with that most dreaded of seditious behaviour, Lollardy. The crown recognized the literary shortcomings of the nation, putting its trust in aural and visual methods to reach the greatest number of people, and where it resorted to the written word, as in Latin proclamations, it saw to it that these were translated into the vernacular.

Government and patronage and the links between them have been of the essence in the volumes of conference proceedings since the earliest days. Recently patronage, in particular, has come under fire[7] and it *may* be that

---

[5] Ibid., p. 15.

[6] C. Carpenter, *Locality and Polity: A Study of Warwickshire Landed Society, 1401–1499* (Cambridge, 1992), p. 205, concludes of her Warwickshire gentry that there is not much evidence of book-ownership but is properly cautious about dismissing them as 'philistines'. It is hard to believe that the successful management of their estates was not partly the result of some level of literacy. See especially chapter 5.

[7] Edward Powell, 'After "After McFarlane": the Poverty of Patronage and the Case for Constitutional History', in *Trade, Devotion and Governance: Papers in Later Medieval History*, ed. Dorothy J. Clayton, Richard G. Davies and Peter McNiven (Stroud, 1994), pp. 1–16.

studies of the system of clientage and how it influences politics will decline. Nevertheless, it is an issue addressed here, in smaller and larger measure, by a number of contributors. Diana Dunn portrays Margaret of Anjou exercising 'good ladyship' in order to demonstrate that whatever she may have done after 1453 the queen conducted herself before that date as 'a dutiful young wife and an effective distributer of patronage'. The exercise of patronage by women across its full spectrum still awaits an historian. That Thomas Tykhill's career was heavily, and ironically, indebted to his Lancastrian patrons is beyond doubt. To the London Tailors, those who were non-tailors were often willingly admitted to the company chiefly as patrons and at least one, Humphrey, duke of Gloucester, did indeed prove a welcome ally in a dispute with the city drapers. Helen Castor, in re-examining the government of East Anglia in the early fifteenth century, looks at how the exercise of patronage by the Lancastrians, in a period in which the local noble families were for various reasons in eclipse, created a strong royalist lordship. Her reconstruction enables her to propose that Thomas Tuddenham and John Heydon, names long synonymous with thuggery in East Anglia, 'had an impeccable pedigree in Lancastrian service'. Dr Castor seeks a new perspective on William de la Pole who, she argues, did not 'exploit his position in central government to subvert established political hierarchies'. This idea may not find widespread acceptance but will not easily be ignored. Dominic Luckett's study examines how, in one example, misjudging the distribution of patronage could be damaging to the crown. He argues that in the south-west opposition to Henry VII in 1497 came in the shires which had initially supported the usurpation, largely through the king's own fault. Henry had relied too much on his closest supporters continuing to back him without much reward. Apparent royal ingratitude and declining vested interest in the Tudor king meant that rebellion broke out in those shires where it was least expected. Wherever the future lies for discussion of questions of patronage, these papers suggest that it is still a profitable area for research.

In every case the contributors here are concerned, quite properly, with people, from kings and queens to nobles, gentry, bureaucrats and townsfolk. Life could be harsh and one's calling precarious and often hazardous, as the history of the Chester alewives shows. Joel Rosenthal and Margaret Wade Labarge drew our meeting to a close in complementary papers which stressed the humanity of our subject. Professor Rosenthal combines the statistical – slow, hard, bare-bones work – with the humane – elusive and important. It is easier to find the grandparents than establish the extent of their influence but it would be foolhardy, for lack of evidence, to set it at nought. Historians must not neglect the elderly. Contemporaries clearly counted them as respected members of the community, as Margaret Wade Labarge shows by close examination of the regimen of Gabriele Zerbi dedicated to Pope Innocent VIII and published in Rome in 1489. She describes it as 'a straightforward treatise, much of whose advice resonates with timeless common sense' even though it ignores the need to care for aged women (a particularly poor show it might be said for a man whose mother was eighty-eight when he met his untimely death), although in his will his provision for her and his wife suggests he was not so misogynistic as his work implies. Zerbi's advice on the need for a balance between diet, exercise and rest, environmental conditions and psychological well-being, in particular, the desirability of a proper caretaker of the elderly – something to which he devoted an entire chapter – suggests he might have approved of the efforts of the London Tailors. Although the latter had no formalized system of nursing, they nevertheless cared for their enfeebled members, probably following the ordinances for Richard Whittington's later almshouse that 'thei that ar myghty and hole of the body . . . helpe and ministre unto ye felawes . . . that ar seke and feble'.

In sum, then, these papers have valuable things to say about important themes in fifteenth-century history. The doubtless somewhat contrived effort of the editor to create a semblance of unity should not, however, constitute the last word. The contributions stand above all as individual studies which, as work in progress, we may hope to see in fuller guise at a later date. They are a credit to their authors.

It is a pleasure to record the debts which were incurred as a result of organizing the conference and preparing the volume for publication. Firstly my thanks go to the Principal of Manchester College, Oxford, the Reverend Dr Ralph Waller, who agreed without hesitation to the proposal to host the conference in Oxford and whose encouragement throughout was unfailing. My very special thanks go to my colleague, Mrs Frances Walsh, for her support and to the College Librarian, Mrs Margaret Sarosi, who put together a special exhibition for the conference of early printed books from the College's collection. The staff at Manchester College – in particular Mrs Anita Owen and Mrs Julie Parkin whose good humour never failed – ensured that everything ran smoothly; two of our history students – Nicholas Fragel and Kate King – helped in many humble, but vital, ways; and Mrs Pat Edwards did more than anyone to keep the editor to the final deadline. It has become part of the standard conference programme to have a 'free' afternoon and on this occasion we were treated to a very special tour of Broughton Castle, near Banbury, which was personally conducted by Lord and Lady Saye and Sele. For the warmth of their welcome and their generosity in showing us parts of their home not normally open to the public, I should like to say thank you from us all. The patience, forbearance and encouragement of Roger Thorp of Alan Sutton Publishing, the company which continues to place its confidence in medieval studies, have been vital in seeing the book to completion. Of course, in the end the greatest debt is to the contributors, to all of whom I offer my warmest best wishes.

Rowena E. Archer

Lady Day, 1995

1

HENRY IV AND THE SHADOW OF RICHARD II

Philip Morgan

ichard II died at Pontefract, probably on St Valentine's day 1400, his
fate surely sealed by the earlier failure of the revolt of the earls in
January.[1] Rumours of his death were already in circulation. The
previous week the privy council had resolved that if he still lived he should be
securely guarded for the safety of the king and realm, and that if he were dead
he should be openly shown to the people.[2] The 14 February date appears in
three independent chronicles and was possibly circulated together with the
apparently official explanation of his death, namely that the former king had
starved himself in despair at the failure of the rebellion on his behalf.[3] Within
days the body was transported to St Paul's in the city of London, having rested
at St Albans, and was taken thence for private burial at Langley.[4]

The circumstances of his confinement had inevitably given rise to rumours.
At the parliament of 1399, charged by Archbishop Thomas Arundel to keep
silent as to their deliberations, the lords had recommended that Richard be kept
in a safe and secure place, *sauvant sa vie*, away from any gathering of people and
without the companionship of any of his familiars.[5] The king had been removed
from the Tower in the autumn of 1399 and sent first to Leeds castle in Kent in
the custody of Sir John Pelham. From there he had been moved to Pickering,

---

[1] David Crook, 'Central England and the Revolt of the Earls, January 1400', *Historical Research*,
LXIV (1991), pp. 403–10.

[2] *PPC*, I, pp. 107–12. The dating of the minutes follows J.H. Wylie, *A History of England under Henry
IV* (4 vols. 1884–98), I, p. 115. See also the discussion of the manuscript in *Chronicon Adae de Usk*, ed.
E.M. Thompson (2nd edition, 1904), pp. 201–2.

[3] *Historia Vitae et Regni Ricardi Secundi*, ed. George B. Stow (Philadelphia, 1977), p. 211 n. 483.

[4] Wylie, *Henry IV*, I, p. 117.

[5] *RP*, III, p. 426.

Knaresborough and finally to Pontefract in the keeping of Sir Robert Waterton and Sir Thomas Swynford.[6]

The received version of events was initially accepted, even in France where the starvation episode featured in Jean Creton's *Metrical History*, known to have been in circulation between November 1401 and March 1402.[7] Negotiations for the return of Richard's queen, the eleven-year-old Isabelle, had begun as early as May 1400, Richard's death being admitted in the diplomatic correspondence, although Henry was to remain *le duc de Lencastre qui se dit roy d'Engleterre*.[8] Another continental writer, a Picard herald formerly attached to the household of John Holand, duke of Exeter, whose own *pièce d'occasion*, the *Traison et Mort de Richard II*, was first composed at this period, invented a story of Richard's murder at Pontefract by the otherwise unknown Sir Peter Exton.[9] Despite the circumstances of his confinement, the fact of Richard's death was not immediately an issue of political significance.

Historians have thus been inclined to dismiss a succession of subsequent risings and civil disorders in Richard's name as foolish and futile, an exercise in the politics of the dispossessed. This was certainly the view of the continuator of the Dieulacres chronicle, for whom, with barely concealed contempt, those who had mustered at Shrewsbury in 1403 in promise of a personal appearance by the living Richard were a 'shoal of fools', *multitudo inbecillorum*.[10] Thomas Walsingham took a kindlier view, stressing the obvious confusion which faced

---

[6] *The Chronicle of John Harding*, ed. H. Ellis (1812), p. 356; BL, Lansdowne MS. 204, f. 203v; *Incerti Scriptoris Chronicon Angliae de Regnis . . . Henrici IV, Henrici V, et Henrici VI*, ed. J.A. Giles (1848), pp. 10–11.

[7] J.J.N. Palmer, 'The Authorship, Date and Historical Value of the French Chronicles on the Lancastrian Revolution', *BJRL*, LXI (1978–9), pp. 151–62.

[8] Frederick C. Wilson, 'Anglo-French Relations in the Reign of King Henry IV of England (1399–1413)' (unpub. McGill Ph.D. thesis, 1973), chapter 2; *Choix de Pièces Inédites Relatives au Règne de Charles VI*, ed. L. Douët d'Arcq (Paris, 1863–4), pp. 185–93.

[9] Palmer, 'Authorship', p. 170. The author of the *Traison et Mort* may perhaps have meant Sir Peter Buckton, Henry IV's steward and familiar, who was steward of Knaresborough castle, for whom see *The History of Parliament: The House of Commons, 1386–1421*, ed. J.S. Roskell, Linda Clark and Carole Rawcliffe (4 vols. Stroud,1992), II, pp. 404–7.

[10] M.V. Clarke and V.H. Galbraith, 'The Deposition of Richard II', *BJRL*, XIV (1930), pp. 177–8.

many, especially the king's *quondam familiares*, as they responded to a proliferation of rumours about the king's survival.[11] The willing suspension of disbelief reached higher levels and Jean Creton, the loyal poet, was despatched by the government of Charles VI on a search for Richard's ghost, probably in April 1402.[12] Accepting the fact of Richard's death, what significance should we attach to a series of advertised appearances by this apparition during the early years of Henry's reign?

Richard II's death and burial did not of necessity signal the end of his lordship. Those whom the historian now casts aside from narrative at the moment of death enjoyed a vicarious existence that might extend across many decades, in images alternately faded and restored by pious successors. Traditional religion has been described as the cult of the living in the service of the dead, the countless small acts, memorials and prayers of intercession which sought to prolong the presence of the dead within the community of the living.[13] What was important in the myriad pattern of great and small lordships, in other communities and solidarities, even within the household, peasant or noble, had a greater resonance for kingship. The authority of a dead king, to borrow James Doig's phrase, might compete with that of his successor.

Contemporaries could look to a range of examples. The dead peopled an imagined landscape and those who survived needed to know its contours, for often its shadows could call men to action. In 1397 it was popularly rumoured that the head and torso of the executed earl of Arundel had been miraculously re-united and crowds flocked to the tomb. Richard commissioned the duke of Lancaster and the earls of Northumberland, Rutland, Kent and Nottingham to investigate the site at night, later ordered the removal of the earl's arms and funeral achievements and demanded that the body be reburied under the pavement of the Augustinian friary where its position would be hidden from crowds. Richard's notorious guard of Cheshire archers was initially seen, in

---

[11] *Annales Ricardi Secundi et Henrici Quarti Regum Angliae, 1392–1406*, ed. H.T. Riley in *Johannis de Trokelowe, Annales* (RS, 1866), p. 363.

[12] Palmer, 'Authorship', pp. 151–4.

[13] Eamon Duffy, *The Stripping of the Altars. Traditional Religion in England, 1400–1580* (1992), pp. 301–3.

Walsingham's account of this incident, as protecting the king from his dreams of the dead earl of Arundel.[14]

Few rulers needed lessons on the political significance of corpses. Attempts to suppress cults, to appropriate the battle sites of factional warfare and to counter the persistent sighting of ghostly claimants are common. The Dictum of Kenilworth of 1266 forbade the circulation of 'vain and foolish miracles' attributed to Simon de Montfort, while the government of Edward II struggled to contain the popular disturbances which met their attempts to suppress spontaneous devotions at the tomb of Thomas of Lancaster.[15] In the aftermath of the Breton civil war the cult of Charles of Blois was encouraged by Louis I, duc d'Anjou, and by the Franciscans who had perhaps organized pilgrims from the royal demesne to the tomb at Guingamp. Despite a papal *bulla* aimed at suppression of the cult in 1368, Duke John IV was driven to mount a lengthy campaign of opposition against the papal commissions to enquire into his late opponent's putative sanctity.[16]

There were a number of well-worn responses to these issues. To permit an outrage to be committed against the corpse, its parts carried abroad, was to assault the concept of the continuing presence of the dead in the world of the living. After the battle of Shrewsbury Henry IV would order the exhumation of Hotspur's body at Whitchurch, to which it had been hastily removed by Lord Furnival, insist upon the mutilation of the corpse, its public display in the

---

[14] *Annales Henrici Quarti*, pp. 218–19; Thomas Walsingham, *Historia Anglicana (1272–1422)*, ed. H.T. Riley (RS, 2 vols. 1863–4), II, pp. 225–6. BL, Additional MS. 35295, f.260r (The Kenilworth Chronicle) perhaps preserves an echo of the same view in its report of the guards' celebrated boast in the vernacular, 'Dycun, slep sicury quile we wake . . .' .

[15] David C. Cox, *The Battle of Evesham. A New Account* (Evesham, 1988), pp. 21–2; J.R. Maddicott, *Thomas of Lancaster, 1307–1322* (Oxford, 1970), pp. 329–30; John Edwards, 'The Cult of St. Thomas of Lancaster and its Iconography', *Yorkshire Archaeological Journal*, LXIV (1992), pp. 103–22.

[16] A. Vauchez, 'Canonisation et Politique au xive Siècle. Documents Inédits des Archives du Vatican Relatifs au Procès de Canonisation de Charles de Blois, Duc de Bretagne (+1364)', *Miscellanea in onore di Monsignor Martino Giusti*, II (Collectanea Archivi Vaticani, VI, 1978), pp. 381–404; Michael Jones, *Receuil des Actes de Jean IV, Duc de Bretagne* (2 vols. 1980–3), I, pp. 170, 191, 213, 221; Michael Jones, *Ducal Brittany, 1364–1399* (Oxford, 1970), p. 53. I owe this account to a paper by Professor Michael Jones at the conference, *Medieval Saints and Hagiography*, York University, 15–16 July 1993.

market place at Shrewsbury and the fixing of the head on the north gate at York.[17] It was, he said, so that men would not say that he still lived. Simon de Montfort's body was likewise first mutilated, the head, testicles, hands and feet dispersed, and the surviving trunk later removed from its tomb in Evesham abbey to a concealed and unconsecrated part of the precinct.[18]

The council of Henry IV could thus not have been ignorant of the issues which faced them on receipt of the news of Richard's death at Pontefract, though their choices were to a degree limited by the late king's own patronage at Westminster abbey. A devotion to the cult of Edward the Confessor, the creation of a private oratory in the chapel of St Mary de la Pew, the commission of the Westminster portrait in the monastic choir and the Wilton diptych, were each part of an indelible link between the king and the abbey which was cemented by the rearrangement of burials around the shrine of St Edward to incorporate, first, the burial of Anne of Bohemia in 1394 and, later, the joint tomb commissioned in 1395 and completed by early 1399.[19] At the same moment the king had founded a perpetual anniversary in the abbey, requiring the distribution of a penny alm to the poor and the recitation of the charter of endowment annually in the chapter. Before his death its annual income was £200.[20] News of the proposed burial-site was widespread. Almost immediately, the continuator of the chronicle of the Cistercian house at Croxden in Staffordshire, incorporating a list of kings with the years of their rule and burial places, noted Westminster as Richard's resting place, though he did not, of course, know the final length of the king's reign.[21]

---

[17] Clarke and Galbraith, 'Deposition of Richard II', p. 181; W.G.D. Fletcher, 'Some Documents Relative to the Battle of Shrewsbury', *Transactions of the Shropshire Archaeological and Natural History Society*, 2nd series, X (1898), pp. 243–5.

[18] Michael Prestwich, *Edward I* (1988), p. 51; Cox, *The Battle of Evesham*, p. 21; J.R. Maddicott, *Simon de Montfort* (Cambridge, 1994), p. 344.

[19] *Age of Chivalry. Art in Plantagenet England, 1200–1400*, ed. Jonathan Alexander and Paul Binski (1987), pp. 393–4, 517–18; Dillian Gordon, *Making and Meaning: The Wilton Diptych* (1993), pp. 22–3, 54, 61–3.

[20] Barbara Harvey, *Westminster Abbey and its Estates in the Middle Ages* (Oxford, 1977), pp. 33–6; *Historia Vitae et Regni Ricardi Secundi*, p. 167.

[21] BL, Cotton MS. Faustina B.vi f.68r.

The decision was instead taken to bury Richard quietly in the Franciscan church at Langley after a mass in St Paul's, no doubt in an effort to avoid the tomb at Westminster serving as a focus for continuing devotion. The penny alm established in 1399 was abandoned.[22] Adam of Usk, who had likened Richard to the builder of the Babylonian temple of Bel, now perhaps echoing the feelings of Henry's councillors, wrote, 'My God! how many thousand marks he spent on burial places of vain-glory for himself and his wives among the kings at Westminster'.[23] During the reign of Henry IV the empty tomb (how telling a phrase) must nevertheless have seemed a perpetual reproach and an invitation to rumour. The seclusion of the burial was to be balanced by the very public nature of Richard's funeral cortège. As a memorandum in King's Bench was later wearily to observe, the king 'has been long time dead and was seen as dead by thousands upon thousands within the city of London and elsewhere within the realm of England'.[24]

On its journey from Pontefract Richard's corpse was displayed with its face, pale, rounded and feminine, uncovered for all to see.[25] The procedure was unlike that which had been observed for his predecessors, though it bears some resemblance to the practice recommended in a text, *De Exequiis Regalibus*, preserved in an early manuscript of the *Modus Tenendi Parliamentum* together with the Steward's Tract. The dead king's body was first to be washed by his chamber servants, perfumed with balsam and aromatic unguents and wrapped in waxed linen bandages in such a way that the beard and face were left open. Dressed as a crowned king, orb and sceptre in hand, the face was to be lightly covered with a silken

[22] Harvey, *Westminster Abbey*, p. 36 n.1.

[23] *Chronicon Adae de Usk*, pp. 43–5.

[24] *S(elect Cases in the Court of) K(ing's) B(ench under Richard II, Henry IV and Henry V)*, ed. G.O. Sayles (*Selden Society*, 7 vols. 1936–71), VII, p. 212.

[25] *Chronicon Adae de Usk*, p. 44; Clarke and Galbraith, 'Deposition of Richard II', p. 174; *Annales Ricardi Secundi*, pp. 330–1; *Eulogium Historiarum sive Temporis*, ed. F.S. Haydon (RS, 3 vols. 1858–63), III, p. 387. The physical description is that of the Evesham chronicler, *Historia Vitae et Regni Ricardi Secundi*, p. 166.

cloth.[26] Edward I's body, though beardless, was treated in like fashion and, when the coffin was opened in 1774, was found to be holding two sceptres and wearing a crown. Before its burial at Westminster it had rested at Waltham abbey, Holy Trinity priory, Aldgate, and at St Paul's.[27] But, neither Edward II nor his son Edward III had been likewise publicly shown. In both cases a wooden funeral effigy served as an image of the late king during the funeral procession.

The practice may have originated as a consequence of the circumstances surrounding the death of Edward II, a king whose deposition and murder were much in the minds of those who helped Henry IV to the throne. Like Richard, Edward II was held captive after his deposition, first at Kenilworth and finally at Berkeley, and he too was the target for attempted rescue.[28] The organization of Richard's funeral owed much to that earlier experience with a dead king. Edward's death at Berkeley on 21 September was officially announced in parliament, but his funeral was delayed for three months until 20 December 1327. This was an impressive state occasion directed by the government of Mortimer. Furnishings and coronation ornaments were supplied from the great wardrobe in London, and the crowds at Gloucester abbey were kept at a distance behind oak barriers.[29] The elaborate royal tomb in the north ambulatory, perhaps an early design of Thomas of Canterbury, may already have been in place before Mortimer's fall in November 1330. Later in the century Abbot Walter Frocester would attribute the rebuilding of the south

[26] BL, Cotton MS. Nero Dvi, f.45v. The earliest manuscripts of the *Modus Tenendi Parliamentum* have been shown to belong to Richard's reign and to have received particular attention at the time of the deposition: James Sherborne, 'Perjury and the Lancastrian Revolution', *Welsh History Review*, XIV (1988), pp. 221–3.

[27] Prestwich, *Edward I*, pp. 558, 566–7; J. Ayloffe, 'An Account of the Body of King Edward the First, as it appeared on opening his tomb in the year 1774', *Archaeologia*, III (1786), pp. 376–413; *Age of Chivalry*, pp. 368–9.

[28] T.F. Tout, 'The Captivity and Death of Edward of Caernarvon', *BJRL*, VI (1921–2), pp. 69–114.

[29] Stuart Archibald Moore, 'Documents Relating to the Death and Burial of King Edward II', *Archaeologia*, I (1887), pp. 223–6; W.H. St John Hope, 'On the Funeral Effigies of the Kings and Queens of England', *Archaeologia*, LX (1907), pp. 530–1.

transept of Gloucester to the income generated by pilgrims to the royal tomb between 1329 and 1335.[30] The short-lived cult of Edward II bears every sign of official sponsorship.

Nevertheless, in March 1330 Edmund Woodstock, earl of Kent, who had been at the Gloucester funeral, was persuaded that Edward was still alive and was arrested after a visit to Corfe castle and executed. The conspiracy included William Melton, archbishop of York, and Stephen Gravesend, bishop of London. The earl's confession pleaded papal encouragement, though John XXII quickly denied any belief in Edward's survival.[31] Later that autumn the judgement against Roger Mortimer charged him with having circulated rumours of Edward II's survival and of having procured Kent's execution.[32] Although Edward III may later have received a letter from Manuele de Fieschi, a papal notary and later bishop of Vercelli, enclosing what was purportedly the last confession of 'Edward II' at the monastery of Sant Alberto di Butrio near Tortona, together with a plausible explanation of his whereabouts between 1326 and his 'death' in 1343, there is no evidence that he was seriously disturbed by his father's ghost.[33]

Whereas many political cults were comparatively short-lived, a focus for opposition to changed or new régimes, the shadow of Richard II was to cloud the whole reign of Henry IV and the early years of Henry V. In an evident attempt to counter persistent rumours of Richard's survival one of Henry's first acts on his accession in 1413 was to exhume Richard's body at Langley and have it reburied at Westminster.[34] Thomas Hoccleve complimented the new

---

[30] Christopher Wilson, 'The origins of the perpendicular style and its development to *circa* 1360' (unpub. London, Ph.D thesis, 1979), pp. 117–21; *Historia et Cartularium Monasterii Sancti Petri Gloucestriae*, ed. W.H. Hart (RS, 3 vols. 1863–7), I, p. 44–6. The importance of pilgrim offerings is challenged in David Verey and David Welander, *Gloucester Cathedral* (Gloucester, 1979), pp. 19–21.

[31] Adae Murimuth, *Continuatio Chronicarum*, ed. Edward Maunde Thompson (RS, 1889), pp. 253–7; *Chronicon Galfridi le Baker*, ed. Edward Maunde Thompson (Oxford, 1889), p. 43; *Foedera*, IV, p. 424; *CPL*, II, p. 499.

[32] *RP*, II, p. 52.

[33] G.P. Cuttino and Thomas W. Lyman, 'Where is Edward II?', *Speculum*, LIII (1978), pp. 522–44.

[34] *The Saint Albans Chronicle, 1406–20*, ed. V.H. Galbraith (Oxford, 1937), p. 77.

king on 'his loving heart' and observed that Richard was 'not fled from his remembrance away'. For the poet, the reburial prophesied the healing of the nation's wounds.[35] The poet of Bodleian Library Digby MS. 102 likewise praised the action in an early advice poem, 'Glade in god, call hom zoure herte'.[36]

The new king would later choose to be buried at Westminster, ignoring the Lancastrian mausoleum to the north of Becket's shrine in Canterbury cathedral which had been created by his father. While the body of Richard II was restored to the tomb which he had himself commissioned, Henry's own effigy would not be erected until the 1420s, when his widow, Joan of Navarre, stepped in to aid the executors of his will.[37] With even greater irony, stories were circulating that Henry's own tomb was empty, the body having been cast overboard during a storm between Barking and Gravesend on its journey from Westminster to Canterbury.[38]

The sightings of Richard's ghost are well documented. While Richard still lived, one of his former household clerks, Richard Maudelyn, who reputedly resembled the king, was used as a surrogate, notably during the revolt of the earls in 1400.[39] From the winter of 1401/2 an impostor, Thomas Ward of Trumpington, established a 'court' in exile, first in the household of Robert III of Scotland and, after 1406, in the household of the regent, Robert Stewart, duke of Albany.[40] Until his death at Stirling in 1419 this Scottish pseudo-

---

[35] *Hoccleve's Works*, I. *The Minor Poems*, ed. Frederick J. Furnivall (EETS, LXI, 1892), pp. 47–9.

[36] *Twenty-six Political and other Poems*, ed. J. Kail (EETS, CXXIV, 1904), p. 50.

[37] Christopher Wilson, 'The Tomb of Henry IV and the Holy Oil of Canterbury', *Medieval Architecture and its Context. Studies in honour of Peter Kidson*, ed. Eric Fernie and Paul Crossley (1990), pp. 181–90.

[38] 'Miscellanea relating to Archbishop Scrope', in *The Historians of the Church of York and its Archbishops*, ed. James Raine (RS, 3 vols. 1879–94), II, p. 311; Stephen K. Wright, 'The Provenance and Manuscript Tradition of the *Martyrium Ricardi Archiepiscopi*,' *Manuscripta*, XXVIII (1984), pp. 100–2.

[39] For his career see Chris Given-Wilson, *The Royal Household and the King's Affinity: Service, Politics and Finance in England, 1360–1413* (New Haven, 1986), pp. 179–81.

[40] Walter Bower, *Scotichronicon*, ed. D.E.R. Watt (9 vols. Aberdeen, 1987 *et seq.*) VIII, pp. 28–9, 64–7, 115.

Richard was the focus of professed homage during many of the assaults on the kingship of Henry IV and Henry V and his reputation may have overwhelmed the claims of other apparitions, occasionally reported at Westminster, Berwick and in Wales.[41]

Since the fact of Richard's captivity at Pontefract was well known it proved necessary that there be an escape. The earliest version is provided in the evidence of John Prittlewell during the countess of Oxford's rising. He had heard the story from one of the countess's servants, Robert Boleyn, during mass at Beeleigh abbey (Essex) on 16 February 1404, namely that Richard had been smuggled from Pontefract castle by three priests and a serving woman of Sir Robert Waterton and from thence to the Isles.[42] Here, according to the much later account of Walter Bower's *Scotichronicon*, he was discovered 'in the kitchen of Donald lord of the Isles by a certain jester'.[43] Andrew of Wyntoun attributed the discovery to Donald's Anglo-Irish sister-in-law who had seen Richard in Ireland and recognized him.[44] From there Richard was sent by Sir John Montgomery of that Ilk, lord of Ardrossan, into the keeping of Robert III. Naïve servants, suborned locksmiths and pliant serving women, the unknown heroes of Edward II's 'escape', of Constance, Lady Despenser's failed freeing of Edmund and Roger Mortimer in 1405 and of Richard II's flight to the Isles, are the inevitable supporting cast of such escapes and form part of the common typology of pretender legends.

After the failure of the rising of the earls in February 1400, Richard's ghost seems to have slumbered until early 1402. This two-year silence is of particular importance to our understanding of his significance. Its breaking coincided with

[41] The claim that Thomas Ward had died in 1413/14, advanced in T.B. Pugh, *Henry V and the Southampton Plot* (1988), pp. 100, 107 n.29, is erroneous. A John Lancaster 'piper' claimed to have seen Richard at Berwick in the spring of 1402, see PRO, Palatinate of Chester, Indictment Rolls, Ches 25/10, m.10d.

[42] PRO, Exchequer, King's Remembrancer, Miscellanea, E163/6/28 (12). Prittlewell's testimony is printed from this document in the *Chronique de la Traison et Mort de Richart Deux Roy Dengleterre*, ed. Benjamin Williams (English Historical Society, 1846), pp. 269–73.

[43] *Scotichronicon*, VIII, pp. 28–9.

[44] *The Original Chronicle of Andrew of Wyntoun*, ed. F.J. Amours (6 vols. 1903–14), VI, p. 390.

a French mission to Scotland to seek news of the risen Richard, the first record of the Scottish pseudo-Richard and with the arrest of Sir Roger Clarendon, Richard's illegitimate half-brother, as part of a conspiracy amongst several minorite houses which claimed that Richard was still alive.[45] Later in the year, in his letter to Sir John Greyndour, Hywel Fychan and the community, *touts les gentielx et comunes* of the lordship of Radnor and Presteigne, Sir Edmund Mortimer claimed that the Welsh rising of Glyn Dŵr would seek to restore Richard, 'if he was alive'.[46] Richard's ghost was to be the focus of internal dissent and the mascot of external enemies in France, Wales and Scotland.

While many of those who gave support to rumours of Richard's survival can be identified as former members of his affinity and household, his household clerks, noble, gentle and yeomanly retainers, his ghost was not the creation of a displaced political clique. Nor is its significance to be understood in such simplistic terms. It was, of course, not necessary to believe that Richard was alive in order to muster in his service. To do so merely challenged Henry IV's title and defined political opposition within a tradition of loyalist rebellion. Such a tradition might provide a legitimizing framework, both for redress of grievance in times of social, political or economic distress, or for a programme of religious or political change. The emphasis which Henry's government was to place on the physical facts of Richard's death and burial was deliberately to misread the grievances of those who adopted his cult. In anatomizing the apparent nostalgia for Richard's rule, the pseudo-Richard symbolized the power of a lost and just king under the unjust rule, of his usurper. He belongs, and is to be understood, in the same context as other pretender kings, the pseudo-Baldwin IX and the resurrected Frederick II.[47]

---

[45] *CCR, 1399–1401, p. 570; Foedera*, VIII, p. 261; Chris Given-Wilson and Alice Curteis, *The Royal Bastards of Medieval England* (1984), pp. 143–6 for Clarendon's career; *Eulogium Historiarum*, pp. 388–94 contains the principal narrative account of the friars' conspiracy; the legal records are printed and discussed in R.L. Storey, 'Clergy and common law in the reign of Henry IV', in *Medieval Legal Records edited in memory of C.A.F. Meekings*, ed. R.F. Hunnisett and J.B. Post (1978), pp. 342–408.

[46] *Original Letters Illustrative of English History*, ed. Henry Ellis, 2nd series (1827), I, pp. 24–6.

[47] Norman Cohn, *The Pursuit of the Millennium* (1957), pp. 79–81, 107–23.

The logic of this tradition of loyalist rebellion was succinctly put by Roger Frisby, a Leicester friar cross-examined by Henry in 1402; 'I do not say that he lives', Frisby is reported to have said, 'but if he lives he is the true king of England'. Henry's retort that Richard had resigned and been deposed, and that he had been duly elected in his place was passionately dismissed. The king would not have resigned had he been free, his kingdom accordingly taken by force of arms and his throne usurped; and the election could not be valid while the legitimate king lived. If he was dead, Henry had been responsible for his death and had thus lost all right to the title and to power in the realm.[48]

The 'rebellion' of the friars in 1402 set the tone and style of the response to resurrection rumours by the government of Henry IV. According to the Canterbury continuator of the *Eulogium Historiarum*, 'the people began to grudge against King Henry because he took their goods and did not pay for them'. A comet in a bad aspect prophesied the events which would result in the execution of sixteen people in June 1402, including eleven minorites from houses at Leicester, Aylesbury, Northampton and Nottingham. A knight, possibly Sir William Heron, had advised the king that the 'ceaseless clamour that Richard lived' would not be silenced until the friars were themselves silenced.

The judge, William Gascoigne, accused the friars of having urged those who had listened to their false preaching to seek Richard in Scotland, and of advising those who made confessions to seek him in Wales.[49] Yet, aside from a 'great council' at Leicester, at which sixteen of those indicted (but only five of those executed) were present, there is scant evidence of a single conspiracy. That against Sir Roger Clarendon, in the confession of Walter Walton, a Leicester friar, was restricted to a reported conversation in the former's Southwark house. Nor do the confessions reveal the existence of a conspiracy with the king's external enemies in Scotland and Wales. The friars' confessions make no reference to the Scottish pseudo-Richard and, while two Leicester friars were sent to Wales to seek him, the former king was also reportedly seen at St James's hospital in Westminster and at 'Wodesere'.

---

[48] *Eulogium Historiarum*, pp. 391–2.
[49] Ibid., pp. 389–94.

A single conspiracy and a threat to the safety of the realm posed by the Scots featured only in the collective charge levelled at those arrested in the spring of 1402 and coincided with the first official attempts to counter rumours of the Scottish pseudo-Richard which had been reported to the king from the diocese of Carlisle.[50] After careful analysis of the legal record, Professor Robin Storey concluded that the indictments had been designed as 'official propaganda', William Gascoigne's closing argument conflating several apparitions of the former king into a single ghost.[51] Gossip and seditious rumour was said to give aid and encouragement to the external enemies of the nation, and to threaten the final destruction of the whole realm; those who campaigned against the crown under the protection of a tradition of loyalist rebellion had become the enemy within. Even so, the several juries proved reluctant to convict all those who had been indicted; the continuator of the *Eulogium* claimed that those at Highgate and Islington sought the forgiveness of those whom they had condemned.

The endeavour to associate expressions of dissent, articulated in support for Richard II, with a wider conspiracy against the realm was to be a characteristic of Henry's government. But, once a telling example had been made of the minorites in 1402 clemency was often invoked. Robert Westbroom of Bury St Edmunds, who had repeated the rumours of Richard's survival there at Whitsun, was pardoned in the summer since it was not the king's intention to punish those 'who happened to hear such lies and innocently told the same'. John Bernard, a ploughman of Offley (Herts.), was likewise pardoned for repeating a rumour of Richard's survival, and plan to emigrate to Brittany, to two of his neighbours, the three agreeing to meet Richard at Atherstone (Warks.)[52]

The threat to the realm must have seemed real enough during these years. The parliament which opened in the painted chamber at Westminster in

---

[50] *Calendar of Documents relating to Scotland* (4 vols. 1881–8), IV, p. 126; *CPR, 1401–5*, p. 125; *CCR, 1399–1401*, p. 570; *Foedera*, VIII, p. 261.

[51] Storey, 'Clergy and common law', p. 356.

[52] *CCR, 1399–1402*, p. 548; *CPR, 1401–5*, pp. 99–100.

January 1404 was summoned to deal with the Welsh rebellion of Owain Glyn
Dŵr, the aggressions of Louis, duc d'Orleans and the comte de St Pol, the perils
faced by Calais and Guyenne, wars in Ireland and Scotland, and the rebellion
of the Percies.[53] Both the French and the Scots had espoused the cause of
Richard's ghost. The Lancastrian dynasty was both embattled and imperilled.

Initially the French court had itself felt threatened by Henry's accession,
which appeared to cast into doubt the truce established in 1396. Jean, duc de
Berri, writing to Philip the Bold, ruefully observed that the usurpation would
lead to a very great evil for France; 'you know that the Duke of Lancaster
governs by the voice of the English commons, and the commons only ask for
war'.[54] In such circumstances, and as early as October 1399, the government of
Charles VI adopted a policy of opposition to Henry IV based on a refusal to
recognize the new king's title, a willingness to sponsor internal rebellion in
Wales and Guyenne, military and naval aid for Robert III in Scotland, and
semi-official approval of channel piracy.[55] In 1402, after the same two-year
hiatus, Charles VI too responded to rumours of Richard's apparent survival,
arguing in an *ordonnance* establishing an enormous *aide* that *inter alia* it was
commonly reported that Richard II was alive in Scotland and required help
from France.[56]

Belief in the reality of the risen Richard was short-lived but French policy
continued to espouse his cause and to speak in his name. Henry IV remained
the *soi-disant roi* throughout his reign. Conventionally this hostility is viewed
pragmatically, both as an inevitable response to the opportunity created by
England's danger, and as the consequence of political intrigue and the
polarization of diplomatic policy options at the court of Charles VI. But there is

---

[53] *RP*, III, p. 522.

[54] Francoise Lehoux, *Jean de France, Duc de Berri. Sa vie, Son Action Politique (1340–1416)* (5 vols.
Paris, 1965–7), II, pp. 420–1, n.6.

[55] Wilson, 'Anglo-French Relations', pp. 29–47; Stephen P. Pistono, 'The Accession of Henry IV:
Effects on Anglo-Flemish Relations, 1399–1402', *Tijdschrift voor Geschiedensis*, LXXXVI (1976), pp.
465–74; C.J. Ford, 'Piracy or Policy: The Crisis in the Channel, 1400–1403', *TRHS*, 5th ser. XXIX
(1979), pp. 63–77.

[56] Lehoux, *Jean de France*, II, pp. 473–5, 518; R.C. Famiglietti, *Royal Intrigue. Crisis at the Court of
Charles VI 1392–1420* (New York, 1986), p. 26.

little doubt that the deposition of Richard had also raised alarm in France where Charles's madness might have offered its own enticing pretext for deposition or assassination. The nearly contemporary deposition of a French ally, the Emperor Wenzel IV, in August 1400 did little to assuage fears of a disordered Europe. The long-recognized Ricardian voice of contemporary French chronicles was grounded in a profound and widely-held disquiet.[57]

Perhaps the earliest French account of the deposition and of attitudes to later rumours of his death is to be found in the diplomatic instructions given to Arnaud-Amanieu, the Sire d'Albret, dispatched to Guyenne in early 1400 in response to rumours that many of the Gascon nobility were reluctant to acknowledge the rule of Henry IV. Richard, who had ruled *en bonne justice et transquilité*, had been deposed by force and in fear of his life, consigned to a hard prison without hope of ever leaving, and here *desja dient aucuns qu'il le a fait mourir*. The founding of the Lancastrian dynasty and the duke's culpability for Richard's death, so the Sire d'Albret was to argue, was offensive to all reasonable people, an assault on the king's lineage and amity, and had no parallel even in ancient scriptures.[58] An anonymous marginal in a late fourteenth-century manuscript of Simon de Hesdin's French translation and commentary on Valerius Maximus ironically likened the reception of Henry of Lancaster in Paris in 1398 to that of King Demeratus of Lacedemonia at the court of Xerxes, as described by Justinus: an exile who nevertheless warned his country of impending attack. Henry had instead brought about the death of his lord and threatened the ruin of his nation.[59]

The Old Testament was, of course, replete with similar instances of empires founded in violence and by usurpation. Although no French king had ever been assassinated, there were innumerable contemporary examples of illicit violence,

---

[57] Palmer, 'Authorship', pp. 145–81, 398–421.

[58] J. de la Martinière, 'Instructions secrètes donées par Charles VI au sire d'Albret pour soulever la Guyenne contre Henri IV', *Bibliothèque de l'Ecole des Chartes*, LXXIV (1913), pp. 329–40; M.G.A. Vale, *English Gascony, 1399–1453* (Oxford, 1970), p. 29.

[59] John Rylands University Library, Manchester, French MS. 63, f.56 printed in Moses Tyson, 'Hand-list of French and Italian Manuscripts in the John Rylands Library, 1930', *BJRL*, XIV (1930), p. 585.

both real and fictional. The French mind at this moment, recently explored by Bernard Guenée, dreamt of order and peace but lived in reality amongst disorder and violence: a violence which was not always blameworthy but was always deplorable. The remedies of justice, alliances and oaths were seen as a safeguard against the descent into disorder and a means of preserving honour.[60] They had been characteristic of the involvement of the French court in the final years of Richard's rule and bolstered the insecure truce established after the failure of a final peace in 1396. Charles VI had, for instance, sent an embassy to persuade Richard to cancel the duel between Bolingbroke and Mowbray in August 1398, and in October had provided an honourable exile for the duke of Hereford with Richard's agreement. The duke's marriage to Marie de Berry, countess of Eu, was briefly contemplated.[61] In June 1399 he and Louis, duc d'Orléans, signed an alliance of love and friendship, the agreement to operate without injury to the relationships which both parties had with their sovereign, kinship, affinity, vassalage or in previously contracted alliances.[62]

The deposition in effect dissolved many of the marital and familial ties which had been so carefully nurtured since 1396 and inhibited the early forging of new relationships. An English mission which had sought a marriage between the children of Henry IV and Charles VI in November 1399 had been rebuffed.[63] Richard's queen, Isabelle, remained in England. Careful negotiations for her return to France, *considéré son joenne age et que le dit feu roy Richart est alé de vie*, occupied the diplomatic missions of 1400 and early 1401 but, as Charles VI observed in a letter of August 1400 to Robert III, Henry could not imagine that the French crown would give even close-mouthed approval of his title or the lordship which he had thus usurped.[64] The Scottish

---

[60] Bernard Guenée, *Un Meurtre, une Société. L'Assassinat de Duc d'Orléans 23 Novembre 1407* (Paris, 1992), pp. 87–100.

[61] Lehoux, *Jean de France*, II, 406–7; BL, Additional Charter 3066; J.J.N. Palmer, *England, France and Christendom, 1377–99* (1972), pp. 217–18.

[62] E. Jarry, *La Vie Politique de Louis de France Duc D'Orléans, 1372–1407* (Paris, 1889), pp. 226–9; Guenée, *Un Meurtre*, pp. 112–13.

[63] Lehoux, *Jean de France*, p. 422.

[64] Wilson, 'Anglo-French Relations', ch. II; *Choix de pièces*, p. 188.

king had in fact recognized the Lancastrian title as early as March 1400, but disapproval of the usurpation was widespread. In the autumn of 1401 Anglo-Scottish negotiations at Kirk Yetholm broke down immediately after the bishop of Glasgow had enquired whether the commissioners of the English king were willing to place Henry's right to the realm of England under arbitration.[65]

The elaboration of French policy was often in the hands of Louis, duc d'Orleans, whose growing network of friendships and alliances made him an increasingly formidable power. In 1401 he had entered into an elaborate friendship with Guillaume I de Juliers, duc de Gueldre, who in the late 1380s had been an ally of Richard II.[66] In January 1402 he retained David Lindsay, earl of Crawford, for life at one thousand marks a year and later helped to equip a fleet with which the Scottish admiral would harass English shipping between March and July 1402.[67] Crawford's following included at least thirty French men-at-arms, amongst them Jacques de Heilly, a veteran of Nicopolis, and Rasse de Renty. Heilly and three other French knights were amongst those listed as killed or captured after the battle of Humbleton Hill in September 1402, amongst the first French supporters of Richard II on English soil.[68]

In the early summer of 1402 Louis began his own personal campaign against Henry. On 19 May seven followers of the duke had successfully challenged seven 'English' knights at Montendre, north of Bordeaux. The *Religieux de St Denis*, Michel Pintoin, while noting the reluctance of the abbey to offer prayers

---

[65] E.L.G. Stones, 'The Appeal to History in Anglo-Scottish Relations between 1291 and 1401; part II', *Archives*, IX (1969), pp. 80–3; idem., *Anglo-Scottish Relations, 1174–1328* (1965), pp. 181–2.

[66] Guenée, *Un Meurtre*, p. 109; Palmer, *England, France and Christendom*, pp. 91–2; Richard Vaughan, *Philip the Bold. The Formation of the Burgundian State* (1962, reprinted 1979), pp. 98–101.

[67] Francisque-Michel, *Les Écossais en France. Les Français en Écosse* (1862), pp. 101–2; Ford, 'Piracy or Policy', pp. 72–5. The fleet's presence at Corunna in May is briefly noticed in *The Canarian, or, Book of the Conquest and Conversion of the Canarians in the year 1402, Jean de Bethencourt*, ed. Richard Henry Major, *Hakluyt Society*, 1st ser. XLVI (1872), pp. 4–6.

[68] *Historia Vitae et Regni Ricardi Secundi*, p. 174; Somerset County RO, Taunton, DD/1 P40/6 gives *le sire de Heillye franceys, Jaket de Haplee* and *Piers de Haresby chivalers Franceys* amongst those at Humbleton. The list is printed in *HMC*, 15, 10th Rep. VI, pp. 77–8. The capture of Pierre des Essarts is noticed in *Chronique du Religieux de Saint-Denys*, ed. M.L. Bellaguet (6 vols. Paris, 1839–52), III, pp. 44–6.

for victory, also reported how the French knights had taunted their adversaries with the ignominious manner of Richard II's death and attributed the implacable hatred of the French for the English to the inexcusable assassination of Richard and the indecorous expulsion of his queen.[69] On 7 August the duke issued the first of a series of personal challenges to Henry IV, suggesting a larger combat on the borders between Bordeaux and Angoulême.[70]

The three challenges, issued between August 1402 and October 1403, and the military campaigns of 1404 to 1406 are traditionally seen as idiosyncratic, what Bertrand Schnerb has described as 'une politique très personnelle'.[71] The *greffier* of the Paris parlement, enrolling the third challenge in November 1403, described it as 'he littere verbose et ventose, absque fructu et discretione'. Michel Pintoin, writing before 1420, felt that the audience of his chronicle would require only a few phrases to give the flavour of their texts; they had had, he explained, less result than the quarrels of old women.[72] But, frontier jousts and tournaments were common in England, Scotland and France in the years after the 1396 truce. In his more sympathetic introduction to the exchanges, Michel Pintoin recalled that since open war was not permitted during the Anglo-French truce and, since the duc d'Orleans could not allow the usurpation to go unavenged, the challenge provided an acceptable remedy. The second challenge, in March 1403, implied that Henry had been responsible for Richard's death; that of Waleran, comte de St Pol in November repeated the accusation. Both were by then part of a familiar litany in which the French too would resurrect Richard, championing the cause of a just king who would restore peace. In 1404, asked by islanders on the Isle of Wight why they had come, a French raiding party answered that they had come in the name of King Richard and Isabelle.[73]

---

[69] Ibid., III, pp. 30–4; Jarry, *Louis de France*, p. 285.

[70] *Chronique du Religieux de Saint-Denys*, III, pp. 54–60. The texts of two of the challenges, with Henry's replies, and a challenge of Waleran de St Pol, are printed in *Chroniques d'Enguerran de Monstrelet*, ed. L. Douët-d'Arcq (6 vols. Paris, 1857–62), I, pp. 43–57. A third is noted by Lehoux, *Jean de France*, II, pp. 523–4 who also corrects some of Monstrelet's dates.

[71] Bertrand Schnerb, *Les Armagnacs et les Bourguignons. La Maudite Guerre* (Paris, 1988), pp. 64–7.

[72] Lehoux, *Jean de France*, II, p. 523 n.8; *Chronique du Religieux de Saint-Denys*, III, p. 60.

[73] *Annales Henrici Quarti*, p. 381.

It has been argued that the changing character of the naval war from the summer of 1403, with raids on the Channel Islands, Plymouth, Dartmouth, Hornsea and the Isle of Wight, simply showed the formalization of hostility rather than its renewal.[74] But, French activity had seldom been on a greater scale. In August 1403 Robert of Bavaria wrote to Henry IV, warning that Louis, duc d'Orleans, had been urging German princes to provide troops for service against England.[75] From the winter of 1403 a naval squadron under Jean d'Espagne harassed English garrisons on the coasts of Wales, the treaty between Charles VI and Owain Glyn Dŵr in July 1404 promised a common league against Henry of Lancaster and in August 1405 a Franco-Welsh army advanced on Worcester.[76] This same period, beginning in the summer of 1402, also coincided with internal dissent on a massive scale. Here too the government of Henry IV saw the hand of the French and the shadow of Richard II.

The conspiracy of the countess of Oxford, memorably characterized by James Wylie as 'the commotion in Essex', did not in fact reach the level of public disorder.[77] Bartholomew Bourgchier and Sir William Coggeshall, the sheriffs of Essex and Hertfordshire, were appointed in the summer of 1404 to enquire into treasons and felonies committed in Essex after 28 November 1402. Inquisitions were held at Braintree and Colchester, and in January 1405 some twenty-five people appeared in King's Bench at Westminster.[78] Those implicated included Maud de Vere, countess of Oxford and members of her household, Henry Despenser, bishop of Norwich, the abbots of St John and St Botolph in Colchester, of St Osyth and Beeleigh, and a few Essex men from the vicinity of Colchester and Great Bentley. All were pardoned their involvement, a few, including the bishop of Norwich, not even indicted.

[74] Ford, 'Piracy or Policy', p. 77; G.A. Knowlson, *Jean V duc de Bretagne, et l'Angleterre* (Cambridge, 1964), pp. 42–5.

[75] Lehoux, *Jean de France*, pp. 520–1.

[76] J.E. Lloyd, *Owen Glendower* (Oxford, 1931), pp. 77–88, 101–6.

[77] Wylie, *Henry IV*, I, pp. 417–28. The incident is not considered in L.R. Poos, *A Rural Society after the Black Death: Essex 1350–1525* (Cambridge, 1991), pp. 231–62.

[78] PRO, E163/6/28; King's Bench, Coram Rege Rolls, KB27/575 mm.3, 4d, 5, 11; *SKB*, VII, pp. 151–5.

The substantive part of the conspiracy occurred over seven days in December 1403, first at the countess of Oxford's hall at Great Bentley. Here on 22 December, according to the confession of John Staunton, one of the countess's servants, he was ordered to ride with William Blith to Ipswich, showing him the country and the coast, the great bridges and, from Caldwell Hill, the road from Harwich along which a French army would ride on 28 December. On the appointed day he and Blith were to cast down the coastal beacons and to guide the army towards Northampton where the risen Richard II would meet them.[79] On the following day the two attended mass at St John's abbey in Colchester. According to the abbot of Beeleigh, who had been intercepted on his journey home from London, Abbot Geoffrey invited him to the abbey 'there for to syng a masse in þe forsayde abbey for there schold be al þe gentylis of þe contrey because of a solemn othe that þe forsayd abbot schold swere in declaration of his chirche.' Rather, the abbot preached on the subject of a prophecy that was shortly to be fulfilled.[80]

The conspiracy coincided with the French assaults on the south coast in December 1403 and the projected rising was planned to coincide with a landing by the duc d'Orleans, the comte de St Pol and Queen Isabelle in the Orwell. Newly-made signs of the white hart were distributed at Great Bentley and news of Richard's survival was preached at Colchester and in the Colne valley. Although no French landing took place, the conspiracy continued in the spring of 1404, the participants preaching that Richard would come out of Scotland to meet Owain Glyn Dŵr at Northampton.

The shrieval enquiry had, however, cast its net further afield than the two or three meetings in Essex, and the final presentment claimed that the invasion had been planned as early as November 1402.[81] The motivation behind the commissions had clearly been to reveal the extent of a wider conspiracy connecting the events in Essex with other risings against Henry in Richard's name, much as the Franciscan conspiracy of 1402 had been

---

[79] PRO, KB27/575, m.5d. The erection of *bekones* is noted in *Incerti Scriptoris Chronicon Angliae*, p. 36.
[80] PRO, E163/6/28 (15).
[81] *SKB*, VII, p. 151.

conflated into a single rebellion. Thus, the shrieval file comprised a series of other allegations which were not to find a place in the final indictment, including examinations of the monks at the Cistercian house at Revesby (Lincs.). Here John Boston claimed that the abbot, Henry Kay, had preached in June 1404 that there were 10,000 in England who believed that Richard was alive.[82]

Of events in Essex, Philip fitz Eustace claimed that the prior of St Botolph's in Colchester had ordered him to purvey horses at the time of the battle of Shrewsbury because all the country in the north had risen against the king, saying that Henry was not the true king, having been chosen by the mob of the city of London (*villanos civitatis*).[83] Simon Ward, one of the countess of Oxford's servants questioned at Halstead, asserted that Thomas Somerton, a London sadler, had known of the rebellion of Thomas Percy, earl of Worcester and Sir Henry Percy a long time before the event, and that John Russell, a servant of William Ayleway from Wixoe Hall in Suffolk, had told many people in Halstead that Richard was alive and would come with an army of Scots, Welsh and French on 28 June 1403.[84] The abbot of Beeleigh, confessing to a meeting with Blith in February 1404, reported that Blith had come to him in the guise of a knight on the advice of the earl of Northumberland. John Prittlewell too claimed that Blith had told him that he had fought at Shrewsbury with Sir Henry Percy and been knighted by him.[85]

Blith had himself implicated Henry Despenser, bishop of Norwich, claiming that the recorder of Southampton volunteered that were the French to land there in the name of King Richard they would be well received, and by the countess of Oxford in Essex and the bishop of Norwich in Suffolk.[86] Blith's allegation against Bishop Despenser was also put to John Prittlewell, at whose house the earl of Huntingdon had been arrested in 1400, but it was clearly

[82] PRO, E163/6/28 (8).
[83] PRO, E163/6/28 (6).
[84] PRO, E163/6/28 (13).
[85] PRO, E163/6/28 (12).
[86] PRO, E163/6/28 (16).

rejected. Indeed, the bishop's involvement seems highly unlikely.[87] Walsingham and the continuator of the *Eulogium* report that the abbots of St John's in Colchester and of St Osyth were implicated but make no mention of the bishop.[88] Had letters passed between the countess and Louis, duc d'Orleans and the other conspirators? This too seems unlikely.

Blith claimed to have seen the late king in Scotland and was clearly familiar with the arrangements made there for the keeping of the pseudo-Richard. Walsingham further attributed the countess's gullibility to forged signet letters issued by William Serle, one of Richard's former chamber esquires, who had fled first to the French court and then to Scotland. Letters, purportedly from Richard, were received in the Westminster parliament early in 1404, provoking the king to challenge any who said that Richard still lived.[89] In retrospect, Serle's confession, that he had stolen Richard's signet on the journey through Wales in September 1399, that the Scottish pseudo-Richard was an impostor, and his gruesome execution in the early summer of 1404, seemed to Walsingham to bring to an end to the 'chatter which had formerly flourished, not only amongst the crowd, but even in the king's own household'.[90] The continuator of the *Eulogium* was less sanguine, observing that the Scots stoked further rumours.[91]

Although the government of Henry IV had searched for evidence of conspiracy, it seems likely that there was often little more than a coincidence of common purpose and exculpation amongst those who espoused Richard's cause. The drift of the Percy family from support for Henry IV to rebellion in Richard's name is especially telling. Henry Percy, earl of Northumberland, and

---

[87] R.A. Edwards, 'Henry Despenser: the Fighting Bishop', *The Church Quarterly Review*, CLIX (1958), p. 36. Some of his private correspondence has survived, including a remarkable letter to a nephew in which he denied complicity in the rising of the earls in 1400. The nephew was not to speak of his defence since it seemed better not to rouse *le chien que dort*. *Anglo-Norman Letters and Petitions from All Souls MS. 182*, ed. M. Dominica Legge, *Anglo-Norman Text Society*, III (1941), pp. 113–15.

[88] *Historia Anglicana*, pp. 262–3; 416–17; *Eulogium Historiarum*, pp. 401–2.

[89] *Eulogium Historiarum*, p. 400.

[90] *Annales Henrici Quarti*, pp. 390–1.

[91] *Eulogium Historiarum*, pp. 402–3.

his son, Sir Henry Percy known as Hotspur, were amongst the chief actors in Richard's deposition. They had been witnesses to Henry's oath at Doncaster, and had perhaps earlier sought an oath on the relics at Bridlington to the effect that he had no ambition to take Richard's crown; the earl had been the chief instrument in bringing Richard into Henry's power between Conwy and Chester.[92] There is little sign that they had given credence to the movement for Richard's return or the promise of French aid before 1403.

In this context Henry, earl of Northumberland's two letters of May and June 1403, to the privy council and the king himself, warning of the military threat to the northern border from the overbearing pride of the Welsh, Scots and French, have been seen as somewhat disingenuous.[93] The first challenges of Louis, duc d'Orleans proposing a combat on the border of Guyenne had, however, perhaps been balanced by another proposing a combat on the Scottish border. The earl's response to such a challenge delivered by Guillaume du Chastel, the Breton lord later killed in the assault on Dartmouth in 1404, bears no hint of collaboration.[94] Like Henry's own response of December 1402, the earl's reply stressed that such a combat would be beneath the royal dignity and promised instead to offer the bright sword point of his own office as constable of England and warden of the marches. The language is redolent of the earl's own self-image as the biblical warrior and defender of the kingdom, Mathathias.[95] Nevertheless, at Chester in early July 1403 his son, Hotspur, had issued proclamations to the effect that Richard was alive and would join an army of his supporters, first at Sandiway in Delamere forest in Cheshire, and later at Prees in north Shropshire, in order to overthrow the usurper, Henry of Lancaster.[96]

[92] Sherborne, 'Perjury and the Lancastrian Revolution', pp. 221, 229–32.

[93] *PPC*, I, pp. 203–5.

[94] BL, Add. MS. 24062, Formulary of Thomas Hoccleve, f.140d. The letter is undated. Chastel's death is noticed in *Annales Henrici Quarti*, pp. 382–6.

[95] The Lanercost chronicler had likened Sir Henry Percy to Judas Maccabeus, the son of Matthathias, in his account of the battle of Neville's Cross in 1346, *Chronicon de Lanercost, 1201–1346*, ed. J. Stevenson, *Bannatyne Club* (Edinburgh, 1839), p. 347.

[96] Clarke and Galbraith, 'The Deposition of Richard II', pp. 177–8; BL, Cotton MS. Cleopatra F III, f.145.

The conversion of the Percies to the cause of Richard's ghost posed the single most serious threat to Henry's kingship. Unlike the seditious rumours which had characterized other 'risings', an English army now marched in the late king's name and outside Shrewsbury on 21 July 1403 would fight in his cause in the face of his usurper. Hotspur's neophyte army of warriors for the working day exemplifies the claim of Richard's ghost on the popular imagination. But, in the defiance, reported in the second version of John Harding's chronicle, the three Percies, 'keepers of the public good', rather accused Henry of oath-breaking in his seizure of the throne and of complicity in the king's murder at Pontefract.[97] For its principals, the Percy rising, like others before it, embraced a traditional loyalist agenda of support for the commonwealth, reform of royal government and the appointment of wise counsellors.[98] Richard's ghost was once more a pretext, the emblem for a lost and just king.

Support for Richard's ghost continued to feature amongst the claims of the earl of Northumberland and when in 1405 the earl again rose against the king it was, as the parliamentary Record and Process said, 'to sustain the right quarrel of King Richard, if he is alive, and to avenge his death if he is dead, against Henry of Lancaster regent of England'.[99] Archbishop Scrope too taxed Henry with the manner of his usurpation, accusing him of complicity in the death of Richard at Pontefract in the articles of excommunication issued in 1405.[100] After 1405 such support for Richard had an almost ritual quality amongst the political opponents of the Lancastrian dynasty. Richard, earl of Cambridge's conspiracy against Henry V, 'Henry of Lancaster, usurper of England', was, like the Percy rising of 1405, built on the prospect of the return of the Scottish pseudo-Richard.[101] The manner in which their title to the throne had been established was a perpetual opportunity for those who sought to challenge the Lancastrian kings.

---

[97] *The Chronicle of John Harding*, pp. 352–3.

[98] *Annales Henrici Quarti*, pp. 361–2.

[99] *RP*, III, p. 605b.

[100] Henry Wharton, *Anglia Sacra sive collectio historiarum de archiepiscopis et episcopis Angliae ad annum 1540* (2 vols. 1691), I, pp. 362–8.

[101] Pugh, *Henry V and the Southampton Plot*, pp. 161–2, 165–6, 172–3, 178–85; Christopher Allmand, *Henry V* (1992), p. 76.

By 1404 Henry IV had been afflicted by a ghost of Richard II sponsored by the late king's disenchanted familiars, by the just king of his political opponents, by the pseudo-Richard adopted by his enemies in Scotland and France, but also by a prophetic Richard whose second coming, in some versions, presaged the end of the world. Prophecy, astrology and preaching, that compelling mixture of predictions of the past and histories of the future, often in the service of present action, posed a wider threat than the few active conspiracies against Henry's crown and furnished the most durable of Richard's apparitions. Such was the source of the 'ceaseless clamour' of which Sir William Heron complained in 1402, and of the *continua murmor* reported in the case of John Whitelock in 1413.[102]

Thus far we have seen the degree to which the official response to Richard's ghost organized its apparitions into a series of connected political conspiracies. With the exception of the Shrewsbury campaign, however, the 'risings' in Richard's name seldom reached beyond the level of seditious rumour. What is significant too is the degree to which support for a prophetic Richard was anchored below what would normally be described as political society. John Sparrowhawk, executed in 1402, merely repeated the amateur prophecy of a Baldock tailor's wife about the imminent end of Henry's illegitimate rule: 'See how wet it is and what dreadful weather there is these days and has been all the time of the present king.'[103] A groom and sometime king's yeoman, who escaped the Tower and execution in 1413 for posting bills in support of the Scottish pseudo-Richard, addressed his audience, 'to alle other þat herith or seth this bille, in defaute of a bettir man I, John Wyghtlok'.[104]

The evident gap between the organizing principle of political conspiracy, which the royal courts employed to characterize continuing Ricardian sentiment, and the less precise motives of those indicted is nowhere more

---

[102] *SKB*, VII, p. 212.

[103] Ibid., VII, pp. 123–4; Isabel D. Thornley, 'Treason by words in the fifteenth century', *EHR*, XXXII (1917), pp. 556–61.

[104] *SKB*, VII, pp. 123–4; E. Powell, *Kingship, Law, and Society. Criminal Justice in the Reign of Henry V* (Oxford, 1989), pp. 137–9. Whitelock, it was asserted, had been active in Richard's cause as early as 1406.

evident than in the testimony of Henry Talbot of Easington in 1417. Charged with the abduction of Murdoch Stewart of Fife as part of a conspiracy in support of the pseudo-Richard, Talbot claimed that his 'intention and purpose [was] to destroy sin . . . on the advice of some of his confessors, as well bishops as other ecclesiastics'. To a charge of conspiracy with the Scots, the court record characterized Talbot's defence as 'a lot of oblique and suspicious words counter to the common law of England'. The record allows him one sentence of reported speech, 'As God wills, because God knows it'.[105] In such apparent fatalism we come nearer to an appreciation of the meaning of Richard's ghost.

The nature and significance of the political crises which marked English society in the years between 1381 and 1414 have been much debated by historians.[106] For contemporaries there is little doubt that the deposition and murder of the king were seen as inaugurating a period of profound disorder. But, whereas chroniclers like Walsingham wrote about these times within a narrative framework filled with astrology, prophecy and celestial influences, historians have been accustomed to see such diverse world views as of marginal importance, preferring narrowly to seek explanations in the changing patterns of constitutional politics.[107] Yet, if change and diversity could be explained by the erratic movements of the planets, the spread of prophecy, rumour and 'sedition', against which Henry IV's government apparently struggled, might indeed be a concerted campaign but could likewise represent no more than random but rational readings of the times.

The early years of Henry IV's reign indeed appeared to fulfil the chiliastic prophecies which had circulated during Richard's rule. Thomas Wimbledon, for example, who had preached at St Paul's Cross in 1388, offering in several senses an *ex eventu* comment on the brief first deposition of Richard II, reported

---

[105] *SKB*, VII, pp. 236–9; Powell, *Kingship, Law and Society*, pp. 137, 254.

[106] John Gillingham, 'Crisis or Continuity? The Structure of Royal Authority in England 1369–1422', *Das Spätmittelalterliche Königtum im Europäischen Vergleich*, ed. Reinhard Schneider (Sigmaringen, 1987), pp. 59–80; Powell, *Kingship, Law, and Society*, pp. 117–25.

[107] The point is made by Hilary M. Carey, *Courting Disaster. Astrology at the English Court and University in the Later Middle Ages* (1992), p. 94.

a common prophecy that the world would end in 1400.[108] The king's deposition and death in 1399, and the risings of 1400 appeared as confirmation; an unseasonal storm in 1402 was actually seen as heralding the final judgement. The apparent disorder of political society was matched by the progress of religious radicalism and by economic upheaval, the whole reflected and in part explained by celestial events and other natural prodigies. Thomas Walsingham's account of the year 1402 included reference to thunder storms, hail storms and whirlwinds, devilish apparitions in parish churches in Hertfordshire and Essex, magical devices and the flight of a comet across the northern sky, each presaging political events. The king himself was said to have narrowly escaped death during a hail storm in Wales.[109] In this respect, as John Sparrowhawk had discovered, politics and the weather were intimately connected. In fact, much of northern Europe was to experience unusual weather conditions and high mortality in the first years of the fifteenth century, with poor harvest yields and occasional famine.[110] At such moments prophecy, astrology and magic provided a rational explanation of the present and hope for the future.

The English court, as Hilary Carey has recently argued, was in fact receptive to astrology and seems to have paid some attention to prophetic visions and even to magic. William Norham, a Northumberland hermit, who had been imprisoned by Richard in 1399 after prophesying disaster, was granted similar privileged access to Henry IV at York in the summer of 1403, speaking, as Walsingham reports, with too little prudence at the cost of his life. Walter Bower, who calls him the 'White Hermit of England', tells us that the subject

---

[108] Nancy H. Owen, 'Thomas Wimbledon's Sermon: "Redde racionem villicacionis tue"', *Mediaeval Studies*, XXVIII (1966), pp. 183–4, 193–4. Wimbledon was perhaps the first to compare Richard to Solomon's son, Rehoboam, who had been deposed (1 Kings: 12) after refusing requests to lighten the burden of taxation, and having ignored the advice of his father's counsellors in favour of 'children that weren his pleiferen'. The analogy was later repeated by the Kirkstall chronicler, Adam of Usk and by the poet of *Mum and the Sothsegger*, Hilary M. Carey, *Courting Disaster*, p. 195 n.5.

[109] *Annales Henrici Quarti*, pp. 338–43; *Incerti Scriptoris Chronicon Angliae*, p. 28.

[110] Wilhelm Abel, *Agricultural Fluctuations in Europe from the Thirteenth to the Twentieth Centuries* (1980), p. 59; PRO, KB27/580, rex m.5v, riots in Bishop's Lynn concerning shipments of wheat to Bordeaux in October 1405.

was Henry's unlawful tenure of the crown and necessary abdication.[111] Norham's prophecy, not original, traced the succession to a devil, a saint, a sword and ultimately to oblivion.[112] Both Richard and Henry had also been among the principal supporters of Boniface IX's canonization of John of Bridlington to whom the early fourteenth-century Bridlington prophecies were routinely but mistakenly attributed. The prophecies were widely cited in support both of the deposition and of the return of the pseudo-Richard.[113]

The degree to which the new dynasty itself engaged in prophecy suggests that its importance has been underestimated as part of the diverse world views which shaped English political society. Henry himself featured in similar texts, notably the so-called Ampulla or Becket prophecy, in circulation since at least 1318, in which the Virgin Mary had appeared to St Thomas predicting the succession of an eagle and his coronation with holy oil. The prophecy was associated both with Richard II and with Henry, as prophets and astrologers sought confirmation of the new times.[114] Where such issues were a normal part of political dialogue, the past was always alive.

Astrology and prophecy were not inevitably fatalistic. Change was always possible. Richard's deposition and murder had unbalanced nature and inaugurated a period of disorder and decay to which the only remedy was the

[111] *Annales Henrici Quarti*, pp. 372–3; *Eulogium Historiarum*, p. 397; *Scotichronicon*, VIII, pp. 29, 161; Carey, *Courting Disaster*, pp. 94–5. He is named as William Norham in *Historia Anglicana*, p. 415. Peter McNiven, 'The Problem of Henry IV's Health, 1405–13', *EHR*, C (1985), p. 754, suggests that Bower's 'white hermit' may be identical with Roger Frisby, the master of theology with whom Henry had disputed in 1402, but the reference to a hermit is explicit. He is called the 'white hermit' to distinguish him from the Augustinian Hermits or Canons. Hermits who followed the rule of St Paul wore a brown habit over which a white scapular was worn, Virginia Davis, 'The Rule of Saint Paul, the First Hermit, in Medieval England', *Studies in Church History*, XXII (1985), p. 207.

[112] A similar prophecy, adding a fool between the sword and oblivion, is recorded in a book of prophecies of *c.* 1465 which makes Richard II the recipient; see John Webb, 'Translation of a French Metrical History of the Deposition of King Richard the Second', *Archaeologia*, XX (1824), appendix IV, pp. 256–60.

[113] Jonathan Hughes, *Pastors and Visionaries. Religion and Secular Life in Late Medieval Yorkshire* (Woodbridge, 1988), pp. 302–5; John Taylor, *English Historical Literature in the Fourteenth Century* (Oxford, 1987), pp. 239–42.

[114] Christopher Wilson, 'The Tomb of Henry IV and the Holy Oil of Canterbury', pp. 181–90.

just king who would bring peace and order. Thus Henry received advice on the reform of royal government, Philip Repingdon counselling him to remember the example of Richard II; his political opponents campaigned on manifestos which spoke likewise of the restoration of justice and order as also of retribution for the deposition and death of Richard II, and many could embrace the cause of a prophetic Richard as an overarching symbol of peace.[115] Certainly the politics of Franciscan preaching are more likely to be located here than in the conventional conspiracy to which they have usually been assigned.

Henry's usurpation had been a deplorable but not blameworthy act. His accession promised, but did not bring about, the re-establishment of peace and offered none of the traditional remedies for violence, neither repentance nor the search for pardon. Most of the chronicle accounts of the deposition of Richard II were written during the early years of Henry's reign when these issues were still unresolved; Richard's example, alive or dead, provided the inevitable framework of political debate. Amongst a literate political community Richard could be resurrected to give advice to the new king. Thus the author of *Richard the Redeless* and *Mum and the Sothsegger*, a 'loyal poet', twice reviewed Richard's reign in his advice to Henry IV: the recent past prefiguring the inevitable outcome of misrule, but offering too the possibility of reform.[116]

The risen Richard featured more widely, often as the returning hero, in the texts of prophetic literature which circulated throughout the kingdom.[117] The northern copyist of Laurence Minot's poems in British Library, MS. Cotton

---

[115] *Memorials of the Reign of King Henry VI: Official Correspondence of Thomas Bekynton*, ed. George Williams (RS, 2 vols. 1872), I, pp. 151–4; *The Chronicle of John Harding*, pp. 352–3; Henry Wharton, *Anglia Sacra*, I, pp. 362–8.

[116] Helen Barr, 'The Dates of *Richard the Redeless* and *Mum and the Sothsegger*', *Notes and Queries*, September 1990, pp. 270–5; Diane A. Facinelli, 'Treasonous Criticisms of Henry IV: The Loyal Poet of *Richard the Redeless* and *Mum and the Sothsegger*,' *Journal of the Rocky Mountain Medieval and Renaissance Association*, X (1989), pp. 51–62; Helen Barr, 'A Study of *Mum and the Sothsegger* and its Political and Literary Contexts' (2 vols. unpub. Oxford D.Phil. thesis, 1989), I, pp. 21–86.

[117] Rupert Taylor, *The Political Prophecy in England* (New York, 1911), pp. 58–9, 87–8, 99–100, 155–6.

Galba E IX, hostile to Henry IV, and who was apparently knowledgeable of the
Tripartite indenture of 1405, alludes to Richard's ghost in his 'prediction' of
Richard's rule:

> His voice and his criyng als I understand
> sall be herd swith wele in euerilka land.[118]

While the reception of such texts amongst a popular audience is difficult to
recover, the appearances of Richard's ghost do follow the common typology of
pretender kings. Henry's usurpation was confirmd by the palpable injustice of
his rule and could only be explained by the survival of the true king. Such kings
inevitably wandered at the margins of political society, on this occasion in
Wales, Scotland, Brittany, Berwick and Chester. Remote appearances were
characterized by letters from the dead to the living, by inventive explanations
for absence and by a just and reforming political agenda. Social distress and
political crisis added to a favourable atmosphere for manifestations.[119]

Solutions to the continuing problems of Richard's ghost remained elusive,
and random sightings continued into the reign of Henry V.[120] In the parliament
of 1402 the king had acceded to a Commons' petition, one of fifteen relating to
the political impact of Glyn Dŵr's rising, against poets and minstrels whose
prophecies were blamed for the outbreak of the Welsh rebellion.[121] In the final
session of the 1406 parliament a petition introduced on behalf of Prince Henry
and the Lords, praising the lost peaceable governance of England, associated
those who preached that Richard was still alive with other forms of religious

---

[118] *The Poems of Laurence Minot*, ed. Joseph Hall (3rd ed., Oxford, 1914), pp. 103–11; V.J.
Scattergood, *Politics and Poetry in the Fifteenth Century* (1971), pp. 117–19; *The Poems of Laurence Minot
1333–1352*, ed. Thomas Beaumont James and John Simons (Exeter, 1989), pp. 6–8; Taylor, *The
Political Prophecy*, pp. 48–51, 157–64; Taylor, *English Historical Literature*, pp. 242–3.

[119] I have been influenced here by Philip Longworth, 'The Pretender Phenomenon in
Eighteenth-Century Russia', *Past and Present*, LVI (1975), pp. 61–83. I owe the reference to my
colleague, David Laven.

[120] Allmand, *Henry V*, pp. 18, 76, 287–8, 308–10, 406.

[121] *RP*, III, p. 508b.

radicalism, and sought action against false prophecies. Such temporary measures were reviewed by Archbishop Arundel in 1407 and confirmed in the terms of his Constitutions of 1409.[122]

Episcopal licensing could, of course, do little to control the random preaching and prophesying in communities where Richard's ghost circulated as the unifying rubric of local social and economic discontent. In 1407 bills in support of Richard, who was said to be on the point of return in 'magnificence and glory', were published in London and fixed to the doors of St Paul's.[123] At this moment Archbishop Arundel favoured a pragmatic solution, to the effect that the return of the pseudo-Richard be a condition of Anglo-Scottish negotiations then in progress.[124] His advice was not taken. Indeed, as Henry must have known, it would not have lain the ghost to rest. As the king's confessor, John Tille, reportedly advised him on his death-bed in 1413, penance had to be done for Richard's death and for þe wrong titil of þe crowne.[125] Penance and renunciation were not merely the recurring theme of ecclesiastical commentators. Without that public remedy the shadow of the late king had overlain the whole of his successor's reign.

[122] Ibid., III, p. 583a, b; Margaret Aston, 'Lollardy and Sedition, 1381–1431', in *Lollards and Reformers* (1984), p. 42.

[123] *Historia Anglicana*, p. 276; *The St. Albans Chronicle*, p. 11.

[124] BL, Cotton MS. Vespasian F vii, fo.88, printed in Thomas Amyot, 'A Reply to Mr Tytler's "Historical Remarks on the Death of Richard II"', *Archaeologia*, XXIII (1831), pp. 297–8.

[125] *John Capgrave's Abreuiacion of Cronicles*, ed. Peter J. Lucas (EETS, CCLXXXV, 1983), pp. lxxxv–vi, 238.

2

LANCASTRIAN ROYAL SERVICE, LOLLARDY AND FORGERY: THE CAREER OF THOMAS TYKHILL*

Maureen Jurkowski

Gentry involvement in early Lollardy is a subject which has received some noteworthy attention from historians in the post-McFarlane era.[1] Michael Wilks has recharacterized Lollardy as originally a court-based, lay reform movement,[2] and in a similar vein, Peter McNiven has analysed the political reasons why, while gaining allies among their supporters, the movement failed to find champions in Henry IV and Henry V.[3] Their findings have perhaps come to a logical conclusion in Edward Powell's recent interpretation of the 1414 revolt as a personal vendetta against Henry V, incited by his betrayal of his retainer Sir John Oldcastle.[4] With this background in mind, this paper offers a prosopographical approach to the subject in considering the experience of one individual – the lawyer Thomas Tykhill of Aston-on-Trent, Derbyshire.

* I am grateful for comments on an earlier version of this paper made by Dr Peter McNiven.

[1] In addition to those cited below, an invaluable study to which this paper is much indebted is C. Kightly, 'The Early Lollards: A Survey of Popular Lollard Activity in England, 1382–1428' (unpub. York D. Phil thesis, 1975).

[2] M. Wilks, 'Royal Priesthood: The Origins of Lollardy', in *The Church in a Changing Society: Proceedings of the CIHEC Conference, Uppsala 1977* (Uppsala, 1978), pp. 63–70.

[3] P. McNiven, *Heresy and Politics in the Reign of Henry IV: The Burning of John Badby* (Bury St Edmunds, 1987).

[4] E. Powell, *Kingship, Law, and Society: Criminal Justice in the Reign of Henry V* (Oxford, 1989), pp. 145–9, 156. This diagnosis of the revolt was first made by the chronicler Thomas Walsingham: *Historia Anglicana, 1272–1422*, ed. H.T. Riley (RS, 2 vols. 1863–64), II, p. 297. I thank Professor Christopher Allmand for pointing this out to me.

The origins of the lesser gentry family of Tykhill in southern Derbyshire are obscure but the family was undoubtedly related to the Tickhills of Tickhill in south Yorkshire, three of whose members had been royal clerks in the early fourteenth century.[5] Thomas first surfaces in a 1389 land conveyance in Aston-on-Trent,[6] and clearly belonged to the branch of the family which had settled in nearby Chellaston by the early fourteenth century.[7] During Richard II's reign he acquired legal training, probably at an inn of court or Chancery, and by April 1399 was employed as an attorney by John Burghill, bishop of Coventry and Lichfield.[8] However, like many lawyers from the Midlands, it was the ascendancy of the Lancastrians which brought about the rapid rise in his fortunes. Appointed first to John of Gaunt's 1398 peace commission, he continued to serve as a Derbyshire justice of the peace from 1401 until his arrest in January 1414.[9] The county's predominant landowner, the duchy of Lancaster, paid him to represent its interests at assizes in Derbyshire, Leicestershire and Staffordshire, and to advise its council as an apprentice-at-law from 1409 to 1416.[10]

Much more important, however, was his role in the Prince of Wales's administration. From 1405 to 1414 he was chief steward of the 'north parts' of all the prince's lands in the principality of Wales, the earldom of Chester and the duchy of Cornwall.[11] His Welsh landed income uncollectable during the Glyn Dŵr revolt, the Prince of Wales was forced to rely heavily upon his

---

[5] J.L. Grassi, 'Clerical Dynasties from Howdenshire, Nottinghamshire and Lindsey in the Royal Administration, 1280–1340' (unpub. Oxford D.Phil. thesis, 1960), pp. 486–9.

[6] D(erbyshire) RO, D779B/T72–73.

[7] As a Chellaston tenant he owed suit at the duchy of Lancaster court from 1390: PRO, Duchy of Lancaster, Court Rolls, DL30/45/536, rot. 1d. For the early Tykhills in Derbyshire: DRO, D2375M/101/3; D779B/T71; Sheffield City Archives, Bagshawe Collection, 2469.

[8] *CPR, 1396–99*, p. 531. Appointed during Burghill's stay in Ireland with Richard II, he probably remained a member of the bishop's council until 1405 when Burghill sued him for the return of muniments in his possession: PRO, Court of Common Pleas, Plea Rolls, CP40/577, rot. 7d.

[9] *CPR, 1396–99*, p. 531; *1399–1401*, p. 558; *1401–5*, p. 516; *1405–8*, p. 490; *1413–16*, p. 418.

[10] He was a feed retainer only from 1411: PRO, Duchy of Lancaster, Ministers'Accounts, DL29/730/12, 015; PRO, Duchy of Lancaster, Miscellaneous Books, DL42/17, ff. 72v, 88, 101; PRO, Duchy of Lancaster, Accounts Various, DL28/4/7, ff. 10v, 22v–23; 4/8, ff. 10, 22, 36v, 39; 4/9, ff. 11, 13v.

[11] PRO, Special Collections, Ministers' Accounts, SC6/813/23, ff. 5–5v.

administrative officers to channel revenue from Chester and the duchy of Cornwall to a central fund and 'secret' treasury to finance the war effort and pay the household expenses.[12] A surviving account shows that Thomas Tykhill was very active as chief steward, for which he was paid £20 per annum and expenses. From November 1405 until Christmas 1408 he spent a total of 76 days in Cheshire and 117 days in other counties, although payment of his expenses was far in arrears.[13] His authority and duties as chief steward were manifold and wide ranging. They included appointing local officials, approving payments, holding inquisitions into lands, overseeing sales and purchases, receiving rent monies and imposing peace bonds on tenants.[14] Closely connected was his appointment in 1406 to supervise the mass submission of the rebels in Anglesey. Having travelled with an armed force to retake the island, he later held a grand inquisition to assess the level of fines to be levied on the rebels and the value of the lands of those killed. As more than 2,100 rebels surrendered, this was a large-scale operation.[15] Thomas Tykhill was also a paid member of the prince's council at 5 marks per annum, approving warrants and petitions, and collecting revenue in that capacity.[16] It too was a key role, as the council took a strong hand in matters relating to the prince's lands, particularly in Cheshire during the Welsh war, and was consulted on all major decisions whether residing in Chester or at Westminster.[17]

[12] W.R.M. Griffiths, 'Prince Henry, Wales, and the Royal Exchequer, 1400–13', *Bulletin of the Board of Celtic Studies* (hereafter *BBCS*), XXXII (1985), pp. 204–15.

[13] PRO, SC6/813/23, ff. 5–5v. In 1408 he was owed £48 16s 8d for expenses of 6s 8d per day for duty in Cheshire and 4s elsewhere.

[14] *The Thirty-Sixth Annual Report of the Deputy Keeper of the Public Records* (1875), p. 399; PRO, SC6/775/5, m. 1d; 1216/2, m. 4; 792/5, m. 9d; 775/6, m. 2d; 775/11, m. 2d; 1216/2, m. 2; 1233/1, m. 4d; 1191/7, m. 1; 1191/9, m. 1; 1152/5, m. 5; PRO, Exchequer, King's Remembrancer, Miscellanea, E163/6/41, m. 02; PRO, Palatinate of Chester, Recognisance Rolls, Ches2/78, m. 5; 81, m. 7.

[15] PRO, SC6/775/5, m. 1d; G. Roberts, 'The Anglesey Submissions of 1406' *BBCS* XV (1952), pp. 39–61. He was involved in the effort to collect the fines as well: PRO, SC6/1216/2, m. 2.

[16] PRO, E163/6/41, mm. 00, 01, 022; PRO, SC6/813/23, ff. 1v, 3v, 5; 813/24, m. 1d.

[17] A.E. Curry, 'The Demesne of the County Palatine of Chester in the Fifteenth Century' (unpub. Manchester M.A. thesis, 1977), pp. 39–40.

Meanwhile, in February 1410 Tykhill formally entered into the service of the crown itself when he was appointed the king's attorney in the court of Common Pleas, at an annual fee of £10. He was authorized to prosecute and defend the king's interests in all suits brought before this court and in Exchequer and Chancery proceedings as well.[18] Related to this office was his frequent appointment to judicial and other commissions concerned with the king's revenue; he was no doubt an expert in matters of land law and crown rights.[19] Although it was ostensibly a powerful position, the status of the king's attorney within the hierarchy of law officers was imprecise. He was not on a par with the privileged serjeants-at-law, but Henry IV's grant of a serjeant's livery to him in February 1412 implies a conscious effort to raise the office's prestige.[20]

Although he held these positions of power and prestige, he did not reap substantial financial benefits – certainly not on the scale of many of his contemporaries. There is no evidence that he received any form of landed endowment from the crown, the prince or the duchy of Lancaster, nor was he given custody of any of the wardships or forfeitures vigorously pursued at Westminster by lawyers and clerks. There are likewise few traces of his participation in the common forms of casual employment for men of his ilk – land conveyancing, mainprising, money-lending and other speculative endeavours.[21] To all appearances he was a hard-working and under-rewarded

---

[18] *CPR, 1408–13*, p. 163; *Select Cases in the Court of King's Bench*, ed. G.O. Sayles (Selden Society, VI, 1965) pp. xc–xci; PRO, Exchequer, Exchequer of Receipt, Issue Rolls, E403/6/611, m. 6; PRO, Exchequer, Exchequer of Pleas, Plea Rolls, E13/127, rots. 7d, 18; PRO, Chancery, Early Chancery Proceedings, C1/6/43; PRO, Chancery, Placita in Cancellaria, Tower Series, C44/23, mm. 4, 5.

[19] *CFR, 1399–1405*, pp. 251–4; *CPR, 1408–13*, pp. 172, 182, 227, 431, 475; *1413–16*, p. 148; PRO, Exchequer, Lord Treasurer's Remembrancer, Originalia Rolls, E371/177, rots. 14–15; 179, rot. 21.

[20] *CPR, 1408–13*, p. 371. Technically an apprentice-at-law, he received only half the serjeants' wages. His successor, William Babington, was from 1417 both the king's attorney and a serjeant: PRO, E403/630, m. 4.

[21] The only examples: land agent – PRO, Justices Itinerant, Assize Rolls, JUST1/1514, rot. 48d; *Derbyshire Feet of Fines 1323–1546*, ed. H.J.H. Garratt and C. Rawcliffe (Derbyshire Record Society, 1985), no. 1027; mainprising – *CFR, 1399–1405*, p. 161; PRO, CP40/553, rot. 329d; PRO, JUST1/1514, rots. 5d, 9; PRO, Chancery, Special Bail Pardons, C237/29, m. 86; PRO, Court of King's Bench, Coram Rege Rolls, KB27/594, rot. 16 rex; PRO, CP40/603, rot. 343.

civil servant. At his accession in 1413, Henry V confirmed his tenure of the posts of king's attorney and chief steward[22] but took away one of the few visible privileges which Henry IV had granted to him, by transferring the duchy of Lancaster fishing rights in Melbourne, Derbyshire, to Peter Melbourne, an already well-rewarded duchy officer. Tykhill apparently resented this slight, for the king was forced to write to him, demanding that he allow Melbourne to enjoy these rights.[23]

Information on Thomas Tykhill's landed estate is scant, but a pattern can be discerned of piecemeal acquisition of lands in Aston-on-Trent, Marston, Wilne and the manor of Shardlow, adjoining his patrimony in Chellaston and Melbourne.[24] His Derbyshire estate was assessed for tax purposes in 1412 at £40 annually and was compacted in one small area of the county[25] with a few holdings across the borders in Castle Donington, Leicestershire[26] and Tutbury, Staffordshire. He was married by 1396 to Agnes, who brought him lands previously held by John Duffield of Tutbury (presumably a relation of hers), which included a house in Scropton, a laundry place on the Dove river and a market stall for selling goblets in the town of Tutbury.[27] Chellaston was an important site of alabaster carving and quarrying, and a series of debt suits brought by Tykhill against the well-known carver and exporter, Thomas

---

[22] *CPR, 1413–16*, pp. 9, 107.

[23] The letter to Tykhill is dated 8 October, the grant to Melbourne had been made the previous April: PRO, DL42/17, ff. 1, 72. Henry IV had also provided Tykhill with timber from duchy parks in 1409: DL42/16, f. 260v. For Melbourne's rewards, see PRO, DL42/15, ff. 1v, 6v, 59 and PRO, Special Collections, Ancient Correspondence, SC1/43/156.

[24] From 1389: DRO, D779B/T72–3, 75–87 (Aston); *Inquisitions and Assessments relating to Feudal Aids 1284–1431* (6 vols. 1899), I, pp. 298, 301 (Marston and Wilne); DRO, D779B/T88, 90; PRO, DL42/17, f. 121v (Shardlow); PRO, DL30/45/531, rots. 1, 3; PRO, CP40/551, rot. 560; 903, rot. 338 (Chellaston); PRO, DL42/4, ff. 99 (Scropton); 115; PRO, DL30/46/536, rot. 1d (Melbourne).

[25] *Feudal Aids*, VI, p. 413 (with the exception of an estate in Astwith in Ault Hucknall, 15 miles north-east of Derby: PRO, CP40/548, rot. 75).

[26] PRO, DL42/17, ff. 121v, 134v.

[27] DRO, D779B/T76; PRO, DL42/4, ff. 99, 119. His association with the Duffields dated from at least 1394: Derby Central Library, Every Deed 3203.

Prentys, suggests that he was involved in business relating to this trade.[28] Indeed, he may have owned the 'plaster pit' which existed still in nineteenth-century Aston,[29] and his complaint in 1424 that a labourer named Richard Plasterer had illegally left his service there supports this conjecture.[30]

Other activities imply that Tykhill had less worldly concerns. In 1410 Thomas and Agnes Tykhill began sheltering the Lollard preacher, William Ederyk, who preached throughout southern Derbyshire, specifically in Derby, nearby Chaddesden and in towns where the Tykhills owned property – namely in Aston, Tutbury[31] and Castle Donington. The Tykhills' maintenance of Ederyk was apparently well known, as the chaplain was also called William 'Tykelpriest'. Ederyk preached in various towns in Leicestershire as well, coming to the notice of Bishop Repingdon during the latter's 1413 visitation. At Castle Donington, twelve parishioners stated that Ederyk had preached in the church on Easter Sunday in 1413 and this had brought him at least one disciple, a 'sutor' named John Anneys. Reportedly, Anneys expounded in taverns and other public places that one need not confess all one's sins to a priest and that all bishops and doctors serving the church were fools and everyone knew it. Although he was forced to purge himself before Repingdon and abjure Ederyk's company, Tykhill's protégé was not himself summoned.[32]

Perhaps anticipating such enquiries, in March 1413 Thomas and Agnes Tykhill purchased a papal indult for a portable altar which may have been meant to legitimize their sponsorship of Ederyk.[33] By autumn 1413 open

---

[28] PRO, CP40/608, rot. 10d; 611, rots 10, 344; 615, rot. 604d; 617, rot. 323; 618, rot. 45; 619, rot. 62; 635, rot. 553d; 636, rot. 331; 637, rot. 333d; 638, rot. 69d. Moreover, he had stood surety in 1411 for Prentys's court appearance in another suit: CP40/603, rot. 343. On Prentys, see N.L. Ramsay, 'Alabaster' in *English Medieval Industries: Craftsmen, Techniques, Products*, ed. W.J. Blair and N.L. Ramsay (1991), pp. 30–4.

[29] Aston's quarry is shown on the first edition of the one-inch Ordnance Survey map, Nottingham, Sheet 35 (1836), reprinted by David & Charles (Newton Abbot, 1970).

[30] PRO, CP40/652, rot. 337d.

[31] PRO, Court of King's Bench, Ancient Indictments, KB9/204/1, mm. 59–61.

[32] Kightly, 'The Early Lollards', pp. 32–4, cf. Lincolnshire Archives Office, Visitation Book Vj/o, ff. 10, 14–14v, 16–16v. In addition to having an influential patron, Ederyk could easily slip in and out of Repingdon's jurisdiction.

[33] *CPL, 1404–15*, VI, p. 344.

support of Lollardy had indeed become dangerous, with the arrest, trial and escape of Sir John Oldcastle, and on 30 December, dressed in armour, Ederyk led a party of men to London to participate in the planned revolt. His group was made up of four tradesmen from nearby Thulston, to whom he promised wages of 13s 4d; two other local men are also known to have taken part. Following the rebels' defeat, Ederyk was able to avoid capture and eventually returned to Aston where Thomas Tykhill allegedly gave him shelter on 2 February; he remained at large until the end of 1414 when he was imprisoned in Kenilworth castle by mandate of the king's household steward, Sir Roger Leche.[34] Despite his prominent role and probably through Tykhill's influence, he obtained a pardon in January 1415 and disappeared into obscurity.[35]

By this time Thomas Tykhill had already been dealt with. Removed immediately from his post as king's attorney, he had been arrested by 25 January on the king's special order and imprisoned in the Tower with other suspected gentry sympathizers.[36] He remained there until May 1414, although he was given liberty to live unchained in houses within the Tower after 1,000-mark surety bonds were posted on his behalf in Chancery and he agreed not to attempt to escape.[37] At that point he was released, again under a 1,000-mark bond, pending a promise by mainpernors to have him in Chancery on a prescribed date.[38] It is likely that he appeared on that day, paid a sum to

[34] Significantly, just after Tykhill's acquittal in Michaelmas 1414: PRO, Court of King's Bench, Recorda, KB145/5/2/1; see below. Moreover, Leche was a friend of Tykhill's: see below.

[35] A writ dated 26 January 1415 ordering his transfer from Kenilworth to Westminster noted that he already possessed a pardon: PRO, KB145/5/2/1. Ederyk's group (Thomas Chapman, thatcher; John Lete, smith; Thomas Mason, mason; and John Webster, weaver) was also pardoned: KB9/204/1, mm. 57–66; KB27/614, rots 5, 45 rex; 615, rots 23, 36d rex; 616, rot. 7 rex; PRO, Chancery, Special Bail Pardons, C237/37, mm. 9, 67, 111; *CPR, 1413–16*, p. 200.

[36] *CPR, 1413–16*, p. 150; PRO, KB27/611/13 rex.

[37] *CCR, 1413–19*, pp. 116, 121. His mainpernors included his kinsman Thomas Tykhill, a London mercer who was originally from Tickhill, Yorkshire, and who was involved in 1415 with another Lollard: PRO, Prerogative Court of Canterbury, Registered Copies of Wills, PCC 44 Marche; Kightly, 'The Early Lollards', pp. 520–2.

[38] *CCR, 1413–19*, p. 124; PRO, Chancery, Recognisances, C259/7, m. 5. The exact date of this recognisance is unknown, but was clearly before 22 May.

guarantee his future behaviour and was freed on condition that he purge himself of heresy before his ordinary. His indictment in February 1414 before specially appointed commissioners in both Derbyshire and London-Middlesex thus became a mere formality. The Derbyshire records cite his maintenance of Ederyk, while the Middlesex indictment accused him of complicity in the revolt itself. But by the time the case came to trial in October 1414 he had already satisfied the king in Chancery and the jurors were no doubt instructed to acquit him by the 'serjeant-at-law and his attorneys' present at the trial. Tykhill thus went free on 26 October.[39]

Remarkably, Thomas Tykhill now became the chief steward of the dower lands of Queen Joan, widow of Henry IV, taking over from Sir William Esturmy who had been chief steward since 1411.[40] Tykhill's tenure of this office is revealed in only two sources. The first is the 1414–15 account of the queen's Northamptonshire receiver, where it was stated that the £34 fee farm for the castle and manor of Moor End, which had formed part of the queen's dower since 1408,[41] had not been received because the queen had granted it to her chief steward, Thomas Tykhill.[42] By autumn 1416 Esturmy was again chief steward, as revealed by the expense accounts he submitted for the years 1416 to 1425.[43] From all of Esturmy's expense accounts and the Northampton account we can deduce that Tykhill's tenure was two years, from Michaelmas 1414 to Michaelmas 1416.

The second reference to Tykhill as chief steward occurs in a warrant issued under the king's signet dated 4 January 1417 which made it clear that Tykhill was no longer in the queen's employ. The chancellor was ordered to issue a warrant for his arrest and to have him brought before the chief justice of both

[39] PRO, KB9/204/1, mm. 58–61; KB27/614, rot. 15 rex.

[40] PRO, SC6/1051/16, rots 2, 6–7. Esturmy's annual fee of office had been 100 marks, two robes and a £20 reward for maintenance of his household.

[41] *CPR, 1405–8*, p. 438. On the castle of Moor End see *The History of the King's Works*, ed. H.M. Colvin (3 vols. 1963–75), II, pp. 742–5.

[42] PRO, SC6/948/11.

[43] PRO, SC6/1295/1/3 (1416/17); 1295/1/4 (1417/18); 1051/17 (1419 and 1422 to 1425). For 1411 to 1414: SC6/1051/16.

the Common Pleas and King's Bench, the chief baron of the Exchequer, and the queen's council, to answer complaints which the queen had made against him. She had alleged that while he was chief steward, Tykhill had taken her great seal of office as well as various chests containing account books, letters patent and other evidence from her treasury and that he was still retaining them on his own authority for deceitful purposes.[44] Simultaneously, Joan initiated process against Tykhill in the court of Common Pleas. A *capias* writ returnable in Hilary 1417 by the sheriff of Middlesex, complained that Tykhill was unjustly detaining from her *quendam librum precii mille marcarum*. Neither this nor a second writ compelled Tykhill's appearance but the action was, nevertheless, abandoned after Easter,[45] when the seal and documents were probably returned; the seal had certainly reappeared by December 1417.[46]

However, by Hilary 1419 the queen was complaining of another problem which had undoubtedly resulted from this situation and related to the return of a writ due on a new action she had personally brought in Common Pleas. Here she claimed that Tykhill had conspired with Thomas Davy, a scrivener of Kent, and contravened a 1413 statute by forging deeds threatening her title to the castle and manor of Moor End. By Easter 1419 *capias* writs were being sent without success to both the Derbyshire and London sheriffs, but after Trinity term Joan's attorney failed to appear.[47] This fact does not signify that remedy had been obtained, but rather that, for allegedly plotting the king's murder, the queen was being held in custody in Rotherhithe castle by 1 October and that her dower lands had been confiscated.[48]

What exactly had happened and why? We begin by asking what the duties of the chief steward were and why Thomas Tykhill was appointed to the position. From Sir William Esturmy's 1413–14 expense accounts[49] we see that his duties

---

[44] PRO, Chancery, Warrants for the Great Seal, Series I, C81/1364/24.

[45] PRO, CP40/624, rot. 194; 625, rot. 60d.

[46] It was applied to a warrant on 15 December: PRO, SC6/1062/27.

[47] PRO, CP40/632, rots. 166, 440d; 633, rot. 200. All of the writs were either returned with the endorsement that Tykhill was not found or were not returned at all.

[48] A.R. Myers, 'The Captivity of a Royal Witch: The Household Accounts of Queen Joan of Navarre, 1419–21', *BJRL*, XXIV (1940), pp. 262–84.

[49] PRO, SC6/1051/16, rots 2–5.

were to oversee repairs and building works to the queen's castles, and to negotiate her business with crown officials. His minutely detailed accounts predominantly catalogue food, drink, riding and lodging expenditure, but some payments relate directly to the business he was undertaking. For example, one journey was to Leicester during the parliament of May–June 1414. As ordered by the queen and her council, his purpose was to *prosequend penes regem pro divers arduuo negociis dictam reginam tangent,* and to this end he made a gift of 3*s* 7*d* to the clerk of the privy seal, almost certainly for the purchase of writs authorizing the payment of arrears on various sources of her income.[50] Other journeys included a seventeen-day trip to London in September to consult with the king's council, and attendance at a *novel disseisin* assize in Salisbury.[51]

One item disallowed by the queen's council was for breakfasts purchased in London from 23 to 26 January 1414 for divers justices, serjeants and apprentices-at-law. At these sessions (the medieval equivalent of the American 'power breakfast'), Esturmy showed them various enrolled grants and other evidence of the queen's lands for the purpose of having them amended, copied and re-enrolled, following the accession of the new king. Total expenditure was £10 6*s* 8*d* and Esturmy attached an itemized list of the food and drink consumed. It may have been the lavish scale of the veritable feasts to which the queen's council objected – large quantities of roasted pheasants, birds, meats, game and poultry were served, along with French bread, pasties, and delicate creams and jellies.[52] This extravagance, however, ultimately served little purpose. The queen's dower had been set by parliament in 1406 at 10,000 marks per annum. More than a third of her annual income – some 3,910 marks – had been

---

[50] *CCR, 1413–19*, p. 127 (dated 22 June); PRO, Exchequer, King's Remembrancer, Brevia Baronibus, E208/12 (unnumbered writs dated 26 June), ordering the allowance for payment of arrears in the accounts of the wool customers at the ports of Southampton, Boston and Great Yarmouth, and the petty customers at Southampton, Bristol and London.

[51] At the latter he distributed bribes of 33*s* 4*d* to several apprentices-at-law and jurors: PRO, SC6/1051/16, rot. 2.

[52] The last two items were considered fine dishes: B.A. Henisch, *Fast and Feast: Food in Medieval Society* (Pennsylvania, 1976), pp. 122, 131. It was a good deal more than that spent on breakfasts for the duchy of Lancaster council convened for pleas in 1411, 1412 and 1416: PRO, Duchy of Lancaster, Accounts Various, DL28/4/7, ff. 11, 22v–23; 4/9, f. 13v.

lost by 1414 largely through recoveries at law, and part of Esturmy's task was to seek (or certainly to finalize) compensatory grants for their loss. His success is documented by letters patent enrolled on 27 January.[53] Most of the new revenue was to be derived from lands and possessions of the alien priories, and as the king had decided by early 1415 to reassign the most lucrative of these to support his new religious foundations, and as two of Joan's manors were forfeitures to be restored to the Percy heir, a further dower adjustment was required, effectively nullifying Esturmy's effort. The results of this second adjustment were enrolled on 1 April 1415 and must have been accomplished by Thomas Tykhill, who had by then replaced Esturmy.[54] Esturmy's expense account was not rendered until after Michaelmas term 1415, well after the second adjustment, by which time the queen's council would have been less inclined to allow these expenditures.[55]

These events effectively explain why Esturmy was replaced by Tykhill. The bidding and brokering process by which forfeitures, wardships, and the other spoils of crown patronage made their way from the Exchequer to the Chancery is not entirely clear,[56] but that this process was ultimately controlled by

[53] *RP*, III, p. 577a; *CPR, 1413–16*, pp. 164–7.

[54] *CPR, 1413–16*, p. 340. The alien priories of Ware, Noyon and Neufmarché and the possessions of the Norman abbey of Lyre worth altogether £357 6s 8d were transferred to the Carthusian foundation of Sheen: E.M. Thompson, *The Carthusian Order in England* (1930), pp. 238–9. The alien priory of Otterton and the alien manors of Throwley, Chilham and Molash with a total annual income of £306 13s 4d passed through feoffees to Syon Abbey: *CPR, 1413–16*, p. 395; PRO, Exchequer, Treasury of Receipt, Council and Privy Seal Records, E28/33, m. 73. The Percy manors of Petworth and Heshott together represented £96 per annum.

[55] PRO, SC6/1051/16. He rendered a bulk account covering the period from 1403 to 1415 – as chief steward from 1411 to 1414, and as farmer of two of the queen's manors from 1403 to 1415. A marginal note beside the disallowed item stated that Esturmy had no warrant, but it is very doubtful that he had acted on his own initiative.

[56] Whether or not all negotiations took place before finalization with the king's legal officers in Chancery is uncertain. The procedure followed under Henry IV whereby the queen formally petitioned the king in parliament for new lands (PRO, Special Collections, Ancient Petitions, SC8/23/1116; *RP*, III, p. 632a) had been largely abandoned under Henry V. Both Chancery and the Exchequer were involved in earlier stages, where presumably many deals were made. The initial valuation was commissioned by Chancery, after which the Exchequer barons fixed the rents of custody awards: A.L. Brown, *The Governance of Late Medieval England, 1272–1461* (1989), p. 57.

attorneys in Chancery[57] is evident in the accounts of Esturmy, if nowhere else. A wealthy and influential knight who had served as a household steward and ambassador,[58] he was often appointed to hear appeals from the military and admiralty courts and was undoubtedly knowledgeable in civil law procedure,[59] but he did not have Tykhill's common law court experience or connections. Tykhill must have convinced the queen and her council that he would have more success because of the links he had forged during his long association with the lawyers who oversaw the examination and verification process. Indeed, William Skrene, Richard Norton and William Lodyngton – all named as members of her council in 1413[60] – would have been well aware of Tykhill's prominence in the law courts. Norton was chief justice of Common Pleas, and together with the serjeants-at-law, Skrene and Lodyngton, had served with Tykhill as duchy counsel.[61]

Whether or not Tykhill was able to do much better is open to question. We do not know what expenses he incurred, but we do know the sources of income he secured: the alien lands lost to Sheen and Syon abbeys were replaced by 1,000 marks from the hanaper. This was traditionally a reliable source, but in fact, the queen's receivers experienced difficulty, at least initially, for the arrears

---

[57] This would have been especially true during the *inspeximus* procedure which took place early in the reign of a new king, and particularly under Henry V, when annuities were substantially reduced and 'anyone who petitioned for a grant of land or revenue was required to list all those he already enjoyed': G.L. Harriss, 'Financial Policy' in *Henry V. The Practice of Kingship*, ed. G.L. Harriss (Oxford, 1985), p. 174.

[58] J.S. Roskell, 'Sir William Sturmy', *Transactions of the Devonshire Association for the Advancement of Science, Literature and Art*, LXXXIX (1957), pp. 78–92; *The History of Parliament: House of Commons, 1386–1421*, ed. J.S. Roskell, Linda Clark and Carole Rawcliffe (4 vols. Stroud, 1992), IV, pp. 520–4.

[59] Indeed he bequeathed a volume of *Decretals*: PRO, PCC 7 Luffenham; *CCR, 1399–1402*, p. 314; *CPR, 1402–5*, pp. 118, 315; *1408–13*, pp. 291, 391.

[60] *Kingsthorpiana*, ed. J.H. Glover (1883), p. 17.

[61] Lodyngton had also been a member of the prince's council: PRO, SC6/813/21; PRO, E163/6/4, m. 022. He was moreover Tykhill's predecessor as king's attorney: *Select Cases*, VI, p. xc; *CPR, 1413–16*, pp. 40; PRO, DL42/17, ff. 72v, 88; PRO, DL28/4/7, ff. 10–10v, 22–3; 4/8, ff. 10, 22, 36v, 39; 4/9, f. 13.

were ordered to be paid in October 1415.[62] Compensation for the Percy manors and for part of the 2,000 marks still lacking from the dower was to be 500 marks drawn on the wool and petty customs of Hull and Boston, and 500 marks from the first monies of the proffers of all sheriffs and escheators at the Exchequer receipt. This latter sounds promising enough and indeed was paid (mostly in cash) in both 1415 and 1416,[63] but the actual receipt of customs monies had always been, and continued to be, a problem.[64] Further adjustments of dower took place in June and August 1415,[65] but although they were still short, none occurred thereafter, perhaps effecting his dismissal and explaining also his possession of title documents at that time.

However, the motive for Tykhill's forgery is still not entirely clear, and one of the most amazing features of the whole affair must now be brought to bear upon these events. The fact was that before 16 June 1415 the castle and manor of Moor End had been granted in fee by Henry V to his brother Humphrey, duke of Gloucester, for on this date Humphrey purchased a licence to enfeoff them to a group of creditors headed by his Beaufort uncles and the bishop of Durham.[66] Inexplicably, no record of the grant itself survives in Chancery or Exchequer records. But that the grant was made and that Humphrey died seised of Moor End in 1447 there can be no question, and both the enfeoffment licence on the original patent roll and the inquisition *post-mortem* held at Humphrey's death indicate that the estate was held in fee simple.[67] Its reversion to the crown's hands at his death and later

[62] *CCR, 1413–19*, p. 239. Indeed, contemporary complaints of arrears from this source abound: PRO, King's Remembrancer, Memoranda Rolls, E159/191, rots. 21d–23 (Michaelmas writs), 23–6 (Hilary writs); 193, rots 11–17d (Hilary writs).

[63] PRO, Exchequer, Exchequer of Receipt, Warrants for Issue, E404/31/463; PRO, Exchequer, Exchequer of Receipt, Teller's Rolls, E405/29, rot. 6; 30, rot. 2; 31, rot. 1.

[64] Witness the numerous letters close and writs authorizing payment of the queen's customs arrears from 1413 to 1416: *CCR, 1413–19*, pp. 239–40; PRO, E208/12 (17 unnumbered writs).

[65] *CPR, 1413–16*, p. 351; PRO, SC8/308/15366; *CChR, 1341–1417*, p. 482; *RP*, IV, p. 53.

[66] *CPR, 1413–16*, p. 338. Moor End was re-enfeoffed to a second group of feoffees, but eventually Humphrey re-took possession at their death: *CPR, 1429–36*, pp. 503–6. The grants to Humphrey of all the other crown lands involved in the mortgage were enrolled: *CPR, 1401–5*, pp. 256, 320–1; *1405–8*, p. 191; *1408–13*, p. 415.

[67] PRO, Chancery, Patent Rolls, C66/397/1, m. 4; PRO, Chancery, Inquisitions *Post-Mortem*, C139/127/8.

assignment in dower to Margaret of Anjou were the consequences of his failure to produce an heir.

It would appear that Tykhill collected the £34 for 1414–15 directly from the Moor End farmer.[68] The account for 1415–16 does not survive, but in that of 1416–17, the receiver reported that the fee farm was to be paid this time to the queen at the Exchequer receipt,[69] although unsurprisingly it was not received there. The continuing confusion of the queen and her officers about Moor End is evident from the accounts of all her lands for the years 1418 to 1420 drawn up at the Exchequer in the post-confiscation years. Relying on information in her treasurer's account book kept for the period Easter 1416 to Michaelmas 1418, the resulting (though futile), expectation of Moor End was that the £34 annual fee farm for both 1418–19 and 1419–20 was due from its long-standing farmer, John Sebright.[70] Clearly the queen's treasurer, at least as late as Michaelmas 1418, had no idea that Moor End had been granted to Humphrey.

This confusion is ultimately the key to understanding both the queen's and Tykhill's actions. Tykhill could not have known about the grant to Humphrey or he would not have forged her title documents. It is doubtful that he was able to collect the £34 for the year 1415–16 and he must have either known or suspected that she had made other arrangements for the £34; he certainly had no reason to think that the king had reassigned Moor End. Incensed, he enlisted the aid of the Canterbury scrivener, Thomas Davy (probably the same man who was also an attorney in the Common Pleas court),[71] and together they reauthorized his grant from the queen.

No other scenario seems possible. The sequence of events renders highly unlikely any hypothesis that Tykhill had forged the queen's original grant to him of the £34 fee farm. If he had, the forgery would have been detected upon submission of the Northampton account of 1414–15. Moreover, it would have

---

[68] Inferred from the receiver's statement that *he* had not received it because it had been granted to Tykhill; he did not claim to have paid Tykhill himself: PRO, SC6/948/11.

[69] PRO, SC6/948/12.

[70] PRO, Exchequer, Lord Treasurer's Remembrancer, Miscellaneous Accounts, E358/17, rots. 14d, 15d.

[71] PRO, CP40/631, rot. 1d.

been both foolhardy and unnecessary to retain the queen's documents after his dismissal in 1416. While no firm evidence exists that Tykhill actually perpetrated any forgery, the fact that the queen knew the details of Thomas Davy's involvement, and that Davy had been taken into custody by July 1419, argues against a frame-up theory.[72] For her part, upon discovery of the forgery in late 1418 and until the truth was revealed during her captivity,[73] Joan most likely surmised that it was Tykhill who had been receiving the Moor End fee farm all along. Several unanswered questions remain, but we are left with the impression that while blaming each other (in his case with some justification), both the queen and Thomas Tykhill were in fact unwitting victims of either an administrative oversight or deliberate concealment.

This bizarre episode is not the only example of Tykhill's restoration to royal service following his acquittal of heresy in 1414. His appointment to judicial and administrative commissions in Derbyshire and Leicestershire had also briefly resumed, attesting to the survival of his local influence, and perhaps also to the patronage of Richard, Lord Grey of Codnor (a former friend of Sir John Oldcastle),[74] who headed two of these commissions.[75] As he was paid until 1416 for counsel to the duchy of Lancaster,[76] it is little wonder that he still found favour among its officials, which is indicated by the council's full support of his positon in a fierce property dispute with duchy tenants in Castle Donington in

[72] Davy and another Canterbury scrivener were bound over to appear regularly before the king's council at that time: *CCR, 1419–22*, p. 49.

[73] In April 1420 and on later occasions, she dined with Humphrey at Leeds Castle. Henry Beaufort also visited her: Myers, 'The Captivity', p. 268, 268n; Leeds Castle Kent, MS. ff. 22, 25. My thanks to the Trustees of the Leeds Castle Foundation for their permission to consult and cite their MS.

[74] Oldcastle had served in his retinue in 1400 and the two held adjoining estates in Kent. A Lollard preacher operating from Oldcastle's estate of Cooling preached in Grey's churches of Hoo and Halstow in 1410: PRO, Exchequer, King's Remembrancer, Accounts Various, E101/42/40; W.T. Waugh 'Sir John Oldcastle', *EHR*, XX (1905), pp. 438, 442.

[75] PRO, E159/191, rot. 4d (Hinckley Priory enquiry, Michaelmas term 1414); *CPR, 1413–16*, p. 418 (peace commission, February 1415); pp. 393–4 (administration of Repton Priory, February 1416). Grey had, moreover, headed all the peace commissions to which Tykhill had been appointed during Henry IV's reign: see n. 9.

[76] PRO, DL28/4/9, ff. 11, 13.

1417.[77] Another incident that same year attests to his enduring image as an important lawyer and crown servant. Appearing at an assize in Derby in the guise of 'challenging' on the king's behalf in a deadlocked local land dispute, he convinced the reluctant jury to give judgement for his friend and neighbour Sir Robert Fraunceys, whose interests happened to coincide with the king's.[78] Clearly his local prestige had not suffered. In London, too, he must have retained influence, as he was counsel to the cathedral priory of Ely from at least 1420 to 1424.[79]

In January 1417, the same month in which the fugitive Sir John Oldcastle was sighted in the area,[80] Thomas and Agnes Tykhill purchased the general pardon offered by the king, and in Hilary 1418 finally purged themselves before their ordinary.[81] However, they were not to escape easily the taint of Lollardy, as was demonstrated in the course of a quarrel which developed between Thomas Tykhill and a prominent local lawyer, Peter Pole of Radbourne.[82] St Werburgh's abbey in Chester had long owned the manor of Weston-on-Trent and adjoining lands in Aston, but in July 1418 it was forced to mortgage all its Derbyshire property to the bishop of Durham for twelve years.[83] A tenant of the abbey in Aston,[84] Thomas Tykhill had probably been the abbot's Derbyshire steward,

[77] PRO, DL42/17, ff. 121v, 134v. In November 1416 the council approved Tykhill's petition to hold an inquisition in his presence into lands he claimed as part of his manor of Shardlow. The inquisition evidently found in his favour, for in February 1417 he complained that these same tenants were deliberately starving 38 of his 'beasts' in a Castle Donington chase. The council duly ordered their return to him.

[78] PRO, KB27/615, rot. 29.

[79] He had probably held the post since he was king's attorney (the relevant records for 1411 to 1419 do not survive): Cambridge University Library, Ely Dean and Chapter Archives, Ely Cathedral Priory, Treasurer's Accounts, EDC 5/13/12. I owe this reference to Dr Nigel Ramsay.

[80] PRO, Justices Itinerant, Gaol Delivery Rolls, JUST3/195, rots. 37, 50d.

[81] PRO, Chancery, Pardon Rolls, C67/37, m. 4; PRO, KB27/627, rot. 12d rex.

[82] Pole then dominated the county bench: PRO, Exchequer, Lord Treasurer's Remembrancer, Miscellaneous Rolls, E370/160/3, m. 22d.

[83] CCR, 1413–19, pp. 518–19, 521–2; D. Jones, The Church in Chester 1300–1540 (Chetham Society, VII, 1957), p. 86.

[84] According to a 1401 rental, Tykhill possessed a freehold at an annual rent of 13s 4d and may have acquired more of its property later from other tenants listed in the rental, who subsequently sold land in Aston to him: S(taffordshire) RO, D(W)1734/J/2005; DRO, D779B/T81–2, 85–7.

but Pole now became the new landlord's steward – much to his consternation. On 4 October 1419 five juries presented before Pole and other justices of the peace that, at his father's prompting, Thomas Tykhill junior and several other men had ambushed Pole at Aston two days earlier, as he returned home from holding the bishop's court at Weston.[85] One of the five indictments attempted to cast the affair in an entirely different light and this was inevitably the text given to the King's Bench court filacer for enrolment. The mesne process roll thus read that twelve men were ordered to appear *coram rege* in November for having committed 'divers trespasses, insurrections and congregations'. In addition to the two Tykhills another gentleman was named, John Prynce of Windley '*alias* John Prynce, *lollardus*', who had also recently purged himself after indictment for teaching Lollard opinions in 1414. Three of the others were the elder Tykhill's servants, one of whom was Thomas, 'brother of William Idrych, chaplain and lollard', and all the rest were undoubtedly tenants of the Tykhills at Aston and Chellaston. Outlawry process continued against them unsuccessfully until at least Easter 1423,[86] but they were never vigorously pursued; the imputations of Lollardy were probably not taken seriously.[87] Nevertheless, Tykhill did receive a letter from the king early in 1420;[88] he did not, however, move to clear himself until Easter term 1422.[89]

Concern over his declining status may have lain behind Tykhill's protective enfeoffment of his manor of Shardlow to local men in 1421;[90] his local position had certainly deteriorated by March 1425 when justices delivered him from

---

[85] PRO, KB9/1056, mm. 33–5. Pole was still steward in 1427: SRO, D(W)1734/J/1999.

[86] PRO, KB27/634, rot. 32 rex; 635, rot. 15 rex; 638, rot. 8d rex; 640, rot. 7d rex; 641, rot. 23 rex; 643, rot. 13d rex; 648, rots. 4–4d. For Prynce's indictment for Lollardy and 1418 purgation: PRO, KB9/204/1, m. 59; PRO, KB27/627, rot. 9d rex.

[87] Tykhill and his son Thomas sued and stood surety at Westminster with impunity while they were wanted men: PRO, CP40/636, rots. 68, 69d; PRO, KB27/634, rot. 17d rex.

[88] On 8 March 1420 a messenger was paid for delivery of the letter sent from France under the king's signet: PRO, E403/643, m. 23.

[89] He then paid a one-mark fine and process against him ceased; two of his tenants similarly paid half a mark each in 1423: PRO, KB27/644, rot. 1d fines; 648, rot. 1 fines; 649, rot. 1 fines; 651, rot. 1 fines.

[90] DRO, D779B/T90.

Nottingham Castle gaol after a malicious indictment before justices of the peace on the nonsensical charge of harbouring his son Richard, who had allegedly stolen £40 from him. His enemies added insult to injury by describing Thomas in the indictment as 'loller', no doubt intended as a term of abuse. On such a ridiculous charge, Tykhill's acquittal before the circuit judges, John Cokayne and James Strangeways, was inevitable, and by the careful selection of jurors for this gaol delivery session it was assured;[91] the panel included at least two of his friends.[92] Nevertheless, grounds for his acquittal were to be found in the very aspersion cast upon his name, as indicated by the small comment on the sheriff's calendar: *dicit quod nomen suum non est lollardus*.[93] Not only did the claim of misnomer disqualify his indictment as a violation of the 1413 Statute of Additions,[94] but it served also as an emphatic protest that he would not allow his position in local society to be thus undermined. Both this incident and the tactics employed by Peter Pole highlight what can only have been a worsening problem for gentry Lollards. That Lollardy's disreputable status could be wielded as a weapon in the local disputes which plagued the fifteenth-century gentry signalled its imminent demise in that quarter.

From this last known incident in his life, what conclusions can be drawn about Thomas Tykhill's Lollardy? This scrutiny of his career basically supports the betrayal theory of the Oldcastle revolt, as his important role in the prince's administration during the Welsh rebellion placed him within the latter's inner circle of retainers, many of whom became disillusioned by Henry's abandonment of Oldcastle to the Church authorities and rose against him accordingly.[95] There is no doubt that during both Henry IV's and Henry V's reigns, Tykhill identified and

---

[91] See also the observations in: E. Powell, 'Jury Trial at Gaol Delivery in the Late Middle Ages: The Midland Circuit, 1400–1429', in *Twelve Good Men and True, The Criminal Trial Jury in England, 1200–1800*, ed. J.S. Cockburn and T.A. Green (Princeton, 1988), pp. 82–6.

[92] Thomas Bradshaw (one of his feoffees in 1421: DRO, D779B/T90) and Richard Prynce (who bequeathed a reversionary interest in his estate to Thomas Tykhill's heirs in 1431: BL, Wolley Charter, I, 85).

[93] PRO, JUST3/13, rot. 1; JUST3/203, rot. 33.

[94] *SR*, II, p. 171. I am grateful to Dr Paul Brand for bringing this fact to my attention.

[95] McNiven, *Heresy*, pp. 155, 195–6, 223–6. The prince's former chief steward of the 'south parts', William Stourton (died in 1413), should be added to this group: K.B. McFarlane, *Lancastrian Kings and Lollard Knights* (Oxford, 1972), p. 215; PRO, SC6/813/23, ff. 2–2v, 5v.

commonly associated in his private business with those who also served (or had served) the Prince of Wales – namely, Sir Roger Leche (household treasurer), Hugh Mortimer and Peter Melbourne (both chamberlains and councillors), and John Makworth (chancellor).[96] He may have had personal, financial reasons for supporting the revolt, but his sponsorship of William Ederyk and the effective sacrifice of his career imply that he had not been spurred purely by hopes of private gain. Like Oldcastle, any personal or political aims were inextricably bound up with his religious beliefs and he must have convinced the king of his primarily pious motives when brought before him in Chancery in 1414. That he was a crown administrator is significant also in the context of that most critical of Oldcastle's demands, the disendowment of the Church. Possessed of an intimate knowledge of the lay and clerical estates of the realm, the law of real property and rights of the crown, he was just the sort of man to put valuable information into the hands of those who drew up the 'Disendowment Bill' presented in parliament in 1410.[97]

The reasons for the forgery have already been analysed, but one further point is worth making. The forgery bore some relation to his heretical activities: both were forms of seditious behaviour, as both thwarted royal authority and betrayed trust placed in him as an official, and both involved taking the law into his own hands to enforce his own brand of equitable justice. Neither would have been contemplated without the confidence and arrogance acquired with his ability to read and write, and both employed the literacy skills which had always been his most effective tools in advancing himself.[98] This study is perhaps ultimately an unsubtle reminder

---

[96] PRO, JUST1/1514, rot. 48d and PRO, C1/9/330 (Leche and Mortimer); DRO, D779B/T72, 80–4 (Melbourne); *Derb. Feet of Fines*, no. 1027 and PRO, C1/16/52 (Makworth); Northamptonshire RO, C. 2998 (Leche and Makworth). It may have been as part of such a coterie that Thomas (and Agnes) Tykhill joined the Holy Trinity guild at Coventry – the prince and other members of his household belonged: *The Register of the Guild of the Holy Trinity, St Mary, St John the Baptist and St Katherine of Coventry*, ed. M.D. Harris (Dugdale Society, XIII, 1935), pp. 13, 41, 79.

[97] Its authors' calculations were relatively accurate: A. Hudson, *Selections from English Wycliffite Writings* (Cambridge, 1978), pp. 204–6.

[98] Forgery was, moreover, only from 1413 an offence with common law remedy; the mesne process was fixed by statute following a petition coincidentally presented in the October 1419 parliament: *SR*, II, pp. 170–1, 202; N.R. Ramsay, 'Forgery and the Rise of the London Scriveners' Company', in *Fakes and Frauds, Varieties of Deception in Print and Manuscript*, ed. R. Myers and M. Harris (Winchester, 1989), p. 99.

that such skills were the means by which the gentry class, in providing invaluable service as lawyers and administrators, came to ever-increasing prominence in fifteenth-century England.

Thomas Tykhill was dead by 1431,[99] but family traditions continued. In 1445, a Robert Tykhill, 'gentleman, late of Aston-on-Trent', was pardoned of outlawry for forging title deeds at Tutbury to the manor of Shardlow.[100] Perhaps the skill was passed like an heirloom as that other valuable possession – knowledge of the law – had been. An interest in religious questions was no less a part of the Tykhill legacy, for in the early sixteenth century, a Thomas Tykhill was investigated for heresy in Lincoln diocese upon the report that he had lent someone a copy of the gospels in English – a volume which could well have been in the family for generations.[101]

---

[99] Only Agnes Tykhill of Tutbury, gentlewoman, was assessed for tax purposes in that year: *Feudal Aids*, I, pp. 298, 301, 304–5.

[100] *CPR, 1441–6*, p. 393.

[101] *The Acts and Monuments of John Foxe*, ed. G. Townsend and R.S. Cattley (8 vols. 1837–9), IV, p. 233.

3

THE DUCHY OF LANCASTER AND THE RULE OF EAST ANGLIA, 1399–1440: A PROLOGUE TO THE PASTON LETTERS*

Helen Castor

D uring the 1440s, regional politics in the counties of Norfolk and Suffolk were dominated by the controversial figure of William de la Pole, earl, and later duke, of Suffolk. The character of his local regime during these years – what Colin Richmond has called the 'systematic and illegal exploitation of his position by the duke of Suffolk'[1] – has become perhaps the single most potent example adduced by historians seeking to demonstrate the corruption of political society under the ineffective rule of Henry VI. Not only are Suffolk and his supporters alleged to have abused their local dominance to manipulate the law and obstruct justice, but the very fact of their local dominance has been cited as evidence of the extent to which the duke's undue influence in central government allowed him to subvert legitimate political hierarchies in the regions. Suffolk's stranglehold on the royal administration and his malign influence over the malleable king, it is argued, allowed him a degree of regional control which was unwarranted by his own territorial stake in East Anglia. This made it possible for him to overwhelm established structures of power in the area, temporarily eclipsing the 'inherent landed strength and traditional authority' of the Mowbray dukes of Norfolk, to

---

* I am indebted to Dr Christine Carpenter for her advice in the preparation of this essay.
[1] C. Richmond, *The Paston Family in the Fifteenth Century* (Cambridge, 1990), p. 235.

whom local leadership naturally belonged.[2] Thus, the rule of the region was 'usurped' by members of the royal household, men such as the 'notorious' Sir Thomas Tuddenham and the 'professional desperado' John Heydon.[3]

This portrait of a household clique trading on its influence at court to intrude into established patterns of legitimate authority owes much to the abundant and compelling evidence provided by the Paston Letters. The correspondence undoubtedly offers a unique insight into the workings of fifteenth-century local politics. It may be, however, that the very wealth of the Paston evidence has had a profound effect on the portrayal of East Anglian society which it has inspired. There is, for example, a striking contrast between the range of studies of Suffolk and his henchmen in the years from 1440 onwards – the point at which the Paston evidence begins in earnest – and the scarcity of work dealing with the politics of the region before that date.[4] The nature of the established pattern of regional influence which Suffolk is supposed to have overturned has largely been taken for granted; it has seemed no more than a happy coincidence that his 'reign of terror'[5] began at the date from which the evidence describing it survives. This essay is intended to test this account of the basis of Suffolk's authority in East Anglia during the 1440s by investigating the structures of power in the region in the four decades before the correspondence begins. Without the Pastons as guides, the operation of local political society has had to be examined through analysis of formal records, both private and public. In this way, an attempt has been made to establish a broader context in which to set the version of events of the 1440s provided in such vivid detail by the letters.

---

[2] Quotation from R. Virgoe, 'The Crown, Magnates and Local Government in Fifteenth-Century East Anglia', in *The Crown and the Local Communities in England and France in the Fifteenth Century*, ed. J.R.L. Highfield and R. Jeffs (Gloucester, 1981), p. 84. See also B.P. Wolffe, *Henry VI* (1981), pp. 121–3.

[3] Quotations from Wolffe, *Henry VI*, p. 122; E.F. Jacob, *The Fifteenth Century* (Oxford, 1961), p. 503.

[4] Exceptions are G.E. Morey's M.A. and Ph.D. dissertations, which offer a wealth of biographical information, but relatively little detailed political analysis: 'The administration of the counties of Norfolk and Suffolk in the reign of Henry IV' (unpub. London M.A. thesis, 1941); 'East Anglian society in the fifteenth century: an historico-regional survey' (unpub. London Ph.D. thesis, 1951).

[5] R.L. Storey, *The End of the House of Lancaster* (1966), p. 54.

One element in East Anglian power structures which has received little sustained attention hitherto is the political role played in the region by the duchy of Lancaster in the years after 1399. The duchy lands, a compact group of estates in northern Norfolk, were both extensive and valuable.[6] Indeed, the duke of Lancaster was the only magnate with a territorial stake substantial enough to support a viable claim to the rule of a shire characterized by fragmented tenurial patterns and an unusually independent gentry society.[7] However, John of Gaunt had shown little appetite for the challenge of establishing his rule in Norfolk, preferring instead to exploit his East Anglian revenues to support his political activities elsewhere. During the late fourteenth century, therefore, the Lancastrian presence in the region, though by no means negligible, took the form of a disparate collection of retainers whose allegiance was not – indeed, was not required to be – exclusive, and whose local influence as a coherent and identifiable group was, at most, occasional.[8]

In 1399, Henry of Bolingbroke inherited his father's estates and retinue. At almost exactly the same time, he succeeded to the throne in place of his deposed cousin, Richard II. The task of combining his personal and private lordship of the Lancastrian affinity, whose support had won him the crown, with his newly acquired public responsibilities in the realm as a whole, was a formidable one; the tensions inherent in this volatile compound of public and private authority played a significant role in provoking the disorder which plagued 'duchy' areas such as the north Midlands during the

---

[6] The average clear annual value of these lands during Henry IV's reign was *c.* £960, a figure exceeded within the duchy only by receipts at the great Lancastrian strongholds of Tutbury, Lancaster and Bolingbroke, and the particularly rich conglomeration of manors known as the 'South Parts': PRO, Duchy of Lancaster, Ministers' Accounts, DL29/728/11987–8, 11991; 729/11993–7, 11999, 12001–2, 12004–5; 730/12006–9, 12011–15; 731/12016–18.

[7] S.K. Walker, *The Lancastrian Affinity* (Oxford, 1990), pp. 182–4; A. Hassell Smith, *County and Court: Government and Politics in Norfolk, 1558–1603* (Oxford, 1974), pp. 3–14; B.M.S. Campbell, 'The Complexity of Manorial Structure in Medieval Norfolk: a case study', *Norfolk Archaeology*, XXXIX (1986), pp. 225–61.

[8] Walker, *The Lancastrian Affinity*, pp. 182–209.

latter part of his reign.[9] In Norfolk, on the other hand, the fact that his father had previously made little political capital out of his extensive estates offered the new king an unusual opportunity to develop a Lancastrian lordship in the shire which, from its inception, could be unequivocally royal.

This political *carte blanche* was rendered even more significant by the contrasting tenurial situation in Suffolk. The duchy held only a few manors in Suffolk and, whereas in Norfolk the territorial presence of the non-Lancastrian nobility was relatively insubstantial, Suffolk was composed of a complex of interlocking magnate estates. The lands of the Mowbrays and the de la Poles formed large territorial blocs; the Mortimer honour of Clare gave the earls of March (and subsequently the duke of York) a substantial foothold in the county, and the sphere of influence in northern Essex of the de Vere earls of Oxford extended into southern Suffolk.[10] In the years after 1399, however, an extraordinary combination of dynastic misfortune and political miscalculation meant that virtually all these noble interests were temporarily in abeyance. The Mowbrays had acquired the rich East Anglian estates of the dukedom of Norfolk on the death of Margaret of Brotherton in 1399, but the unfortunate effects of two minorities, of participation in the Scrope rebellion, and of over-generous dower settlements meant that no adult Mowbray controlled the bulk of these lands until 1425.[11] The earls of March and Oxford, and Lord Scales, who held lands in Norfolk and Suffolk as well as in Essex and Cambridgeshire,

---

[9] For conflict involving members of the duchy of Lancaster affinity which developed in Staffordshire and Nottinghamshire during these years, see E. Powell, *Kingship, Law, and Society: Criminal Justice in the Reign of Henry V* (Oxford, 1989), pp. 208–16, 224–8; S.J. Payling, *Political Society in Lancastrian England: The Greater Gentry of Nottinghamshire* (Oxford, 1991), pp. 189–95; and H.R. Castor, 'The Duchy of Lancaster in the Lancastrian Polity, 1399–1461 (unpub. Cambridge Ph.D. thesis, 1993), ch. 6.

[10] R.E. Archer, 'The Mowbrays: Earls of Nottingham and Dukes of Norfolk, to 1432' (unpub. Oxford D.Phil. thesis, 1984), appendix I; L.E. James, 'The Career and Political Influence of William de la Pole, First Duke of Suffolk, 1437–50' (unpub. Oxford B.Litt. thesis, 1979), pp. 231–2, 234; P.A. Johnson, *Duke Richard of York, 1411–60* (Oxford, 1988), p. 14; D. MacCulloch, *Suffolk and the Tudors: Politics and Religion in an English County, 1500–1600* (Oxford, 1986), p. 55.

[11] *GEC*, IX, pp. 600–6; R.E. Archer, 'Rich Old Ladies: The Problem of Late Medieval Dowagers' in *Property and Politics: Essays in Later Medieval English History*, ed. A.J. Pollard (Gloucester, 1984), pp. 28–9.

all died between 1398 and 1402; all three left minor heirs.[12] Thomas, Lord Bardolf, one of the few nobles with a relatively substantial interest in Norfolk, also joined Scrope's rebellion and forfeited his estates to the crown.[13] Of the regional nobility, only Michael de la Pole, earl of Suffolk, was of age and in full possession of his inheritance, but, perhaps chastened by the dramatic end to his father's meteoric career as Richard II's favourite, his political ambition and certainly his influence seem to have been extremely limited.[14]

In 1399, therefore, no identifiable structure of power in East Anglia remained. This remarkable political vacuum meant that Henry had a rare chance to exploit his Lancastrian territorial interests from his new position as king without having to accommodate the authority of those with rival claims to local lordship, and with his own landed interest reinforced by control of a handful of forfeitures and wardships. He was supported in this task by the service of a relatively disparate group of Lancastrian retainers, made up of a few eminent members of the greater gentry, most notably his close companion Sir Thomas Erpingham, and many more lesser gentlemen with a tradition of administrative service to the duchy.

Henry chose to make no radical changes in the management of his local resources, but to put his trust in what traditions of Lancastrian service already existed in the region, limited though they were. Nevertheless, even though the personnel of the duchy administration remained static, the size of their rewards and the scale of their influence increased significantly, and this in itself had a profound impact on local society. The lawyer John Winter of Town Barningham, for example, had long combined professional service to the duchy with minor office in local government.[15] His duchy employment was by no means exclusive; he also acted for the Staffords in the area, as well as using his

---

[12] *GEC*, VIII, pp. 449–50; X, p. 233–4; XI, pp. 503–4.

[13] Ibid., I, p. 420.

[14] Ibid., XII, i, p. 441; R. Virgoe, 'The Crown and Local Government: East Anglia under Richard II', in *The Reign of Richard II*, ed. F.R.H. Du Boulay and C.M. Barron (1971), p. 226; A.L. Brown, 'The Reign of Henry IV: the establishment of the Lancastrian regime', in *Fifteenth-Century England, 1399–1509*, ed. S.B. Chrimes, C.D. Ross and R.A. Griffiths (Manchester, 1972), p. 7.

[15] Winter was receiver of the Lancastrian estates in Norfolk from 1396, and served as escheator in 1392 and 1397. Walker, *The Lancastrian Affinity*, p. 289; *List of Escheators for England and Wales* (PRO Lists and Indexes, LXXII, 1971), p. 86.

legal expertise in the service of the city of Norwich.[16] Nevertheless, his connections with other Lancastrian servants combined the professional, both within the duchy and in other contexts, with the personal. His sister married the esquire John Reymes, who had been retained by Gaunt since 1392, and he himself married the sister-in-law of Bolingbroke's butler, John Payn.[17] In this he was typical; and for him, and for the other Lancastrians, 1399 brought greater responsibility and greater eminence, and therefore endowed the personal and professional network within which they operated with a correspondingly greater significance. Winter was appointed to every commission of the peace in Norfolk for the first six years of the reign, and by 1411 had represented the shire in parliament five times.[18] In 1408, he became steward of the duchy in East Anglia.[19]

His rapid promotion has many parallels among his Lancastrian associates. John Payn, who had been appointed chief butler of England immediately on Henry's accession, served in parliament and as a JP in 1401. In September 1399 he was granted the constableship of Norwich castle, and on his death in 1402 he was succeeded in this office by John Reymes, who sat in the parliaments of 1404 and 1406.[20] John Gournay, son and heir of Gaunt's local

---

[16] Walker, *The Lancastrian Affinity*, p. 192; *The Records of the City of Norwich*, ed. W. Hudson and J.C. Tingey (2 vols. Norwich, 1906–10), II, pp. 41, 53.

[17] Walker, *The Lancastrian Affinity*, pp. 194, 279; E.L.T. John, 'Sir Thomas Erpingham, East Anglian Society and the Dynastic Revolution of 1399', *Norfolk Archaeology*, XXXV (1970), p. 103; Richmond, *The Paston Family*, p. 72.

[18] He was not appointed to the peace commissions of 1407–8, but served again from 1410 until his death in 1414. *CPR, 1399–1401*, p. 561; *1405–8*, p. 494; *1408–13*, p. 483; *Return of the Name of Every Member of the Lower House of the Parliament of England, 1213–1874*, Parliamentary Papers, LXII, pts. i–iii (1878), pp. 261, 265, 272, 274, 277.

[19] R. Somerville, *History of the Duchy of Lancaster, vol. I, 1265–1603* (1953), p. 594. Winter also received an annuity of 5 marks from the duchy from 1399: PRO, DL29/738/12096, m. 9.

[20] *Return of the Name*, pp. 261, 265, 269; *CCR, 1402–5*, pp. 241–2; *CPR, 1399–1401*, p. 561; John, 'Sir Thomas Erpingham', p. 103; *Calendar of Signet Letters of Henry IV and Henry V (1399–1422)*, ed. J.L. Kirby (1978), p. 55. John Payn received an annuity of 10 marks from the duchy lands in Norfolk from 1399. John Reymes was granted £20 a year from the customs of Great Yarmouth in 1399; in July 1405 this, and the three pipes of wine he also received there, were replaced by a duchy fee of £30, paid at the Norfolk receipt, on top of the £10 he already received from the duchy: Norfolk and Norwich RO, Norfolk Record Society, NRS 11071, m. 3; NRS 3347, m. 4; PRO, Duchy of Lancaster, Miscellaneous Books, DL42/16, pt. 2, f. 9v; *CCR, 1399–1402*, pp. 12–13.

steward Edmund Gournay, served as escheator in 1401, as sheriff in 1399 and 1408, and as knight of the shire in 1399 and 1404.[21] Edmund Oldhall, receiver of the duchy lands since 1398, joined Gournay in parliament in 1404, and was elected again with Winter in 1411. He sat on the Norfolk peace commission from 1406, and held office twice as escheator and twice as sheriff.[22] Sir Robert Berney had acquired the stewardship of Gimingham from Gaunt in 1398, and Henry granted him a duchy annuity of £40. Berney was appointed sheriff in 1406 and 1410, and served on three peace commissions and in two parliaments during the reign.[23]

The influence of these Lancastrians was overwhelmingly concentrated in Norfolk, where the duchy interest they represented was based, and where such rapid advancement could be accommodated fairly readily by an already relatively heterogeneous county society. Their activities did not, in general, extend into Suffolk. G.E. Morey remarks that the surviving administrative records of the reign from the two shires 'convey the impression that each led an exclusive existence'.[24] Nevertheless, even though the duchy had no territorial stake in Suffolk, and though an adult earl of Suffolk, however uninfluential on the wider political stage, was resident and active there, Lancastrian interests were not completely absent from the rule of the shire. Suffolk was represented in parliament three times during the reign by Sir John Strange, a Lancastrian retainer since the 1370s, who became controller of the royal household in 1406; twice by Sir Andrew Botiller, whose wife was Thomas Erpingham's niece; and

---

[21] Morey, 'The administration of . . . Norfolk and Suffolk', p. 268; Somerville, *History of the Duchy*, p. 377; *List of Escheators*, p. 86; *List of Sheriffs for England and Wales* (PRO Lists and Indexes, IX, 1898), p. 87; *Return of the Name*, pp. 258, 267. Gournay died in office as sheriff in 1408; his replacement, at the king's suggestion, was Ralph Ramsay, for whom see below, n. 25: *Calendar of Signet Letters*, p. 150.

[22] Oldhall held the escheatorship in 1405 and 1411, and the shrievalty in 1401 and 1413: Somerville, *History of the Duchy*, p. 596: *Return of the Name*, pp. 267, 277; *CPR, 1405–8*, p. 494; *1408–13*, p. 483; *List of Escheators*, p. 86; *List of Sheriffs*, p. 87.

[23] He sat in the parliaments of 1399 and 1401, and on peace commissions in 1399 and twice in 1410: Walker, *The Lancastrian Affinity*, p. 289; PRO, DL42/15, pt. 2, ff. 56, 59v; PRO, DL29/738/12096; *List of Sheriffs*, p. 87; *CPR, 1399–1401*, p. 561; *1408–13*, p. 483; *Return of the Name*, pp. 258, 263.

[24] Morey, 'The administration of . . . Norfolk and Suffolk', p. 34.

once by Ralph Ramsay, a relation by marriage of Sir Robert Berney, who had
been retained by Henry before his accession.[25] If the duchy presence in East
Anglia in the years before 1399 had been 'ill-defined',[26] the establishment of the
new regime threw it into sharp focus, as Henry placed increasing
responsibilities in the hands of the men who had administered his father's
interests. However, it was to become a yet more significant force in the politics
of the region. The affinity, such as it had existed in 1399, evolved into a
connection which assimilated Henry's private territorial influence to his public
authority as king, a connection broader than the duchy interest, though
incorporating and intrinsically linked to it, which was to dominate East Anglia
during the following decades.

Fundamental to this process was the presence of Sir Thomas Erpingham,
unquestionably the most eminent local Lancastrian. His home manor of
Erpingham lay in the heart of duchy territory in northern Norfolk, and his
history of Lancastrian service was long and distinguished.[27] By 1399 he was
already receiving an annuity of 100 marks from Henry, and two fees of £20 and
40 marks from Gaunt, besides holding the Norfolk hundred of South
Erpingham by grant of the duke. Under the new regime, he was rewarded with
a number of financial and territorial grants which substantially increased both
his resources and his authority in his native area. From 1400 he received

[25] Strange sat as an MP in 1404 (twice) and 1406, Botiller in 1404 and 1410, and Ramsay in
1402: *Return of the Name*, pp. 264, 266–7, 270, 275; Walker, *The Lancastrian Affinity*, p. 282; A. Rogers,
'The Royal Household of Henry IV' (unpub. Nottingham Ph.D. thesis, 1966), p. 680; John, 'Sir
Thomas Erpingham', pp. 102, 104. Ramsay also served twice as sheriff, while Strange served twice
as escheator and on Norfolk peace commissions in 1401 and 1406: *List of Sheriffs*, p. 87; *List of
Escheators*, p. 86; *CPR, 1399–1401*, p. 561; *1405–8*, p. 494. *The History of Parliament: The House of
Commons, 1386–1421*, ed. J.S. Roskell, Linda Clark and Carole Rawcliffe (4 vols. Stroud, 1992), II,
III, IV, for recent biographies of all the MPs.

[26] Walker, *The Lancastrian Affinity*, p. 206.

[27] Erpingham had been retained by Gaunt in 1380, and served in his company in Scotland and
Spain before moving into the retinue of the earl of Derby, whom he accompanied to Prussia and the
Holy Land in the early 1390s. In 1398 he followed Henry into exile, and in October 1399 was
appointed chamberlain of the household by the new king: *Dictionary of National Biography*, ed.
L. Stephen and S. Lee, suppl. XXII, p. 614; John, 'Sir Thomas Erpingham', pp. 96–8; Rogers,
'The Royal Household of Henry IV', appendix C, pp. 678, 687.

additional annual sums of £80 from the issues of Norfolk and Suffolk and £40 from the fee-farm of Norwich, and from 1402 another 100 marks from the fee-farm of Cambridge; in 1405 he was granted the alien priory estate of Tofts.[28] Most significantly, he was a major beneficiary of the crop of noble minorities in the first year of the reign. The keeping of the central Mowbray estate of Framlingham castle was committed to Erpingham in November 1399.[29] Four years later, he was also granted custody of the castle and honour of Clare and all other Mortimer lands in Norfolk, Suffolk and Essex during the minority of the earl of March.[30] During the early years of the reign, therefore, Erpingham was controlling the major part of the territorial interests of two of the greatest landowners of the region, vastly extending his sphere of influence from his own estates in the duchy heartlands of northern Norfolk across East Anglia into Suffolk.

This increased territorial power was reflected by Erpingham's role in the public affairs of the region. Named to every commission of the peace in Norfolk, he also figured prominently on a wide variety of other local commissions.[31] In 1403, for example, he was appointed with the earls of Northumberland and Worcester and the keeper of the privy seal to settle a long-standing dispute between the bishop of Norwich and the town of King's Lynn.[32] His appearance in such select company reflects his closeness to Henry and his consequent eminence at court, but the fact that he was the only local representative on the commission also demonstrates the implications of that eminence for his regional influence. Moreover, this participation in royal administration involved Erpingham in a public context with the members of the

---

[28] PRO, DL42/15, ff. 22, 67v; *CPR, 1399–1401*, p. 274; *1401–5*, p. 47; *1405–8*, p. 18; *CCR, 1399–1402*, p. 460.

[29] *CPR, 1399–1401*, pp. 93, 224; *1401–5*, p. 16; *CFR, 1399–1405*, pp. 31, 47, 62.

[30] Erpingham was originally one of the group of trustees, headed by the earl of Northumberland, to whom custody of all the Mortimer lands was granted. Northumberland acquired sole control in 1401, but Erpingham was granted the keeping of the East Anglian estates in November 1403. *CFR, 1399–1405*, pp. 22, 233–4; *CPR, 1401–5*, pp. 256, 326.

[31] *CPR, 1399–1401*, p. 561; *1401–5*, pp. 128, 274, 280, 503; *1405–8*, pp. 152, 154, 200, 494; *1408–13*, pp. 65, 181, 205, 222, 226, 483.

[32] *CPR, 1401–5*, p. 274.

emerging Lancastrian connection in the region, and this shared role reinforced personal associations which were already close and long-standing. John Winter, John Strange, John Gournay, Robert Berney, Edmund Oldhall and Nicholas Wichingham, steward of the duchy by 1401,[33] all acted as mainpernors or trustees for Sir Thomas, and Winter, Berney and Andrew Botiller each held office as his deputy constable of Dover castle.[34] Erpingham repaid this service in kind, acting as feoffee, for example, for Strange, Botiller and Wichingham, and as supervisor of the will of Winter's father.[35] Indeed, these names recur again and again, associated in various combinations and various capacities in the legal transactions which were the stuff of local landed society. Entirely characteristic were Botiller's feoffment of 1401, when his trustees included Erpingham, Strange, Berney and Winter, and Winter's feoffment of 1409, when his quitclaim of Town Barningham to a group including Berney and Oldhall was witnessed by, among others, Erpingham.[36]

These most prominent Lancastrian retainers formed the core of a network which extended throughout East Anglian society, embracing other men whose connections with the duchy itself were less close or less active, but who nevertheless acted consistently in association with the same interests. The esquire Oliver Groos, for example, who had been retained by Gaunt during the 1390s, was less prominent in local administration, but joined Erpingham and Reymes as a witness for John Winter.[37] However, the new-found efficacy of

---

[33] Somerville, *History of the Duchy*, p. 594.

[34] *CFR, 1399–1405*, pp. 31, 233; *1413–22*, p. 12; *CCR, 1399–1402*, p. 170; John, 'Sir Thomas Erpingham', pp. 103–4; Morey, 'The administration of . . . Norfolk and Suffolk', pp. 250, 302. Botiller was later to become one of the executors of Erpingham's will: *The Register of Henry Chichele*, ed. E.F. Jacob and H.C. Johnson, Canterbury and York Society (4 vols. Oxford, 1938–47), II, p. 380.

[35] Erpingham also witnessed deeds for Winter himself. *CCR, 1399–1402*, pp. 332, 392; John, 'Sir Thomas Erpingham', pp. 103–4; *CCR, 1405–9*, pp. 522, 524.

[36] *CCR, 1399–1402*, p. 392; *1405–9*, p. 524. See also BL, Additional Charter, 14128; *Historical Manuscripts Commission, Report on the Manuscripts of the Marquis of Lothian* (1905), pp. 52–3; *CCR, 1399–1402*, p. 305; *1405–9*, pp. 279, 385, 462–3. For earlier associations between this group, see Magdalen College, Oxford, Guton deeds 23A and 1566; Norfolk and Norwich RO, Le Strange, A16, and Phillips, Phi/23.

[37] Groos held office only as sheriff, in 1409: *List of Sheriffs*, p. 87; *CCR, 1405–9*, p. 522.

Lancastrian interests in shaping regional affairs did not obliterate the wealth of non-Lancastrian local connections which duchy retainers had formed before 1399. Henry was promoting in the rule of the shire the relatively small group of men with whom he had previous associations; the logic of this situation meant that *their* associates would in turn benefit, and these men too must be included in any analysis of the emerging 'Lancastrian' network. Sir Simon Felbrigg is perhaps the most obvious, and most prominent, example of this process. He had been among the East Anglian knights most closely associated with Richard II during the 1390s, becoming in 1395 the king's standard bearer and a knight of his chamber, and securing a collection of valuable grants in Norfolk.[38] The change of regime in 1399 stripped him of most of this acquired wealth and influence,[39] but seems to have left unaffected his association with Thomas Erpingham, whose home at Erpingham lay only a few miles from Felbrigg Hall in northern Norfolk. Despite the dramatic divergence of their political careers in that year – while Erpingham joined Henry in exile, Felbrigg accompanied Richard to Ireland – the two men remained closely involved with each other in their local context both during and after the crisis.[40] This naturally connected Felbrigg with the network developing around the duchy and dominating the county administration. He was a feoffee, for example, for both Botiller and Winter in the transactions cited above, which was characteristic of his associations during the reign, and he was a regular member of the peace commission from 1407.[41] Indeed, this

[38] Felbrigg had served abroad under Gaunt in the 1380s, but by the following decade had followed his father into Richard's service. The grants he received included the constableship of Framlingham castle in 1399, which he was to lose to Thomas Erpingham only months later. C. Given-Wilson, *The Royal Household and the King's Affinity: Service, Politics and Finance in England, 1360–1413* (New Haven, 1986), pp. 165, 201–2, 283; J.D. Milner, 'Sir Simon Felbrigg KG: The Lancastrian Revolution and Personal Fortune', *Norfolk Archaeology*, XXXVII (1978), pp. 85–6.

[39] Henry confirmed Felbrigg's annuity in November 1399, but he lost his offices: John, 'Sir Thomas Erpingham', p. 102.

[40] Felbrigg was one of the trustees to whom Erpingham entrusted his estates before his departure in 1398: John, 'Sir Thomas Erpingham', p. 102; Milner, 'Sir Simon Felbrigg', p. 86.

[41] See above, n. 36; *CPR, 1405–8*, p. 494; *1408–13*, p. 483.

Ricardian knight[42] eventually became a direct beneficiary of duchy patronage when in 1410 he received a life grant of a licence to hunt in all duchy lands.[43]

Thus, during the previous reign, when the duke of Lancaster had only occasionally attempted to direct regional affairs, a variety of associations had been forged within the political community. After 1399, when the sudden reordering of priorities gave duchy connections prime significance, the Lancastrians who acquired a new eminence did not jettison old allies. Crucially for its ability to represent the region, the political network which emerged therefore did not depend solely on previous association with the new king, but was shaped also by the dynamics of the local society within which it operated. In this process, Thomas Erpingham remained a key figure, filling a role which complemented his eminence in the duchy. One of the few new retainers, for example, to be granted an annuity by Henry in the area after his accession was Erpingham's nephew and heir, Sir William Phelip.[44] As Trevor John concludes, Sir Thomas was 'the centre of a web of influence and connection stretching from the central government to local society, and binding them together'.[45]

However, although Erpingham's regional authority vastly increased in the years after 1399, and despite his control of the Mowbray and Mortimer inheritances, the ability of a knight to dominate such a disparate society would

---

[42] Milner argues that Felbrigg was never reconciled to the new Lancastrian regime which, Milner asserts, rejected and ostracized him. In the light of Felbrigg's close and continuing involvement with the Lancastrians of East Anglia, as well as the fact that he received several substantial grants from the Lancastrian kings (though admittedly never rivalling the scale of his acquisitions under Richard II), this argument seems overstated. However, it is true that, very unusually, when Felbrigg made his will in 1440 he left masses to be said for Richard's soul, and made no mention of the dynasty he had served since 1399: Milner 'Sir Simon Felbrigg', pp. 86–7, 89–90; Norfolk and Norwich RO, Ketton-Cremer, WKC1/336/1a.

[43] BL, Add. Ch. 70687.

[44] Phelip was the son of Erpingham's sister Juliana, who had married Sir William Phelip of Dennington, Suffolk. He was granted £20 a year from the duchy receipt in Norfolk in 1403: John, 'Sir Thomas Erpingham', p. 104; PRO, DL29/310/4981; DL42/16, f. 43; Norfolk and Norwich RO, NRS 11061 m. 3.

[45] John, 'Sir Thomas Erpingham', p. 104. See also Richmond, *The Paston Family*, p. 69n.

always remain limited.[46] As the reign progressed, Erpingham's influence became one part of a hierarchy of lordship in the area, created through, and remaining fundamentally connected to, the authority of the crown. The duchy played an integral role in this process, though not an exclusive one. The arrival in the area of the king's half-brother, Thomas Beaufort, for example, was the result not specifically of involvement with the duchy, but of his acquisition of forfeited noble estates. However, he rapidly became associated in local affairs with the increasingly influential 'Lancastrian' connection headed by Erpingham.

Beaufort had acquired some connections with East Anglia and with the duchy in the area before Henry's accession. In 1398 Richard II granted him the Fitzalan lordship of Castle Acre in Norfolk which had been forfeited by its temporary holder, Thomas Mowbray, and in January of the following year Gaunt assigned his annuity of 300 marks at the Norfolk receipt of the duchy.[47] His active involvement in the region, however, dates only from 1405, when he was granted the estates in western Norfolk forfeited by the rebel Thomas, Lord Bardolf.[48] These lands, centring on the honour of Wormegay, were not outstandingly valuable or extensive, certainly in comparison to the estates of the duchies of Lancaster and Norfolk or the earldom of Suffolk.[49] Nevertheless, despite Beaufort's close relationship to the new king, he had, as the youngest son of a recently legitimized family, inherited a very limited landed estate.[50] For

[46] Despite his custody of the Mowbray lands in northern Suffolk and the Mortimer estates in south-west Suffolk, for example, Erpingham never sat on the peace commission in the county; his authority seems to have remained firmly concentrated in Norfolk.

[47] PRO, DL42/15, f. 69; DL42/16, pt. 2 f. 1v; *CPR, 1396–9*, p. 414.

[48] Custody of the lands was committed to him in August, and he obtained a life grant from the following October: *CFR, 1399–1405*, p. 316; *CPR, 1405–8*, p. 105.

[49] The estates, which included the manors of Stow Bardolph, Runcton and Fareswell in Fincham, were valued in the grant at 250 marks annually. For a slightly later listing and valuation of the Bardolf estates, see National Library of Wales, Aberystwyth, Peniarth MS. 280, pp. 56–7.

[50] Gaunt had left Thomas 1,000 marks in cash, but lands worth only £17 per year in reversion. His wife's lands in Lincolnshire and Yorkshire were worth a further £40 *p.a.*, although she did not come into possession of her inheritance until 1413. A.J. Elder, 'A Study of the Beauforts and their Estates, 1399–1450' (unpub. Bryn Mawr Ph.D. thesis, 1964), pp. 69–71; G.L. Harriss, *Cardinal Beaufort: A Study of Lancastrian Ascendancy and Decline* (Oxford, 1988), pp. 6–7; *CFR, 1413–22*, pp. 22–3.

him, therefore, the Bardolf inheritance constituted a highly significant territorial interest, which, despite his later eminence in government, was to remain his greatest stake in the localities.[51]

With many of the noble interests in the area in abeyance, and with duchy influence effectively in the hands of men of significantly lesser status, Beaufort's lordship rapidly became a force to be reckoned with across the entire region. His new authority was most immediately felt in the area around the Bardolf lands. By February 1406 he was already heading a commission to investigate insurrection in the nearby town of King's Lynn, an appointment which he shared with the Lancastrians Erpingham, Winter, Gournay and Oldhall.[52] However, the royal grants he acquired during these years suggest a willingness on his own part and on that of the king to establish his authority more securely in East Anglia as a whole.[53] Most significantly, in May 1408 his life grant of the Bardolf lands was converted into an hereditary estate.[54] Since Beaufort's death without issue in 1426 could not reasonably have been anticipated eighteen years earlier, it seems likely that Henry intended his half-brother's presence in East Anglia to be permanent. Certainly, his consistent appointment to every commission of the peace in Norfolk from 1406 and in Suffolk from 1411, for example, made him the highest-ranking JP in the region apart from the duke of York in Norfolk, and the earl of Suffolk who was appointed in both counties.[55] The fact that the authority of both these men was to some degree compromised – York's by the marginality of the region to his territorial interests and Suffolk's by his lack of influence at court – made Beaufort's presence all the more significant. Moreover, his authority

---

[51] Harriss, *Cardinal Beaufort*, pp. 162–4, 353.

[52] The other commissioners were the lawyers John Cokayn and William Lodyngton, and the local knight John Inglesthorpe: *CPR, 1405–8*, p. 152.

[53] From September 1406 until October of the following year, during the vacancy of the see of Norwich, Beaufort had the keeping of the temporalities of the bishopric, and in April 1407 he secured the farm of the town of Dunwich in Suffolk: *CFR, 1405–13*, pp. 45, 71–2; *CPR, 1405–8*, p. 445.

[54] *CPR, 1405–8*, p. 443.

[55] *CPR, 1405–8*, pp. 494, 497; *CPR, 1408–13*, pp. 483, 485.

was from the first closely associated with Thomas Erpingham and the local Lancastrians. William Phelip, Erpingham's nephew, entered Beaufort's service, and it was presumably through the latter's influence that Phelip was by 1407 married to the daughter and coheiress of Lord Bardolf.[56] This alliance ensured that, even should the Wormegay estates revert from Beaufort control to their previous owners, they would still fall within the Lancastrian sphere of influence in the region.

The final element in the hierarchy of authority connecting the power structures which represented and ruled the region with the power of the crown was the local involvement of the Prince of Wales. His duchy of Cornwall lordship of Castle Rising in western Norfolk lay close to the Bardolf estates belonging to Beaufort, his uncle, with whom his association in government became ever closer in the latter half of the reign.[57] The prince's authority might therefore be expected to have buttressed Beaufort's attempts to establish himself in East Anglia, and this undoubtedly proved to be the case. However, Henry's personal involvement in the region – in terms both of his landed interest and of his association with the leading local gentry – also became much deeper during the following years.

Thomas Erpingham, whose prominence among the closest associates of the king had been marked in the early years of the reign, became increasingly associated at both a national and a regional level with the emerging interest of the Prince of Wales. In 1405 Erpingham lost the custody of the Mowbray castle at Framlingham, and in 1409 he surrendered the keeping of the Mortimer lands. However, the new beneficiary in both cases was Prince Henry, and it seems that the grants reflected and underpinned his growing links in the region, in which Erpingham's service played a key role,[58] rather than any fall from grace of the latter, who retained possession of three Mowbray manors in Norfolk, and received an annuity of 100 marks from the prince at

---

[56] *William Worcestre: Itineraries*, ed. J.H. Harvey (Oxford, 1969), p. 355; *GEC*, I, p. 420. Phelip would later become chief executor of Beaufort's will: *CCR, 1435–41*, pp. 374–5.

[57] Harriss, *Cardinal Beaufort*, pp. 16, 43–67.

[58] *CPR, 1405–8*, p. 23; *CFR, 1405–13*, pp. 150–1.

Framlingham.[59] Moreover, Erpingham was not the sole East Anglian presence in the prince's retinue. One of John Winter's professional interests was the stewardship of the duchy of Cornwall, an office he held until 1402, and this connection brought him into the service of Prince Henry, from whom he held several key appointments.[60] In the early years of the reign he was controller of the prince's household, an office he exchanged in 1403 for that of receiver-general.[61] The man with whom he exchanged office was John Spenser, a Norfolk esquire who had been attached to Henry's household since at least 1401.[62] The keeping of the prince's 'secret treasury' was entrusted to another Norfolk esquire, John Wodehous, whose service with the prince on campaign in Wales was rewarded in his native area with his appointment as steward of Castle Rising.[63] This East Anglian element was further afforced by the presence in Henry's household of Erpingham's nephew John Phelip, the younger brother

[59] *CFR, 1399–1405*, pp. 315, 320–1; *CPR, 1405–8*, p. 21; PRO, Special Collections, Ministers' and Receivers' Accounts, SC6/997/20. In 1409, in return for the offices of constable of Dover castle and warden of the Cinque Ports which he also surrendered to Henry, Erpingham was granted a further £100 a year assigned on the prince's Lincolnshire estates: *CPR, 1408–13*, p. 57; W.R.M. Griffiths, 'The Military Career and Affinity of Henry, Prince of Wales, 1399–1413' (unpub. Oxford M.Litt. thesis, 1980), p. 208.

[60] For Winter's career in Lancastrian service, see above, at nn. 15–19.

[61] From 1403 Winter also received a fee of £20 assigned at Kirton-in-Lindsey, the same Lincolnshire estate from which Erpingham was to receive a fee of £100 later in the reign: Griffiths, 'The Military Career . . . of Henry, Prince of Wales', pp. 116–17, 217.

[62] In 1403, when Spenser took over from Winter as controller, the prince granted him £20 a year from the part of the tollbooth in King's Lynn held by the duchy of Cornwall. On Henry's accession to the throne in 1413, Spenser became cofferer of the royal household and subsequently keeper of the great wardrobe. Ibid., pp. 116–17, 215; E. de L. Fagan, 'Some Aspects of the King's Household in the Reign of Henry V' (unpub. London M.A. thesis, 1935), pp. 191, 246.

[63] Wodehous was acting as Henry's treasurer in 1401 and again in 1407–8. He received an annuity of £40 from the prince. Griffiths describes Wodehous as a 'close friend of the prince and king': Griffiths, 'The Military Career . . . of Henry, Prince of Wales', pp. 121–4, 174, 217. He may also have been related to Thomas Erpingham through his paternal grandmother, though the exact relationship is not clear: F. Blomefield, *An Essay towards a Topographical History of the County of Norfolk* (11 vols. 1805–10), VI, p. 414.

of Beaufort's retainer William.[64] Unsurprisingly, it is clear that at a local level Phelip, Spenser and Wodehous fitted seamlessly into the network in which Erpingham and Winter were so prominent. When John Phelip was granted an alien priory estate in Norfolk in 1409, for example, his mainpernors were Sir John Strange and John Spenser.[65] Spenser had also acted as surety the year before for a group including Simon Felbrigg and Edmund Oldhall in a local transaction involving Erpingham, William Phelip and John Gournay.[66] When, in 1413, the bishopric of Norwich fell vacant, the temporalities were committed to Erpingham, Winter, Wodehous and Spenser, for whom Oldhall acted as mainpernor.[67]

It is clear that Prince Henry had developed a much closer association with the Lancastrian network in East Anglia than in many other areas of the duchy, and also that this association was stronger than his father's links with the region. The prince's local involvement formed part of a hierarchy which connected the gentry of East Anglia, through various interests including that of the duchy, to the royal power of the crown. Henry's accession to the throne in 1413 allowed this expanding network to dominate the entire region. The blossoming of this local connection both during the reign of Henry V and under the rule of the lords he appointed to govern after his death took place very clearly under the lordship of Thomas Beaufort, who had been granted the earldom of Dorset in 1412 and whom Henry created duke of Exeter four years later.[68] Not only did the eminence of his new estate mean that he headed every peace commission in Norfolk and Suffolk from 1416 until his death ten years later, but from 1418 until 1423 in Norfolk, and from 1417 until 1422 in Suffolk, he was the only

---

[64] John Phelip's association with the prince can be dated to the early years of the reign, since his annuity was increased in 1406 from its previous level of £10 to 40 marks: Griffiths, 'The Military Career . . . of Henry, Prince of Wales', p. 213; *CPR, 1413–16*, p. 92.

[65] Phelip shortly afterwards surrendered Horstead in favour of his uncle, Erpingham, while retaining the reversion: *CFR, 1405–13*, p. 145; *CPR, 1408–13*, pp. 80–1.

[66] *CCR, 1405–9*, p. 385.

[67] *CFR, 1413–22*, p. 12.

[68] *GEC*, V, p. 201; *CPR, 1416–22*, p. 53.

nobleman named as a JP.[69] In 1415 he became formally involved with the duchy when he was named as one of the feoffees to whom Henry committed part of the Lancastrian estates, a settlement which included the East Anglian lands.[70] His local influence was further reinforced in 1417 when he was granted custody of the estates of the earl of Oxford during the minority of the latter's son and heir, who became a member of Beaufort's household.[71] In 1425, he added to this wardship the keeping of the Mortimer lands in East Anglia, which again passed to the crown during the minority of Richard, duke of York.[72]

William Worcestre's note of the members of Beaufort's household gives ample testimony to the influence of the latter's lordship in both Norfolk and Suffolk. Apart from William Phelip and the earl of Oxford, the East Anglian knights and esquires in Beaufort's service also included William Oldhall, William Calthorp, John Carbonell and his son Richard, William Wolf, John Shardelowe, William Drury, Robert Clifton, John Curson and Gilbert Debenham.[73] Beaufort's increased eminence in the government of his nephew does seem to have meant that he became a more remote figure in local politics; certainly his appearances on local commissions other than those of the peace dwindled as his responsibilities at court grew. However, the extensive following he commanded among the leading local gentry represented his authority effectively in the region, and, in turn, their local influence was reinforced by connections with his regional lordship and Henry's royal overlordship.

[69] *CPR, 1416–22*, pp. 456, 460; *1422–9*, p. 566. This isolation on the peace commission owed much to the fact that other potential noble JPs were fighting in France. Nevertheless, Beaufort continued to be appointed despite his own service abroad from 1418 to 1422. Moreover, he seems to have taken some pains to maintain contact with East Anglia. The accounts of the corporation of Norwich record payments made in 1416 and in 1420 to messengers bringing letters and news to the city from Beaufort in France. Harriss, *Cardinal Beaufort*, pp. 101–4; *Records of the City of Norwich*, ed. Tingey and Hudson, II, pp. 62–3.

[70] Somerville, *History of the Duchy*, pp. 199, 339.

[71] *CPR, 1416–22*, p. 110; *CCR, 1413–19*, p. 395; *Worcestre: Itineraries*, ed. Harvey, p. 355.

[72] In the same year Beaufort also reacquired the temporalities of the see of Norwich during another vacancy: *CFR, 1422–30*, pp. 85, 108.

[73] *Worcestre: Itineraries*, ed. Harvey, p. 355.

At the head of this group, Erpingham and his family also reaped local benefits from the change of regime. In 1415, after the deaths of Michael, earl of Suffolk and his eldest son at Harfleur and Agincourt respectively, custody of the de la Pole estates was granted to the dowager countess together with Erpingham and William Phelip.[74] Erpingham continued his regular membership of the Norfolk peace commission, and from 1423, under the rule of the lords of the minority council among whom Beaufort was prominent, Phelip was regularly appointed to the Suffolk bench.[75] John Phelip, William's younger brother, benefited particularly from his personal connections with the king,[76] although his political activity in East Anglia was more circumscribed than that of his brother. As a younger son who would inherit neither the Phelip lands at Dennington nor the Erpingham estates, John focused his territorial interests, greatly increased by several royal grants, elsewhere.[77] Nevertheless, he remained closely associated both with his older brother and with Beaufort. In 1415 John too became a feoffee in the duchy, and in the same year he married the daughter and heiress of Thomas Chaucer, the Beauforts' cousin and close ally. Phelip's career was cut short a few months later, however, by his death at Harfleur.[78] John Wodehous was another of the East Anglian group whose service to Henry brought him advancement. In 1413 he was appointed chancellor of the duchy, and was named a feoffee and executor in Henry's will two years later; he was appointed chamberlain of the exchequer for life in 1415, and later became chancellor to Queen Katherine.[79] This activity at court did

---

[74] *CPR, 1413–16*, pp. 383–4.

[75] *CPR, 1413–16*, p. 421; *1416–22*, p. 456; *1422–9*, pp. 566, 570; *1429–36*, p. 625; *1436–41*, pp. 590–1.

[76] See above, at n. 64.

[77] Phelip remained a member of Henry's household after 1413: PRO, Exchequer, Various Accounts, E101/407/10. For grants to Phelip of custody of lands see, for example, *CPR, 1413–16*, pp. 67, 131–2, 257, 328, 361 (properties in Berkshire, Bedfordshire, Dorset, Gloucestershire, Buckinghamshire, Sussex, Southampton, Kent and Suffolk).

[78] Somerville, *History of the Duchy*, p. 339; *CPR, 1413–16*, p. 356; *GEC*, XI, p. 395; J.H. Wylie and W.T. Waugh, *The Reign of Henry the Fifth* (3 vols. Cambridge, 1914–29), II, p. 47.

[79] *CPR, 1413–16*, pp. 336, 365; Somerville, *History of the Duchy*, pp. 199, 389.

not disrupt his involvement in regional affairs. He represented Norfolk in
parliament three times during the reign, and was appointed to the peace
commission in the shire from 1415, while, again, royal grants helped to enhance
his local territorial interests.[80]

It seems that the multiplicity of Lancastrian connections within the disparate
political society of East Anglia, combined with a hierarchy of authority which
linked the region directly with the crown itself, meant that the affinity offered
sufficient scope for the realization of interests and the settlement of conflict
within the region as a whole. It is not easy to interpret judicial records as
quantitative evidence of conflict within political society during the first two
decades of the century, since the king's bench records, the major source for
disputes involving landowners, are somewhat sparse for these years and may not
be complete.[81] However, even allowing for possible losses, the fact that both the
surviving records of the king's bench and the relatively full series of assize rolls
contain almost no major cases from the region does suggest that the dominance
of the Lancastrian connection did not provoke instability and confrontation.
Rather, the complex web of public and private authority which supported the
affinity seems to have allowed it to develop into an extraordinarily broad and
cohesive network which had a credible claim to represent the full range of
regional interests.

There were, of course, changes within this affinity. John Winter, for example,
died in 1414, and was succeeded in the local stewardship of the duchy by his
colleague, John Wodehous.[82] Nevertheless, it is clear that the connection was
maintaining its coherence as a younger generation emerged within the same
political orbit. John Winter's nephew-in-law, John Heydon, for example, was
retained as legal counsel by the duchy, and rose to prominence in the service of

---

[80] In 1413, for example, Wodehous was granted the keeping of alien priory estates at Welles,
Norfolk and Paunfield, Essex: *CPR, 1413–16*, pp. 52, 421; *1416–22*, p. 456; *Return of the Name*,
pp. 284, 290, 297.

[81] C. Carpenter, *Locality and Polity: A Study of Warwickshire Landed Society, 1401–1499* (Cambridge,
1992), pp. 364, 707.

[82] Richmond, *The Paston Family*, p. 72; Somerville, *History of the Duchy*, p. 594.

William Phelip.[83] In 1425, John Wodehous relinquished his stewardship of the duchy in East Anglia to make way for his son-in-law, Sir Thomas Tuddenham, a member of Beaufort's household.[84] The names of Thomas Tuddenham and John Heydon are familiar – indeed, notorious – from their leading role in the Pastons' account of East Anglian politics in the 1440s. However, the context in which they appear here seems entirely unexpected. Tuddenham and Heydon, that 'unruly pair' usually identified as prime culprits in the hijacking of regional affairs by members of a court clique during the 1440s,[85] in fact had an impeccable pedigree in Lancastrian service which predated any association with the earl of Suffolk, and were among the legitimate heirs of a political connection which had peacefully dominated the region since the beginning of the century.

This conclusion provides the first indication that some aspects at least of the familiar picture of Suffolk's local rule in the 1440s may not in fact be entirely accurate. Moreover, the case for a new perspective is substantially supported by analysis of the greatest changes which overcame the Lancastrian network in the region during the 1420s and 1430s. In 1426 Thomas Beaufort died, leaving no direct heirs to take over his estates at Wormegay, and his death was followed two years later by that of the veteran knight, Thomas Erpingham.[86] Active royal direction had been lost with the death of Henry V in 1422; now the existing leadership of the East Anglian connection had also been removed. At the same time, the political vacuum in Suffolk – the circumstance which had allowed the essentially Norfolk-based duchy connection to broaden its scope across the entire region – was coming to an end as a new generation emerged among the East Anglian nobility. The hierarchy of authority in the region, and the relationship between public and private interests which had been so successfully

---

[83] Richmond, *The Paston Family*, pp. 89–90; W.J. Blake, 'Fuller's List of Norfolk Gentry', *Norfolk Archaeology*, XXXII (1961), p. 272; Somerville, *History of the Duchy*, p. 425. Phelip and Heydon were associated certainly by 1431; *CFR, 1430–7*, p. 59.

[84] R. Virgoe, 'The Divorce of Sir Thomas Tuddenham', *Norfolk Archaeology*, XXXIV (1969), p. 406; PRO, DL42/18, pt. 2 f. 61; *Worcestre: Itineraries*, ed. Harvey, p. 355.

[85] R.A. Griffiths, *The Reign of Henry VI: The Exercise of Royal Authority, 1422–1461* (1981), p. 342.

[86] *GEC*, V, p. 204; *DNB*, suppl. XXII, p. 615.

negotiated during the first three decades of the century, were again in flux on
the newly repopulated East Anglian stage.

John Mowbray, for example, retrieved a substantial part of his estates in the
region in 1425 on the death of his mother, and in the same year was restored to
the dukedom of Norfolk. However, it appears that he visited East Anglia – a
region where the Mowbrays had yet to establish themselves as a political force –
relatively rarely, and that, in the brief periods which he spent in England
between military campaigns in France, he continued to regard Lincolnshire as
his home. He died in 1432 having apparently made little political impact in
Norfolk and Suffolk, leaving an heir aged only seventeen.[87] William de la Pole,
earl of Suffolk, on the other hand, returned to England in 1430 after more than
a decade spent fighting in France,[88] and plunged immediately into East Anglian
affairs. This could no longer be a straightforward resumption of inherited
power, since the rule of the two shires had, since the early part of the century,
passed to a close-knit group of men whose authority remained intrinsically
connected both to the crown itself and to the crown in the particular guise of
the duchy. Moreover, the cohesion of this connection had not been immediately
undermined by the loss of Beaufort and Erpingham, since it was so broadly
based and deeply rooted in the gentry society of the region. The way was open
for any contender for local rule to attempt to win the service of this powerful
but now leaderless affinity; indeed, success in the attempt was essential if any
nobleman was to impose his authority on the region.

The obvious candidate to take over the leadership of the affinity was perhaps
William Phelip, as the heir of Sir Thomas Erpingham, as one of Beaufort's
closest associates, and because he had a claim to Beaufort's Wormegay estates
through his wife Joan Bardolf. However, from the moment of Suffolk's return to
England, the latter also allied himself firmly with the powerful association of
regional interests which had developed around Beaufort and Erpingham. In

---

[87] *GEC*, IX, pp. 606–7; for these points, and fuller discussion of the Mowbrays' situation in East
Anglia, see Archer, 'The Mowbrays', pp. 177, 190, 261–4, 282–7; Castor, 'The Duchy of
Lancaster', pp. 115–20.

[88] *GEC*, XII i, pp. 444–5.

1430, Suffolk married Alice Chaucer, who had been the wife of John Phelip until his death in 1415, and whose father Thomas was one of the closest allies of his cousins, the Beauforts.[89] In the following year, when the Bardolf estates at Wormegay were granted at farm, it was Suffolk, not William Phelip, who secured their possession.[90] Through this grant, the earl gained control of the territorial stake which had underpinned Beaufort's regional authority. Moreover, the estates greatly increased his own local landed interest, since the de la Pole properties in Norfolk consisted only of scattered individual manors. His mainpernors for the Wormegay grant included the Suffolk knight John Shardelowe and the Norfolk esquire Thomas Hoo, both of whom had been members of Beaufort's household.[91] In other words, Suffolk was immediately picking up the threads of the local Beaufort connection to which his marriage had given him access, in terms of both land and personnel. His association with Thomas Tuddenham, for example, was already close by 1435, when the earl became Tuddenham's chief feoffee in his Norfolk manor of Oxburgh.[92] Moreover, since the broad political connection associated with the duchy and the Lancastrian crown had not lost its coherence in the region in the few years since the deaths of Beaufort and Erpingham, Suffolk's rapid acquisition of the service of prominent individuals such as Tuddenham brought him into contact with a wider local network, besides giving members of that network access to his lordship.

Suffolk's increasing authority in East Anglia, intrinsically linked as it was to his burgeoning association with the duchy–crown affinity, represented a significant challenge to the regional influence of William Phelip, who had both a specific

---

[89] *CPR, 1429–36*, p. 86.

[90] *CFR, 1430–7*, pp. 33, 60–1.

[91] See n. 90 above; *Worcestre: Itineraries*, ed. Harvey, pp. 355, 359 (Shardelowe); *A Collection of all the Wills . . . of the Kings and Queens of England*, ed. J. Nichols (1780), p. 262 (Hoo). Hoo was Suffolk's chief steward at Costessey in 1431–2, and was the only person outside the earl's family to whom the latter was paying an annuity in 1436: Richmond, *The Paston Family*, p. 239n; PRO, Exchequer, King's Remembrancer, Miscellanea, E163/7/31, pt. 1. Shardelowe and Hoo were both in fact already closely associated with Suffolk by October 1430, when they served as feoffees for the earl, and acted with him in his negotiations for Alice Chaucer's hand: PRO, Exchequer, King's Remembrancer, Ancient Deeds, Series D, E210/5796; BL, Harleian Charter, 54.1.9.

[92] *CCR, 1429–35*, pp. 361–2. For Tuddenham's service to Beaufort, see above, at n. 84.

claim to the Wormegay estates which were now in Suffolk's possession, and a general one to the political legacy of Beaufort and Erpingham. Phelip had, with Erpingham, held the custody of Suffolk's lands during his short minority,[93] but there is little evidence of further direct association between the two in a local context in the years immediately after the earl's return to England – the time at which the latter was securing his stake in the political connection left by Beaufort, which Phelip might have hoped to inherit. Their relationship was by no means straightforwardly antagonistic; they had too many associations in common, as leading officeholders in the king's household and at a local level through their Beaufort connections, for their interests to diverge sufficiently for any rivalry to become overt opposition. Nevertheless, their respective authorities continued in uneasy parallel within East Anglian politics until 1437. In that year, a series of manoeuvres resulted in an accommodation which extended Phelip's territorial stake in the area, while establishing Suffolk's authority as the dominant regional lordship.[94] In November 1437 Suffolk surrendered his farm of the Wormegay lands so that an hereditary grant could finally be made to Phelip; two days later, Phelip surrendered the lordship of Swaffham in Norfolk, the farm of which he had recently acquired, so that it could be granted for life to Suffolk.[95] It is hard to avoid the conclusion that an exchange had been negotiated to allow Phelip to recover his wife's inheritance, while preserving the earl's enhanced authority in Norfolk.

This interpretation is supported by the reorganization of the duchy administration in the same year, in which accommodation was again reached between the rival claims of Suffolk and Phelip. The earl became chief steward of the north parts of the duchy, and Phelip was granted the equivalent office in the south.[96] The local stewardship of the duchy lands in East Anglia, which Phelip had acquired earlier in the 1430s, was transferred back to its former

[93] See above, n. 74.

[94] For full details of these manoeuvres, see Castor, 'The Duchy of Lancaster', pp. 100–4; J.L. Watts, 'Domestic Politics and the Constitution in the Reign of Henry VI, c. 1435–61' (unpub. Cambridge Ph.D. thesis, 1990), pp. 180–2.

[95] *CPR, 1436–41*, pp. 117–18, 133; *CFR, 1430–7*, p. 336. It seems to have been with the Wormegay estates that Phelip acquired the title of Lord Bardolf: *GEC*, I, pp. 420–1.

[96] PRO, DL42/18, ff. 47–47v.

incumbent, Thomas Tuddenham, who had been a member of Beaufort's household at the same time as Phelip, but had rapidly become associated with Suffolk during the 1430s.[97] These settlements seem to have represented a watershed in the development of the political relationship between Suffolk and Phelip, and only from 1437 were their regional interests fully assimilated into a single political connection. It was not until this point, for example, that John Heydon, Phelip's deputy as chief steward of the south parts of the duchy, and later executor of his will, began to forge his close and later infamous association with Suffolk.[98]

Nevertheless, the very fact that co-operation had been achieved left Suffolk with the upper hand. Grants of office and land may have been divided equally, but in the region where the territorial interests of the two men were concentrated the extent of the earl's lands overshadowed Phelip's collection of estates. On top of this, by 1437 Suffolk was clearly in the ascendant at court.[99] The latter observation brings this discussion back to its starting-point: Suffolk's influence in government and its role in buttressing his regional power in East Anglia. Examination of the structures of local authority in the first four decades of the fifteenth century has demonstrated that Suffolk's eminence in government during the 1440s cannot be regarded as the *sine qua non* of his local rule. Nor can it be maintained that his followers, men such as Tuddenham and Heydon, were interlopers deriving illegitimate power in the region from their position in the king's household. Rather, the earl's authority in national government merely served to reinforce a position of local dominance which he had already achieved during the 1430s. He had built on the territorial advantages his extensive estates gave him in Suffolk by establishing his lordship over an exceptionally broad, cohesive and powerful political network, which had developed since the beginning

---

[97] PRO, DL42/18, f. 94.

[98] Somerville, *History of the Duchy*, p. 430; *Register of Henry Chichele*, II, p. 598. In 1440 Suffolk supported Heydon unequivocally when he incurred the enmity of the duke of Norfolk: see *CCR, 1435–41*, p. 381; Storey, *End of the House of Lancaster*, pp. 226–7; Castor, 'The Duchy of Lancaster', pp. 124–6.

[99] Harriss, *Cardinal Beaufort*, pp. 270–1, 293–4; Griffiths, *Henry VI*, pp. 233–4; Wolffe, *Henry VI*, p. 104.

of the century around the duchy of Lancaster estates under the auspices of royal authority. Tuddenham and Heydon enjoyed their influence in East Anglia originally as representatives of this 'Lancastrian' connection. Their local authority in fact predated that of Suffolk himself; the acquisition of their service helped to secure Suffolk's regional power, rather than the other way around. By 1440, therefore, Suffolk and his wide-ranging and broadly representative affinity embodied traditional structures of power in East Anglia, as the legitimate successors to the 'royal' connection which had evolved around the duchy under the lordship of Thomas Erpingham, Thomas Beaufort and Henry V.

   In other words, some aspects of the accepted picture of Suffolk's 'systematic and illegal exploitation of his position'[100] in East Anglia in the 1440s stand in need of revision. The earl did not exploit his position in central government to subvert established political hierarchies in the region; rather, he himself represented those hierarchies. Against this background, it may be important to re-examine other aspects of his role, and the role of his affinity, in East Anglian society. Did Suffolk in fact systematically and illegally exploit the position of regional authority which was legitimately his? The credibility of the Pastons as our chief witnesses needs to be tested thoroughly against the full range of surviving evidence before their account of East Anglian politics can be accepted as authoritative. The de la Pole connection had inherited its substantial and long-standing local authority from traditional and legitimate structures of power in the region. With this in mind, it is perhaps worth considering the thought that the version of events portrayed in the letters may have been profoundly coloured by the fact that it was the Pastons, and not the earl of Suffolk, whose claim to a prominent place in local landed society was of recent origin and uncertain provenance.[101]

---

[100] Richmond, *The Paston Family*, p. 235.

[101] See *The Paston Letters, 1422–1509*, ed. J. Gairdner (6 vols. 1904), I, i, pp. 28–31, and Richmond, *The Paston Family*, pp. 2–42, for the meteoric rise during the early decades of the century, via a successful legal career, of William Paston, the son of a mere husbandman (possibly even a bondman). For fuller consideration of these issues, and of the local politics of the period 1440–61, see Castor, 'The Duchy of Lancaster', chs. 4 and 5.

4

PROPAGANDA, PUBLIC OPINION AND THE SIEGE OF CALAIS IN 1436*

James A. Doig

The congress of Arras in 1435 marks a watershed in late medieval English history. As one contemporary observed, the rupture of the English alliance with Burgundy was 'a singler help in al the Conquest of Normandy and of Fraunce'.[1] From the moment when the English delegation swept out of the conference hall after rejecting the final French offer of peace, leaving France and Burgundy to compose their differences, the fragility of the dual monarchy was exposed. Some English commentators were openly critical of the intransigence of the Lancastrian embassy, and Hugh de Lannoy, governor of Holland, in a letter to the duke of Burgundy in September 1436, probably provides an accurate gauge of English opinion at the time:

> the common people of England are so tired of war that they are more or less desperate. It is true that they have experienced important disputes among themselves, for the majority of people blamed the royal council for not achieving a general peace at the congress of Arras, and for refusing the offers made to them immediately after it.[2]

* I would like to thank Professor R.A. Griffiths for critically reading a draft of this paper.

[1] *The Brut or the Chronicles of England*, ed. F.W.D. Brie (2 vols. EETS, CXXXI & CXXXVI, 1906–8), II, p. 503. On the congress, see J.G. Dickinson, *The Congress of Arras, 1435* (Oxford, 1955).

[2] *Brut*, II, p. 503; G.L. Harriss, *Cardinal Beaufort: A Study of Lancastrian Ascendancy and Decline* (Oxford, 1988), p. 255; R. Vaughan, *Philip the Good* (1970), pp. 104–5.

The consequences of Arras tested the public relations of the crown in two respects. Firstly, the crown found it necessary to justify its hard-line policy at the congress, a policy which was based largely on a strict adherence to the terms of the treaty of Troyes. Henry V had widely publicized the treaty and from 1422 royal propaganda had emphasized the glory of the dual monarchy; however, the rupture of the Anglo-Burgundian alliance indicated to many that peace with France was the preferable option.[3] Secondly, faced with a public opinion apparently divided about the prospects of continued war, it was essential for the crown to fortify the resolve of its subjects, particularly now that Burgundy could no longer be relied on to shoulder part of the burden of supplying men and arms. In the months which followed the congress of Arras, a propaganda offensive was launched which vilified the duke of Burgundy and his allies and stressed the threat which they posed to England and the dual monarchy.

By the fifteenth century there were numerous channels of political communication at the disposal of the crown; most of them were well-tried and efficient. The crown had long harnessed the institutions of central and local government and of church and parliament to reach the mass of the king's subjects. From the reign of John, when government records begin to survive in significant numbers, the importance of political communication in national politics is much in evidence. *Magna Carta* was proclaimed throughout the kingdom in the vernacular and Henry III's decree declaring allegiance to the provisions of Oxford was drawn up in French and English and similarly widely declaimed. Henry III used sophisticated arguments to counter the claims of Simon de Montfort and the barons; Edward I appealed directly to his subjects for support when he embarked on his military expeditions against the Scots and Welsh; and Edward III successfully popularized his military and political ambitions in France. In the late fourteenth and fifteenth centuries, the extension of literacy significantly increased the use of the written message and had a marked influence on expressions of political dissent. Nevertheless, while increased literacy enhanced the sophistication of political communication, it did

---

[3] On royal propaganda and the dual monarchy, see R.A. Griffiths, *The Reign of King Henry VI: the Exercise of Royal Authority, 1422–1461* (1981), pp. 217–28, and the references there.

not increase the number of people influenced by political messages. The mass of the population continued to be reached through aural and visual media.

Perhaps the most effective method of broadcasting the royal will was by proclamation. Sheriffs were ordered to make proclamations 'in your full county court and in cities, boroughs and markets' where the greatest numbers of people would gather. Sometimes a wider area of publication was requested; in 1346, for example, sheriffs were instructed to proclaim the news of Edward III's successes in Normandy *in pleno comitatu tuo, quam in Feriis, Mercatis, et aliis locis publicis, in Balliva tua, infra Libertates et extra.*[4] It was difficult, if not impossible, for the crown to police the sheriffs who were responsible for promulgating royal decrees; thus, the writs of proclamation frequently included threats of amercement or forfeiture if the proclamations were not made. At other times the writs would include an appeal to the sheriffs' sense of national duty, such as 'order upon his allegiance, as he loves the king and his honour and desires the defence of the realm, to cause the proclamation to be made'.[5] The text of a proclamation was written in Latin and was translated into English, presumably by the sheriff's clerk, for promulgation.[6] As it was desirable that the text be followed as closely as possible, it was preceded by instructions to cry the edict *in haec verba* or *in forma sequenti.* Often a note to the sheriff to omit nothing in the text concluded the writ. Again, these instructions frequently appealed to his public duty to the crown; thus, a writ of proclamation of array against Owain Glyn Dŵr in 1402, read: *Et hoc, super Fide et Ligentia tuis, ac sicut Nos et honorem nostrum Defensionemque Regni nostri Angliae diligus, nullatenus omittas.*[7] One effective

---

[4] *Foedera*, II, iv, p. 203.

[5] Ibid., IV, i, p. 49, from a writ of proclamation to array troops against an expected invasion of the Welsh and French in 1405.

[6] There is little doubt that the text was translated into the vernacular; it is improbable that proclamations were cried in Latin. Furthermore, there is no evidence to suggest that translations were provided by the government; the number of local dialects would have made them largely unintelligible. Only after 1450 were writs of proclamation drawn up in English, and up until the accession of Edward IV this occurred only rarely, see A. Allan, 'Royal Propaganda and the Proclamations of Edward IV,' *BIHR*, LIX (1986), p. 153.

[7] *Foedera*, IV, i, p. 30.

method of ensuring that a proclamation was made in accordance with the instructions set out in the writ was to order the sheriff to return the writ to the royal chancery endorsed with the dates and places where the proclamation was made. The surviving returns indicate that general proclamations, that is, those promulgated throughout the kingdom, were heard in over 200 places in the realm.[8] They also show that proclamations were made quickly in the counties. In Yorkshire, for example, a proclamation of 1398 ordering the duke of Norfolk to appear before the king was heard in eighteen towns within five days of the sheriff receiving the writ; a proclamation of 1404 suspending annuities was heard in fourteen towns within a week.[9] In London, the latter decree was made, apparently in a single day, at the Standard in Cheap, at the Leadenhall above Cornhill, at the Grasschurch in Langbourne, at the wharf of Woolkey in the Tower Ward, at the wharf at Billingsgate, at Bridgestreet, at Stodies Lane in the Vintry, at the Wharf at Queenhithe, and the suburbs of Aldgate, Bishopsgate, Cripplegate, Aldersgate, Smithfield, Holborn and Fleet.[10] The proclamation was certainly an effective news service and a useful instrument for propaganda. Military victories, invasion warnings, diplomatic expeditions, the agreement of truces, and measures against Lollardy and dissent were regularly broadcast throughout the kingdom. Statutes and ordinances were similarly proclaimed, and their preambles could have an avowedly propagandist intent.[11] It should be noted, however, that whatever the efforts of the crown, there was no guarantee that proclamations would be heard in areas dominated by its opponents. Hence, it is impossible to gauge the effectiveness of proclamations against the barons in 1261 and the duke of York and his supporters in 1460.[12]

[8] J.R. Maddicott, 'The County Community and the Making of Public Opinion in Fourteenth Century England,' *TRHS*, 5th series, XXVIII (1978), pp. 34–6.

[9] PRO, Chancery, Taxes and Rolls Chapel Series, Miscellaneous Files and Writs, C255/3/7/18; 8/25. Note that in the boroughs it was probably the responsibility of the hundred bailiffs to ensure that the writs were executed.

[10] C255/3/8/20.

[11] See, for example, a statute of 1452–3 making void the acts of Jack Cade, *SR*, II, p. 360.

[12] *Foedera* (Record Edition), I, p. 408; *Foedera*, V, ii, p. 97.

Another efficient method of informing and influencing public opinion which would affect all church-goers was the sermon. The crown frequently enlisted the help of the church to order prayers, sermons and processions for the success of military and diplomatic expeditions, and the well-being of the king and kingdom.[13] In the Lancastrian period alone requests for such religious devotions number at least seventy, and their frequency suggests that they were a permanent feature of the religious calendar.[14] They range from prayers for the Emperor Sigismund in 1415 and 1416, to prayers against spells and black magic directed against Henry V, to prayers for the restoration of the health of Henry VI and the expulsion of the Saracens from Byzantium in 1453.[15] Devotions invariably took place on Wednesdays and Fridays, and parishioners were encouraged to attend by the offer of a 40-days' indulgence. The prayers used on such occasions were taken from the relevant votive mass from the Sarum Missal such as the *missa pro rege* or the *missa contra adversantes*.[16] They were probably conducted in Latin, a language beyond the understanding of most people; however, the sermons were undoubtedly declaimed in English and some survive in the occasional

[13] H.J. Hewitt, *The Organization of War Under Edward III* (Manchester, 1966), pp. 160–5; W.R. Jones, 'The English Church and Royal Propaganda During the Hundred Years War', *Journal of British Studies*, XIX (1979), pp. 18–30; A.K. McHardy, 'Liturgy and Propaganda in the Diocese of Lincoln during the Hundred Years War', *Studies in Church History*, XVIII (1982), pp. 215–27.

[14] The mandates requesting prayers survive in bishops' registers. For some unpublished examples for the reigns of Henry IV and Henry V, see London Guildhall Library RO, MS. 9531/3 (register of Robert Braybrooke), ff. 301^v–302 (16 October 1399), ff. 303^v–304 (7 June 1400), ff. 305^{r-v} (1 June 1401); ibid., MS. 9531/4 (contains the registers of Roger Walden, Nicholas Bubwith, Richard Clifford, John Kemp and Robert Fitzhugh), ff. 12 (30 August 1405), 20^v (23 July 1407), 142 (1 December 1408), 150^v–151 (26 August 1412), 155–156 (21 January 1413), 152 (23 October 1413), 161 (9 April 1415), 161^v–162 (7 June 1415), 165^{r-v} (2 August 1416), 167^v–168 (16 December 1416), 168^v (8 May 1417), 185^v (4 April 1418), 186 (8 August 1418), 188^{r-v} (26 October 1418), 187^v–188 (5 September 1419).

[15] *The Register of Philip Repingdon*, ed. M. Archer (3 vols. Lincoln Record Society, 1963–82), II, pp. 127–8; III, pp. 57, 289; *Foedera*, IV, ii, p. 169; *Concilia Magnae Brittaniae et Hiberniae, A.D. 466–1718* ed. D. Wilkins (4 vols. 1737), III, pp. 563–4.

[16] *The Sarum Missal*, ed. J.W. Legg (Oxford, 1916), pp. 397, 411.

sermon collection.[17] The third element of these devotions was the procession. Any gathering of folk, such as at fairs and markets, facilitated the exchange of views and information, and presumably processions were no exception. However, unlike other forms of co-operative action, these processions focused the collective mind in an act of piety which engendered feelings of national solidarity.

In the fifteenth century requests for special devotions were usually initiated by the archbishops, although the decision to mobilize the clergy was probably made in the royal council chamber.[18] In the province of Canterbury archiepiscopal mandates ordering prayers were usually sent to the bishop of London, the dean of the province, who, in turn, relayed the instructions to the dioceses. At the diocesan level, the request was transmitted by the bishops to their subordinates, whether the commissary general or the archdeacons and their officials. They conveyed the request to the lesser clergy and made sure that the devotions were carried out in conventual churches, chapels and parish churches throughout the diocese.

As with the sheriffs, the assiduousness of the bishops and their officials was monitored. Bishops were required to certify that each request had been carried out and to provide the archbishop with details of dates and places. On 1 September 1412, for example, Robert Hallum, bishop of Salisbury, received a mandate from Richard Clifford, bishop of London, transmitting a mandate from Thomas Arundel, archbishop of Canterbury, dated 14 August; it requested prayers for the military expedition of the duke of Clarence. The bishop of London was expected to notify the archbishop of the action taken before 14 September. Subsequently, Bishop Hallum sent copies of the mandate to the

---

[17] R. Haines, 'Church, Society and Politics in the Early Fifteenth Century, as viewed from an English Pulpit', *Studies in Church History*, XII (1975), pp. 143–57; idem, ' "Our Master Mariner, Our Sovereign Lord," a Contemporary Preacher's View of King Henry V', *Medieval Studies*, XXXVIII (1976), pp. 85–96. A vernacular sermon *pro pace* is in *Middle English Sermons*, ed. W.O. Ross (EETS, 1940), pp. 206–14. Also see G.R. Owst, *Preaching in Medieval England* (Cambridge, 1926), pp. 222–30.

[18] However, it is evident that bishops could order prayers on their own initiative; see McHardy, 'Liturgy and Propaganda', pp. 223–4. Sometimes prayers were ordered by means of a royal writ; see *Foedera*, IV, i, pp. 81, 189; ii, pp. 169, 187; iii, p. 45.

dean of Salisbury, requesting appropriate prayers in Salisbury cathedral, and to Geoffrey Crukoden, canon of Salisbury, who was ordered to execute the request in respect of the diocese. On 7 September notification was sent to the archbishop that his request had been complied with.[19] Such devotions complemented royal proclamations in that they disseminated news of national importance throughout the realm and contributed to a favourable opinion of the Lancastrian regime; indeed their effects were probably more wide-reaching, for the tentacles of ecclesiastical administration penetrated to the remotest corners of the kingdom. As H.J. Hewitt observes, the religious devotions helped to 'direct men's mind to the achievements of the royal, and indeed the national, aim'.[20]

The distinguished constitutional historian, Helen Cam, pointed out many years ago that among their other roles, the members of parliament during the middle ages served as 'publicity agents' for the crown. Antonio Marongiu similarly recognized that the purposes of parliament embraced the 'public relations' of medieval kings.[21] The monarchy used parliament to publicize royal occasions such as coronations, weddings, and entries, as well as to promulgate new laws and to publish treaties. The attendance of the nobility and the clergy, the knights and the townsmen, meant that the deeds and decisions of the English kings could be disseminated across a wide social spectrum, and could serve to strengthen the monarchy, popularize a policy or justify the grant of a subsidy. As the king was obliged to seek the assent of his subjects with regard to laws and taxation, it was necessary for the crown to persuade (or cajole) the commons of the justice of its demands and actions.

The chancellor's sermon at the opening of parliament, ostensibly a statement of the business of parliament, was couched in terms designed to elicit a favourable response to the crown's demands. According to the *Modus Tenendi*

---

[19] *The Register of Robert Hallum, Bishop of Salisbury, 1407–1417*, ed. J.M. Horn, Canterbury and York Society (1982), p. 151.

[20] Hewitt, *Organization of War*, p. 163.

[21] H.M. Cam, *Liberties and Communities in Medieval England* (Cambridge, 1944), p. 226; Antonio Marongiu, *Medieval Parliaments*, trans. J. Wolfe (1968), pp. 45, 47–52.

Parliamentum, an anonymous treatise on the nature of parliament usually dated to about 1321, the function of the chancellor's speech was *pronunciae causas parliamenti primo in genere, et postea in specie.*[22] The generalized section of the address was academic and discursive in tone and didactic and conventional in content, taking texts from scripture and expressing political themes which seemed relevant to the specific purposes of the parliament, or to contemporary issues and exigencies. Hence, the sermon served the dual purpose of instructing and informing. The brief was, of course, recorded in the rolls of parliament, which were themselves propagandist documents, compiled selectively by clerks, probably under supervision. They were sometimes circulated, as was the case, most famously, with Henry IV's first parliament, whose record of Richard II's deposition found its way into numerous chronicles.[23] Chroniclers themselves showed a keen interest in parliaments, often reporting when they were held, and sometimes setting down their proceedings at length, occasionally, as with Adam of Usk, as the result of first-hand experience.[24]

Borough representatives were required to report parliamentary proceedings to their constituents. May McKisack found evidence of such reports in the assembly books and Guildhall rolls of King's Lynn.[25] The surviving reports are generally meagre, but it is evident that the burgesses were required to report in some detail; in 1413, for example, the burgesses of King's Lynn said that the chancellor spoke on the text *Ante omnem actum stabile consilium* and discussed his exposition at some length before reporting the specific business of parliament.[26] Other evidence also suggests that the chancellor's homily was widely circulated. The collection of political poems in Bodleian Library, Oxford, Digby MS. 102

---

[22] *Parliamentary Texts of the Later Middle Ages*, ed. N. Pronay and J. Taylor (Oxford, 1980), p. 71.

[23] G.O. Sayles, 'The Deposition of Richard II: Three Lancastrian Narratives,' *BIHR*, LIV (1981), pp. 257–70.

[24] *Chronicon Adae de Usk, A.D. 1377–1421*, ed. and trans. E.M. Thompson (2nd ed., 1904), pp. 9–18, 152–163. For the detailed reports of parliament in fourteenth-century chronicles, see J. Taylor, *English Historical Literature in the Fourteenth Century* (Oxford, 1987), pp. 195–216.

[25] M. McKisack, *The Parliamentary Representation of the English Boroughs During the Middle Ages* (Oxford, 1932, repr. 1962), pp. 139–44.

[26] Ibid., p. 141.

may have been composed by a single author who attended parliament in the first two decades of the fifteenth century; some of the poems appear to reflect the concerns of the parliamentary sermons of that period.[27] F. Taylor and J.S. Roskell have pointed out that works such as the *Gesta Henrici Quinti* expressed views in accord with the chancellor's speech in the parliaments of Henry's auspicious reign, 'often with similar phrasing'.[28] Hence, the opening homily could reach and influence a large audience and, as Professor Chrimes suggested, may have contributed to the political vocabulary of those who attended parliament.[29]

In the late middle ages, as at other times, poetry served the propagandist functions of publicity and persuasion as well as of entertainment. Officially sponsored verse explained the Lancastrian claim to the French throne, exalted Henry V's victories at Agincourt and Rouen, and related Henry VI's triumphant entry into London in 1432 and Queen Margaret's entry in 1445.[30] These poems, composed by such court poets as John Lydgate and Thomas Hoccleve, popularized an unashamedly Lancastrian view of the present, glorifying the deeds of kings and noblemen out of all proportion. The numbers in which they survive suggest that they enjoyed a wide currency. Propagandist verse was, of course, deployed by both Lancastrians and Yorkists during the Wars of the Roses, and a range of literary techniques and devices was used by poets to rally supporters to both sides. The reference to lords by their badges and coats of arms, the punning of names, the insistence on the solidarity of their own faction and on divine favour characterize much of this verse.[31] A novel, if particularly nasty, device was used on the night of 17 September 1456 when the

[27] *Twenty-Six Political and Other Poems*, ed. J. Kail (EETS, CXXIV, 1904); see particularly pp. 55–60.

[28] *Gesta Henrici Quinti*, ed. F. Taylor and J.S. Roskell (Oxford, 1975), p. xxix.

[29] S.B. Chrimes, *English Constitutional Ideas in the Fifteenth Century* (Cambridge, 1936), pp. 305–6.

[30] *Chronicles of London*, ed. C.L. Kingsford (Oxford, 1905), pp. 120–2; *The Historical Collections of a Citizen of London in the Fifteenth Century*, ed. J. Gairdner (Camden Society, new series, XVII, 1876), pp. 1–46; see below, notes 37, 38. Generally on this, see V.J. Scattergood, *Politics and Poetry in the Fifteenth Century* (1971), pp. 35–106.

[31] Ibid., pp. 173–217.

heads of five dead dogs appeared on the standard in Fleet Street, evidently placed there by a Lancastrian partisan; in the mouth of each dog was a paper containing a quatrain revealing how these animals had been sacrificed to the ambitions of the duke of York.[32] It is difficult to say whether these poems were recited or read; the well known 'Collection of a Yorkist Partisan' is a convenient, compact roll, which looks like the sort of thing which was declaimed at political gatherings.[33] Many poems were copied into common-place books, chronicles and anthologies to be perused at leisure, and indicate an enduring interest in their subject matter.

Other forms of political diatribe, such as newsletters, bills and open letters were publicly posted and distributed, as, indeed, were sermons, proclamations and poems.[34] In 1450, 'many strange and woundyrfulle bylle were sete in dyvers placys, sum at the kyngys owne chambyr door at Westemyster, in hys palysse, and sum at the halle dore at Westmyster, and sum at Poulys chyrche, and in many other dyvers placys of London'.[35] For those who could not read, the gist of the bill would be passed on to them by those who could.

In a largely illiterate society, visual propaganda could demand attention and convey a clear meaning. Livery badges, for example, were easily identifiable: in the November parliament of 1450, 'every lorde hadde hys bagge a-pon his harnys, and hyr mayny also, that they myght ben knowe by hyr baggys and leverys'.[36] Pageants and mummings could deal with political themes, as, for example, the tableaux devised to entertain and, evidently, to edify the king and his subjects at royal entries. When, in 1432, Henry VI returned to England after his coronation in France, an elaborate series of pageants was devised,

[32] *Historical Poems of the Fourteenth and Fifteenth Centuries*, ed. R.H. Robbins (New York, 1959), pp. 189–91.

[33] BL, Cotton Roll II, 23; C.L. Kingsford, *English Historical Literature in the Fifteenth Century* (Oxford, 1913), pp. 358–68.

[34] J.L. Kirby, 'Henry V and the City of London,' *History Today*, XXVI (1976), p. 224; Owst, *Preaching in Medieval England*, p. 225.

[35] *The Historical Collections of a Citizen of London*, p. 195. For other examples, see *CPR, 1446–52*, p. 579; *CCR, 1447–54*, p. 396.

[36] *The Historical Collections of a Citizen of London*, p. 195.

possibly by John Lydgate, for the royal procession through London.[37] At the Cross in Cheap, the king encountered two trees which bore the arms of England and France, and the pedigree of Henry going back to Edward the Confessor and St Louis. The other pageants were high-brow allegorical pieces which exemplified certain aspects of kingship which were appropriate to the occasion in view of Henry's recent coronation. In like manner, the pageants devised for Queen Margaret's entry in 1445 were concerned with peace and unity, while those made for Henry V's triumphant entry in 1415 emphasized the king's divinity.[38] These tableaux allowed for the unfolding of a visual sermon on political themes, and steps were taken to ensure that their message was widely understood. In 1432 and 1445 explanatory verses were attached to the pageants which left no doubt as to their meaning, and sometimes the characters explained their own roles in prepared speeches.

By the mid-fifteenth century these methods of political communication were sophisticated and efficient, and in the Burgundian crisis which followed the congress of Arras they were exploited to the full. In the parliament which met late in 1435, the chancellor, John Stafford, railed against Burgundy in his opening speech and indicated the likelihood of war.[39] The text of his sermon was from Ephesians 4: 3 – *soliciti siti servare unitatem spiritus in vinculo pacis* – which, no doubt, referred ironically to Burgundy's *volte face* at Arras. Not surprisingly, Stafford's view of the congress was partisan and a distortion of actual events. He maintained that the duke of Burgundy had chosen a date to treat of peace between England and France at Arras without consulting Henry VI or his council. The English king had nevertheless sent ambassadors to the congress who proposed reasonable and honest terms of agreement, but the French and

---

[37] H.N. MacCracken, 'King Henry's Triumphal Entry into London, Lydgate's Poem and Carpenter's Letter,' *Archiv Für das Studium der Neueren Sprachen und Literaturen*, CXXVI (1911), pp. 75–102.

[38] C. Brown, 'Lydgate's Verses on Queen Margaret's Entry into London,' *Modern Language Review*, XIII (1915), pp. 53–7; *Gesta Henrici Quinti*, pp. 100–13.

[39] *RP*, IV, p. 481.

Burgundians, *non ut pacis, ut protius guerrarum zelatores*, rejected the English offers, and responded with terms which were *trupha et derisoria*. The king was subsequently informed that Philip had treacherously quit the English alliance for the French; hence, Henry VI could either capitulate and lose his crown of France or prepare to defend his rights through war. Stafford concluded that to consider how best to respond to the present circumstances was the reason for the summoning of parliament. The chancellor thus defended the English delegation's actions at Arras, and invoked the plea of necessity in order to justify an appropriate subsidy.[40] Stafford's exhortation appears to have had the desired effect, and the commons responded with a number of petitions implementing sanctions against the Flemings.[41] More importantly, a large subsidy was granted and a special graded income tax on land and offices was introduced.[42]

Henry VI himself fuelled the reaction against Burgundy by publishing a papal bull which he had obtained in July 1435 preventing his vassals from soliciting release from their allegiance to the king.[43] Thus, the king publicly cast aspersions on the papal absolution from his oath to the English crown which Philip had received at Arras. English propaganda was to make much of Burgundy's 'fals foresworn' behaviour. Furthermore, Henry VI, as feudal overlord of the duke of Burgundy by virtue of the dual monarchy, declared forfeit the territories of his rebellious subject. Henceforth, Philip was styled 'him who calls himself duke of Burgundy and count of Flanders' in all official documents, a practice reminiscent of Edward III's references to Philip of Valois.[44] The crisis appears to have prompted Henry VI to assume a more active role in government than heretofore; he attended a meeting of the continual council for the first time in October 1435, and he first authorized a warrant with his own sign manual in

---

[40] On 'necessity', see G.L. Harriss, 'Aids, Loans and Benevolences,' *Cambridge Historical Journal*, VI (1963), pp. 1–19.

[41] *RP*, IV, pp. 491–3.

[42] Ibid., pp. 486–8.

[43] *Foedera*, V, i, pp. 21, 23.

[44] *English Historical Documents, IV, 1327–1485*, ed. A.R. Myers (1969), pp. 67–8. In a similar vein were the duke of Bedford's ordinances against the French in 1423: B.J.H. Rowe, 'King Henry VI's Claim to France in Picture and Poem', *The Library*, XIII (1932–3), p. 77.

July 1436.[45] However, it is unlikely that the fourteen-year-old king masterminded the campaign against Burgundy, though his ire was certainly aroused; upon learning that Philip no longer addressed him as his sovereign, he burst into tears before his assembled council.[46] One experienced campaigner who had long recognized the value of public support to his enterprises was Humphrey, duke of Gloucester. In the recent past he had angered Philip by attempting to take Hainault by force, and now, on 1 November 1435, he was appointed captain of Calais and royal lieutenant of Picardy, Flanders and Artois.[47] His role in the propaganda campaign against Burgundy and the Flemings may have been crucial.

At the end of 1436, Duke Philip was probably still inclined towards peace. Following Arras, he had sent a placatory embassy to England; however, his heralds were lodged in the house of a shoemaker (according to a Burgundian account) and treated with contempt. Worse was to follow when news of Burgundy's defection was made public:

> *Si se mirent ensamble pluiseurs du commun, et alerent en divers lieux parmy ladicte ville pour quérir aulcuns Flamanz, Hollandois, Braibencons, Picars, Haynuyers et aultres des pays dudet duc, qui la estoient pour faire leur merchandise, non eulx doubtans de ceste adventure. Et en ceste fureur, en prirent et occirent aulcuns soubdainement.*[48]

According to the same source, 'no-one who was well bred was sparing of the grossest abuse against the duke of Burgundy'.[49] His messengers, curtly dismissed with only a verbal reply, feared for their lives but managed to escape to the

[45] PRO, Chancery, Warrants for the Great Seal, Series I, C81/1545/55; Exchequer, Treasury of Receipt, Council and Privy Seal Records, E28/57/92. See Harriss, *Cardinal Beaufort*, p. 256; Griffiths, *Reign of King Henry VI*, p. 231; J.L. Watts, 'When did Henry VI's Minority End?', in *Trade, Devotion and Governance: Papers in Later Medieval History* (Stroud, 1994), pp. 125, 136 n.68.

[46] *La Chronique d'Enguerran de Monstrelet . . . 1400–1444*, ed. L. Douët d'Arq (6 vols. Paris, 1857–62), V, p. 192 (hereafter, *Chronique*).

[47] *Foedera*, V, i, p. 23; *RP*, IV, pp. 483–4; *PPC*, V, p. 5.

[48] *Chronique*, V, p. 192–3. Monstrelet maintains that Henry VI quickly put an end to the violence, ibid., p. 193.

[49] Ibid., p. 192.

coast. Anti-alien feeling was, of course, a perennial threat to the numerous foreign merchants inhabiting London in the later middle ages. In 1425 serious outbreaks of violence occurred and anti-Flemish bills were distributed round the city; in 1435–6 the crown's propaganda offensive against Burgundy no doubt prompted a similar reaction.[50]

Although late in 1435 Philip sent the archbishop of Rouen to England to try to prevent conflict, by February 1436 his patience had worn thin. English acts of piracy, raids into Flanders, and Henry's efforts to solicit help from the Dutch and the Emperor Sigismund provoked an angry letter to the king.[51] Henry's reply, addressed to 'him who calls himself duke of Burgundy and count of Flanders', rebutted Philip's charges at length and in turn accused him of fabricating his complaints. A draft of this letter survives showing that references to 'the Flemings' were amended to read 'our subjects of Flanders', corrections designed to emphasize Henry's continuing authority in Flanders.[52] It was sent to various parts of France and Flanders which further incensed the duke, and soon afterwards an English spy's report of a council held in Ghent early in March disclosed Philip's intention to besiege Calais.[53]

The duke of Gloucester himself organized the bid to 'rescow Calais' from the clutches of Burgundy and enormous efforts were made to extract loans and raise a relief force:

Then Humfrey, Duyke of Gloucestre, Protectoure and Deffendoure of England and capetyn of Calais and of Guysnes, send for al the lordes of the Realme, both spirituell and temperell, and for al his feede men, and desired of hem an eyde for the rescowe of . . . Calais.[54]

---

[50] For the events of 1425, see Griffiths, *Reign of King Henry VI*, pp. 74–5. On anti-alien violence in the fifteenth century, see S.L. Thrupp, 'Aliens In and Around London in the Fifteenth Century', in *Studies in London History Presented to P.E. Jones*, ed. A.E. Hollaender and W. Kellaway (1969), pp. 251–72.

[51] M.R. Thielemans, *Bourgogne et Angleterre . . . 1435–1467* (Brussels, 1966), pp. 437–8.

[52] *PPC*, IV, pp. 329–34; J. Le Fevre de Saint-Remy, *Chronique, 1400–44*, ed. F. Morand (2 vols. Paris, 1876–81), II, pp. 374–81.

[53] *Chronique*, V, pp. 211–12; below, n. 55.

[54] *Brut*, II, p. 574.

Late in March the crown appealed to the public at large, circulating throughout the kingdom the report of the spy, together with letters exhorting the king's subjects to contribute to the defence of Calais. They were reminded:

> How grete a jewel the seide towne with his marchies is to us and to our lande; how grete many fold and importable grevys, hurtes and harmes that the sayd towne and marchies did and bare dayly to this lande whiles it was in the ennemys handes and sembely were like to doo. And also to caste this lande out of all reputacion and into perpetuelle reproche, vilanye and shame through the world yf so fell, as with our lordis mercy it never schall falle, that it were getyn by oure ennemys for lak of convenable defense in tyme.[55]

About the same time, commissioners were dispatched to different counties to raise loans and men for the defence of Calais. They were ordered to 'avise such meanes as shalbe thought to theim most expedient and behovefull for the frutefull execucon of their power and thereto appointe suche daies and places within the saide shire to have trety with the inhabitants thereof as theim seme best'. They were directed to proclaim that Calais 'sittith as nigh to the kings hert and to the lordes of his counsail as it may doo', and that if the town were lost 'it sholde be the grettist dishonor rebuke sclaunder and shame that myght grawe to this reame and over that to irrecuperable an hurt to the king and all his subgitts'.[56] Feelings of national pride and honour were generated, and once again the plea of necessity was invoked.

One gauge of the success of the crown's appeals to public opinion is the magnitude of the loans obtained. A number of chronicles provide an account of the crown's efforts to raise finance and men and they accurately reflect the concern and enthusiasm aroused by the crown's appeals.[57] Between 17 April and 11 July sixty-three individual loans netted over £4,000 and, in all, the

---

[55] BL., Additional MS. 14848, f. 190, with f. 190–1 for the spy's report. All references to this source are printed in J.A. Doig, 'A New Source for the Siege of Calais in 1436', *EHR*, CX (1995), pp. 404–16. *Historical Manuscripts Commission, Various Collections*, IV, pp. 197–200.

[56] *PPC*, IV, p. 352, b–e.

[57] For example, *Brut*, II, pp. 468, 505.

amounts raised by loans over the Michaelmas and Easter terms of 1435–6 amounted to more than £48,000.[58] Cardinal Beaufort's contribution was considerable; on 15 February he loaned 20,000 marks for the payment of wages to York, Salisbury and Mortain, and on 23 July he arranged a further loan of 9,000 marks 'for the defence of Calais'.[59] The feoffees of the duchy of Lancaster provided £4,000 early in May, and on 15 May the archbishop of Canterbury loaned over £1,500. The mayor and the city of London contributed £1,333, the people of Bristol and Bath £200 each, and those of Norwich £100. Foreign merchants residing in England gave generously, and those of Venice, Genoa and Florence provided about £800 between them.[60]

It is evident that in England during the later middle ages the royal writ was the crown's preferred vehicle for disseminating propaganda, and between March and July 1436 a rash of writs of proclamation and privy seal letters was dispatched from the royal chancery in response to the growing Burgundian threat.[61] Rumours of Philip's intentions probably caused the anti-Flemish reaction which prompted a proclamation issued on 20 March offering protection to friendly Flemings on condition that they renew their oaths of fidelity to the English crown.[62] The writ was critical of the Flemings for allowing themselves to be 'induced or rather seduced by perverse and treasonable counsels of him who calls himself the duke of Burgundy'. A proclamation dated 18 June requesting free shipping for the earl of Huntingdon, admiral of England, deplored Burgundy's defection at Arras and the threat he represented to the dual monarchy.[63] The Flemings were censured in almost identical phrasing to the earlier proclamation, and the writ emphasized the *injuriam et contemptum* and *magnum opprobium* which would follow the fall of Calais,

---

[58] Harriss, *Cardinal Beaufort*, pp. 257, 260.

[59] Ibid., pp. 258, 260; *Foedera*, V, i, pp. 26, 32; *CPR, 1432–6*, p. 604.

[60] PRO, Exchequer, Exchequer of Receipt, Receipt Rolls, E401/747, 8 May, 10 May, 15 May, 1 May, 17 April, 3 May, 8 May, 30 June.

[61] P.S. Lewis, 'War Propaganda and Historiography in Fifteenth Century France and England', *TRHS*, 5th series, XV (1965), pp. 14–16.

[62] *CCR, 1435–41*, p. 38; *Foedera*, V, i, p. 27.

[63] Ibid., p. 31.

terms once again reminiscent of earlier government directives. On 3 July writs of proclamation were sent to the sheriffs of Essex and Hertfordshire and fifteen other counties, ordering all persons willing to serve with the duke of Gloucester in defence of Calais to assemble at Sandwich by 22 July.[64] As usual, the treachery of Burgundy was invoked, on this occasion with regard to the capture of Oye (*fraudulenter ceperit*), and the consequences of losing Calais are represented in familiar terms:

> *si sic eveniret, nedum in nostri scandalum et opprobrium, verum etiam in utriusque Regnorum nostrorum Francie et Angliae Laesionem et Derogationem tenderet manifesta.*

As the situation in the Calais marches deteriorated, privy seal letters were dispatched to towns and religious houses (and presumably the gentry) in the kingdom asking for men and keeping the king's subjects apprised of developments. Thus, in one letter 'we be credybly enfourmed that the malice of hym that callith hym duc of Burgoigne ne cessith not but contynueth and encreseth fro tyme to tyme'; in another, 'the seid callying hym duc hath take oure fortalice of Oye and slayn at oure soudeours therynne and that the secunde day of Juyll . . . next comyng purposith hym redely to be before . . . Caleys'.[65]

Contemporary local records provide some gauge of the public's response. The town of Salisbury placed a company of twelve 'defensable and habile men' at the king's service; on 23 July the aldermen of Norwich issued an order for the array of forty men for the defence of Calais; the Grocers' Company in London provided 'ii speres and iiii bowes, sowdiers ffor the sauf kepyng of Caleys'; the abbey of Bury St Edmunds provided *personas versus calisiam transmittendas duos videlicet Armorum viros cum viii valettis sagittariis in una secta iuxta eorum statum per omnia uniformes.*[66] Not all were enthusiastic, however; the town of Lydd paid the expenses of Richard Glover to travel to Canterbury to excuse the town from

---

[64] *CCR, 1435–41*, pp. 68–9; *Foedera*, V, i, p. 32.

[65] BL, Add. MS. 14848, f. 191–2. The letters are dated 16 June and 30 June.

[66] *HMC, Various Collections*, IV, p. 198; Norfolk and Norwich RO, case 16, shelf d, f. 1; J.B. Heath, *Some Account of the Worshipful Company of Grocers* (1854), p. 395; BL, Add. MS. 14848, f. 192.

involvement in the expedition.[67] An impressive relief force of almost 8,000 was eventually assembled and under the command of Gloucester it prepared to cross the channel late in July.[68]

A week or so earlier the church was mobilized. On 22 July archiepiscopal mandates were dispatched from London to different dioceses ordering prayers and processions for the success of Gloucester's expedition.[69] In the diocese of Exeter, Bishop Lacy did not receive the mandate until 5 August, but on the following day copies were sent to the archdeacons and their officials. By this time the siege had been raised, and Gloucester had passed Gravelines water to embark on a systematic destruction of Flanders. Devotions were nevertheless to take place on Mondays, Wednesdays and Fridays, *in ecclesiis suis cathedralibus et aliis ecclesiis conventualibus et collegatis tam regularibus quam secularibus necnon parochialibus ecclesiis suarum civitatem et diocesium.* The processions were to be observed *cum omni cordis humilitate, nudes pedes, si qui modo induci valeant,* and alms giving was to be included in the devotions, perhaps indicating the crown's financial need. The explanatory preamble of the mandate censured the duke of Burgundy in familiar terms and sermons based on it were probably declaimed from pulpits throughout the kingdom.

Some reactions at home were less constructive. Anti-Flemish hostility seems to have continued unabated. In response to the proclamation offering protection to friendly aliens, 1,800 Lowlanders of various nationalities came forward to take the oath of allegiance; 400 of them were from the London area.[70] By 21 July, when the siege was in full swing, emotions had reached such a pitch in London that the city government was forced to issue a proclamation forbidding the molestation of Flemish merchants and other foreigners who had taken the oath in April.[71] Earlier, in mid-June, the city government took steps to

---

[67] *HMC, 4th Report*, p. 518.

[68] Griffiths, *Reign of King Henry VI*, p. 204.

[69] *The Register of Edmund Lacy, Bishop of Exeter, 1420–1455*, ed. G.R. Dunstan, Canterbury and York Society (5 vols. 1963–72), II, pp. 15–17; *Registrum Thome Spofford, Episcopi Herefordensis, A.D. 1412–1448*, ed. A.T. Bannister, Canterbury and York Society (1919) pp. 215–16.

[70] *CPR, 1429–36*, pp. 37–9, 541–88; *Foedera*, V, i, p. 28; Thrupp, 'Aliens In and Around London', in *Studies in London History*, pp. 255–6.

prevent a boycott of the Dutch brewing industry which had been crippled by rumours that its produce was 'poisonous, not fit to drink and caused drunkenness'.[72] Invasion rumours also spread through the southern counties. On 22 March, a special Brodhill was held at Romney which ordered that each port should warn the others upon sight of the enemy, and this may have prompted the townsmen of Lydd to purchase two new horns for their watchmen.[73] The Waltham annals record fears of an attack on Maldon, Essex, in June, and earlier, in April, Sandwich prepared for an invasion.[74] In a proclamation of 3 July, troops mustered in the south-eastern counties were ordered to heed only the words of the sheriffs because rumours spread by people dwelling along the coast were causing disturbances. Furthermore, in May government anxiety had been heightened by a campaign of seditious billing, spread by 'children of iniquity in the realm, native and alien'.[75]

Meanwhile, the duke of Gloucester had marshalled the physical and mental resources of the kingdom for a confrontation with Burgundy which, as one commentator astutely observed, he perhaps hoped would make him a worthy successor to Henry V as vanquisher of France.[76] In the end, however, Gloucester's role was negligible. By the time he arrived at Calais at the head of the relief force on 2 August, the siege was abandoned; the heroics of the count of Mortain, the nephew of Gloucester's old adversary, Henry Beaufort, were perhaps decisive in Burgundy's humiliation. Denied the chance of personal glory, Gloucester launched a savage *chevauchée* into Flanders which accomplished little. Yet, on his return to London late in August, he quickly attempted to immortalise his role as the triumphant rescuer of Calais. Indeed the parliament which met in January 1437 commended 'the most esteemed uncle of the king,

---

[71] *Calendar of the Letter-Books Preserved Among the Archives of the Corporation of the City of London*, ed. R.R. Sharpe (11 vols. A–L, 1899–1912), Letter Book K, p. 206.

[72] Ibid, p. 205.

[73] *A Calendar of the White and Black Books of the Cinque Ports, 1432–1955* ed. F. Hull (1966), p. 7; *HMC, 4th Report*, p. 518.

[74] Griffiths, *Reign of King Henry VI*, p. 208.

[75] *CCR, 1435–41*, pp. 68–9, 60; *Calendar of Letter Books*, ed. Sharpe, Letter Book K, p. 204.

[76] Harriss, *Cardinal Beaufort*, pp. 254, 263.

Humphrey, duke of Gloucester and other temporal lords for rescuing Calais and resisting he who calls himself duke of Burgundy, enemy and rebel of the king'.[77]

The four surviving English poems concerning the siege of Calais have been examined at some length by Professor Scattergood and C.L. Kingsford, amongst others, and their strong nationalistic sentiment, reminiscent of Laurence Minot's fourteenth-century verse, is well known.[78] If the chronicles are to be believed, these poems were hugely popular in the celebrations which followed the abandonment of the siege, and they may have been circulated in multiple manuscript copies.[79] Furthermore, the dates of composition of the manuscripts in which they survive suggest that they continued to be read long after the events which they relate.

Two of the poems, 'In Despite of the Flemings' and 'Mockery of the Flemings,' survive in copies of the *Brut* chronicle, appended to accounts of the siege of Calais.[80] 'Mockery of the Flemings' is the most vituperative of all the extant poems; in his jingoistic fervour the poet owes more to Laurence Minot than do the others. It is most interesting as a striking instance of a versifier drawing from a chronicle account. It survives in Lambeth Palace, London, Lambeth MS. 6, a finely illuminated St Albans chronicle, in a hand of the late fifteenth century. It contains the longest and best English narrative of the siege, and the poet borrows freely from this source, as the following example, among many, illustrates:

'Mockery'	*Brut*
ll.36–7. Remembres ye of Brugge, how ye first wan youre shan,/ How ye com forth to scarmyssh upon on aftirnoon/ with pavyses and crossebowes on Saynt Petirs playn.	p. 580. Sone after that, it fell that they of Brugges that lay at Saint Petirs, com from theire tentes down to Bulleyngate ward, some with pavis, and some with crossebowes.

[77] *RP*, IV, pp. 506–7.

[78] Scattergood, *Politics and Poetry*, pp. 83–90; Kingsford, *English Historical Literature*, pp. 240–1.

[79] *Brut*, II, p. 582.

[80] Ibid., pp. 582–4, 600–1.

'In Despite of the Flemings' survives in a unique, late fifteenth-century version of the *Brut*, Lambeth MS. 84, and has been attributed to John Lydgate by H.N. MacCracken.[81] Although its brevity (five eight-line stanzas) is not typical of Lydgate's verse, it shows signs of official sponsorship, and it may have been distributed in bill form. Unlike 'Mockery of the Flemings', the abuse of the Flemings is muted. The poet stresses rather Burgundy's deceit in turning the Flemings against the English: 'But thou ageynward, be fals decepcioun,/ Madest Flaundrys ageyn Ingeland to malygne.' This is similar in sentiment to the proclamations examined earlier, and suggests that the function of the poem was to focus popular outrage on Burgundy and away from the Flemings. The poem has significant similarities of expression and sentiment to a third poem, 'Scorn of the Duke of Burgundy', as the following parallels illustrate:

'Despite'	'Scorn'
ll.14–17: Fyrst to remembre . . ./ How Harry the fifthe, of knyghtly gentylness,/ Had of his [John, Duke of Burgundy] deth manly compassioun.	ll.9–11: Remembre the, Phelippe . . ./ How king Henre the Vte, of veray gentinesse,/ Withoute thy desert he was to the kynde.
ll.22–4. Thou [Philip] madest an oothe, be gret avisynesse./ Uppon the Sacrement at Armyas, in that toun,/ Ay to be trewe, voyde of dobylnesse.	ll.27–9 . . . thou [Philip] madest a solempne vow,/ Using goddes body the holy sacrement,/ To become trew ligeman with gode entent.

'Scorn of the Duke of Burgundy' survives in English College, Rome, MS. 1306, a major Lydgate anthology of the second half of the fifteenth century, and an incomplete version is in the British Library, Sloan MS. 252.[82] MacCracken

[81] H.N. MacCracken, 'A New Poem by Lydgate', *Anglia*, XXXIII (1910), pp. 283–6.

[82] The Rome version is printed in *Historical Poems of the Fourteenth and Fifteenth Centuries*, pp. 86–9; The Sloane version is in *A Collection of Political Poems and Songs Relating to English History, From the Accession of Edward III to the Reign of Henry VIII*, ed. T. Wright (RS, 2 vols. 1859–61), II, pp. 148–9.

seems to have accepted it as by John Lydgate, though he did not include it in his edition of Lydgate's minor poems.[83] It may also have been officially sponsored, concluding with a plea to Philip to reconsider his position and rejoin the English:

> fforsake thy frowardnes and become stable,
> Be trew of promesse and sadde of governance,
> Obey thy ligelord, and be not variable,
> Lest thou be destroied and end with myschance. (ll. 109–12)

The poet proves himself to be sensitive to the issues involved here. The maintenance of the Anglo-Burgundian alliance was economically and strategically crucial to both parties, a fact which was finally recognized in 1439 when links were restored after protracted negotiations. Further evidence of official sponsorship and of Lydgate's authorship may be detected in similarities between these poems and the well-known *Libel of English Policy* and Lydgate's 'Debate of the Horse, Goose and Sheep'.[84]

'The Siege of Calais' is one of the best and most detailed narratives of the siege.[85] It survives in two manuscripts, along with 'Scorn of the Duke of Burgundy' in the Rome MS. and in British Library, Cotton Galba E IX, which also contains Laurence Minot's poems, where it is written on a flyleaf. The anonymous poet offers some unique material and there are a number of similarities of expression and detail with the chronicles. Although the pride and boastfulness of the Flemings are not ignored, the

---

[83] A. Klinefelter, 'The Siege of Calais: A new Text', *Proceedings of the Modern Language Association of America*, LXVII (1952), p. 889 n. 7. Note, however, that MacCracken was unaware of the Rome MS, which links the poem to Lydgate, when he published his edition of the *Minor Poems* in 1934; see R.A. Klinefelter, 'A Newly Discovered Fifteenth-Century English Manuscript', *Modern Language Quarterly*, XIV (1953), pp. 3–6.

[84] On this, see G.A. Holmes, 'The "Libel of English Policy"', *EHR*, LXXVI (1961), pp. 212–14; MacCracken, 'A New Poem by Lydgate', pp. 283–6.

[85] *Historical Poems of the Fourteenth and Fifteenth Centuries*, pp. 78–83.

poem is essentially a celebration of the deeds of the English, with certain individuals singled out for attention. The verse is assured and often light-hearted, with a hint of pageantry about the proceedings, reinforced by the opening evocation of summer, reminiscent of chivalric romance. It is the work of a competent poet and it is tempting to conclude that it was directed towards a courtly audience, if only because it lacks the cutting edge of popular verse, which was notoriously strident when English fortunes were at stake.

Two of these four poems stress the intervention of Gloucester in raising the siege. 'The Siege of Calais' and 'Scorn of the Duke of Burgundy' assert that Burgundy abandoned the siege because of his fear of Gloucester:

> Erly the duk fled away . . .
> Ffor they had verray knowyng
> Of the duc of Gloucester commyng
> Calais to rescow. (ll. 152, 157–9)

And

> . . . duc Humfray at sandwich redy to saille
> To rescow Calais and doo his ligeance,
> Thou flygh away for dred of bataille. (ll. 93–5)

Consider, too, the 'Libel of English Policy,' which Professor Holmes recognized as representing 'roughtly the point of view of the duke of Gloucester':[86]

> For they turned bake and hyede fast
> Milorde of Gloucestre made hen so agaste. (ll. 294–5)

---

[86] Holmes, 'Libel of English Policy', p. 211. The poem is printed in *The Libelle of Englyshe Policye,* ed. G. Warner (Oxford, 1926).

Poems such as these exaggerated the importance of Gloucester's role and may
have been commissioned by Gloucester himself. The 'Libel of English Policy'
almost certainly was, and a four-line tag from it is attached to the version of
'The Siege of Calais' in Cotton Galba E IX. Lydgate, whom Gloucester
commissioned on a number of occasions, may have composed them, but it is
impossible to be certain.[87] One poem which was certainly sponsored by
Gloucester is Titus Livius Frulovisi's 'Humfroidos,' a celebration in appalling
Latin hexameters of Humphrey's deeds from the congress of Arras to his
return to England in 1436.[88] The work survives in a single manuscript in
Seville, in Biblioteca Columbina, MS.7.2.23, which also contains Frulovisi's
De Republica. The sentiments of the poem are familiar: the unchivalric conduct
of Burgundy is frequently alluded to; his refusal to confront Gloucester's force,
leaving his land unprotected, is shameful; the Flemings are repeatedly
described as arrogant and cowardly, and following Gloucester's *chevauchée* they
hang from trees like grapes on a vine. The bravery of the English garrison is
stressed; they are described as fighting lions and appear to the Flemings more
numerous than five hundred strong; throughout the poem the English are
called 'Britons', invoking the legendary origins of Britain. Gloucester, is of
course, the hero of the poem. When he returns to England and a tumultuous
reception, Henry VI declares: 'you most brave hero will now hold the heart of
our house with great glory'.[89] Thus, Gloucester's ambition to become the
triumphant successor of his brothers had been achieved, if only in Frulovisi's
indifferent verse.

The London chronicles have long been recognized as rich repositories of
public feeling and opinion. C.L. Kingsford believed that they were 'perhaps the

---

[87] W.R. Schirmer, *John Lydgate* (1952), *passim*; Holmes, 'Libel of English Policy', p. 215.

[88] Biblioteca Colombina, Seville, MS. 7.2.23, ff. 64–86. On the poem see, R. Weiss, 'Humphrey,
Duke of Gloucester and Tito Livio Frulovisi', in *Fritz Saxl Memorial Essays*, ed. D.J. Gordon (Oxford,
1957), pp. 218–27. Dr Weiss's transcription of the poem is amongst his papers in the Warburg
Institute, London, NAH 8320. Note that the MS. has been refoliated since Weiss examined it: f.62
is now f.64.

[89] F.85ᵛ, ll. 1120–1: *Sed tu fortissimus heros/ Gloria magna domus nostre jam corda tenebis.*

most important for the student of sources of all the original authorities for English history in the fifteenth century'.[90] Professional scribes borrowed freely from different texts to draw out their narratives and cater for the tastes of their clientèle, and they felt at liberty to employ whatever sources were available to them – poems, official newsletters, municipal documents and the reports of eye-witnesses. The siege of Calais generated enormous public interest and there are numerous extant narrative versions composed at different times. Space permits only a cursory examination of the major themes and the more interesting versions.

There is some disagreement in the chronicles about the role of the count of Mortain in raising the siege. Mortain had been countermanded from Maine to Calais around Easter 1436, perhaps at the instigation of Gloucester who may have harboured anxieties over the Beauforts' territorial ambitions in Normandy.[91] Mortain immediately grasped the initiative and launched a series of successful pillaging expeditions around Calais and was awarded the Garter for his efforts.[92] One chronicle version found in 'Gregory's Chronicle', British Library, Cotton Vitellius A XVI, Rawlinson B355, the Great Chronicle of London and Cotton Cleopatra CIV, emphasizes Mortain's role in raising the siege; the decisive event was his destruction of a mobile blockhouse or 'bastille' which the Flemings had constructed to help reduce the fortress-town.[93] This version makes it clear that the report of Mortain's raid was conveyed to London in newsletters and, presumably, thence into chronicles. Other versions emphasize the importance of this event, but no other mentions Mortain's role in its capture, although 'Giles's Chronicle' credits Mortain with raising the siege.[94]

---

[90] Kingsford, *English Historical Literature*, p. 70.

[91] Harriss, *Cardinal Beaufort*, pp. 258–60.

[92] *Brut*, II, p. 575.

[93] See for example, 'Gregory's Chronicle' in *The Historical Collections of a Citizen of London*, p. 179. According to Kingsford the version should be dated to 1440, although the MSS. in which it is found date from a later period, *English Historical Literature*, pp. 78–9, 81.

[94] *Incerti Scriptoris Chronicon Angliae de Regnis . . . Henrici IV, Henrici V, et Henrici VI*, ed. J.A. Giles (1848), pp. 15–16.

In fact, one account of the siege stresses rather the effort of Sir John Radclyf, the lieutenant of the town. This version, in Latin, is inserted in the register of William Curteys, abbot of Bury St Edmunds between 1429 and 1446, and follows a series of privy seal letters requesting help for the defence of Calais.[95] This account concentrates on the deeds of Radclyf who, according to the narrative, was alone responsible for defending Calais and who valiantly raided and destroyed the Flemish blockhouse, prompting Burgundy to flee ignominiously. Two other chronicles also praise Radclyf for raising the siege, the brief accounts in *An English Chronicle* and *Waltham Annals*.[96] There may be some political significance in this discrepancy. Radclyf was a retainer of Gloucester's, and Humphrey may have preferred to see the interests of his lieutenant advanced rather than those of Beaufort; as an honorary canon of Bury St Edmunds one might expect him to enjoy some influence there.[97] Other chronicles credit Gloucester himself with raising the siege; Dr Brie's *Brut* G and both versions of Hardyng's chronicle, perhaps drawing from the poems, claim that Burgundy fled Calais when he noticed the approach of Gloucester's relief force.[98]

Gloucester's *chevauchée* into Flanders was applauded by almost all English contemporary commentators, and their similar phrasing and expression – for example, the destruction of Poperinge and Bailleul – suggest that they largely relied on an official report. Some chroniclers were less enthusiastic. The later version of Hardyng's chronicle, *Brut* G and the late and corrupt Lambeth MS. 84, all composed after 1461, claim that Gloucester achieved little; this may reflect their Yorkist bias. 'Giles's Chronicle' maintains that Gloucester's

---

[95] BL, Add. MS. 14848, ff. 192ᵛ–193. Doig, 'A New Source', pp. 415–16. For the privy seal letters, see above, pp. 93, 95. The MS. also contains the '*Cartae Versificatae*' of John Lydgate, who was, of course, resident at the abbey.

[96] *An English Chronicle of the Reigns of Richard II, Henry IV, Henry V and Henry VI*, ed. J.S. Davies (Camden Society, old series, LXIV, 1856), p. 55; Kingsford, *English Historical Literature*, p. 352.

[97] K.H. Vickers, *Humphrey, Duke of Gloucester* (1907) pp. 241–2. He was admitted to the fraternity in 1433 by Curteys himself; thus he knew Curteys personally.

[98] *Brut*, II, p. 505; BL, Lansdowne MS. 204, f. 219; J. Hardyng, *Chronicle*, ed. H. Ellis (1812), p. 396. Note that *An English Chronicle*, although stressing Radclyf's role, also follows this line: see p. 55.

force was reduced by three companies without repulsing the enemy; in this the chronicler may have had the interests of the Lancastrian court partly in mind.[99]

Naturally, one can detect the influence of royal propaganda in the chronicles. *An English Chronicle* and the Latin *Brut* declare Burgundy a 'fals foresworn man' and 'A Short English Chronicle' mentions him as 'foresworne unto the crowne of England'. His retreat is labelled 'cowardly' in 'Gregory's Chronicle' and this is implied in all the chronicles.[100] The most vituperative is the account in the Bury register which concludes, *Prout in precantibus est plenius declaratum quare de libro deletur vivencium et cum certeris iustis ascribi non meretur.*[101] In substance and attitude the chronicles have much in common, certainly enough to entertain the notion that the authors drew from a store of common knowledge and sentiment. One should not treat them independently from the poems and, indeed, the proclamations and other anti-Burgundian diatribes of the period. These sources interacted and drew from one another to a greater or lesser extent and influenced, and were influenced by, public opinion; even the Grocers' account book speaks of the 'fals pretendyng Duke of Burgogne'.[102]

The threat to Calais, then, roused governmental anxiety which expressed itself in a propaganda offensive that exploited a range of methods of widespread communication. Official communiqués stressed 'the justice of the English cause, while denigrating the character of the enemy'.[103] Poets and chroniclers alike employed official reports and newsletters with the stories of returning soldiers to

---

[99] *Brut*, II, pp. 505, 599–600; Hardyng, *Chronicle*, p. 396; *Incerti Scriptoris*, p. 16. The latter chronicle is not strongly Yorkist, as Kingsford maintains, but is sympathetic to the Lancastrian court party. Kingsford, *English Historical Literature*, pp. 156–7; *Incerti scriptoris*, pp. 39, 41, 44–5, 47. In stressing Mortain's role and disparaging Gloucester, the chronicle may reflect this bias.

[100] *An English Chronicle*, p. 35; *English Historical Literature*, p. 321; *Three Fifteenth Century Chronicles*, ed. J. Gairdner (Camden Society, new series, XVII, 1880), p. 61; *The Historical Collection of a Citizen of London*, p. 179.

[101] BL, Add. MS. 14848, f. 193. The passage refers to Psalms, 69, 28.

[102] Heath, *Some Account of the . . . Grocers*, p. 395.

[103] Griffiths, *Reign of King Henry VI*, p. 222.

paint a picture of the siege which was fundamentally uniform in both detail and emphasis, and which continued to interest the reading public long after 1436. More generally, the consequences of the congress of Arras serve to illustrate that the crown placed the national agenda before the mass of the population frequently and effectively. This is a point which tends to be muted or sometimes contradicted in local studies of the gentry. Such studies are important, indeed crucial, to extending our understanding of the fifteenth century; however, they tend to emphasize the limited horizons and localized concerns of their subjects. The siege of Calais affected to a greater or lesser extent the bulk of the king's subjects, from the illiterate labourer to the powerful nobleman; the kingdom was successfully united against a threat, albeit one which ultimately proved vaporous.

5

MARGARET OF ANJOU, QUEEN CONSORT OF HENRY VI: A REASSESSMENT OF HER ROLE, 1445–53*

Diana Dunn

O f all medieval queens consort, Margaret of Anjou has received some of the harshest criticism from both contemporary commentators and later historians.[1] She shares with an almost equally vilified queen, Isabella of France, the unflattering description 'She-Wolf of France' and there were many similarities in their personal circumstances which gave rise to such unpopularity.[2] Their nationality partly explains the hostile attitude towards them

---

* I am grateful to Professor Ralph Griffiths and Anne Crawford for their comments on an earlier draft of this paper and to Dr Rowena E. Archer for her help and encouragement. My research was facilitated by my colleagues in the History Department of Chester College who gave me time during the summer term, 1993, to work in London and Oxford.

[1] The following studies of Margaret of Anjou have been consulted: M.A. Hookham, *Life and Times of Margaret of Anjou* (2 vols. 1872); A. Strickland, *Lives of the Queens of England* (6 vols. 1891), I; T.F. Tout in the *Dictionary of National Biography*, vol. XII (1909), pp. 1023–33; J.J. Bagley, *Margaret of Anjou, Queen of England* (1948); P. Erlanger, *Margaret of Anjou* (1970); J. Haswell, *The Ardent Queen: Margaret of Anjou and the Lancastrian Heritage* (1976). There are also useful sections in R.A. Griffiths, *The Reign of King Henry VI: the Exercise of Royal Authority, 1422–1461* (1981); B.P. Wolffe, *Henry VI* (1981) and J. Gillingham, *The Wars of the Roses* (1981).

[2] In Shakespeare's play the duke of York describes Margaret of Anjou as the 'She-Wolf of France but worse than wolves of France, Whose tongue more poisons than the adder's tooth!', William Shakespeare, *Henry VI*, pt. 3, Act I, scene 4, lines 111–12. Thomas Gray in 'The Bard', written in 1757, referred to Isabella of France as 'She-Wolf of France, with unrelenting fangs, That tearest the bowels of thy mangled mate'. See also H. Johnstone, 'Isabella, the She-Wolf of France', *History*, XXI (1936), pp. 208–15.

at a time when Anglo-French relations were strained to the point of open war.
Both queens earned disapprobation because they became directly involved in
politics and were seen to be seeking power for themselves, thus acting against
contemporary standards of acceptable behaviour for a queen which demanded
that she be totally subservient to her husband and restrict her spheres of activity
to mediation and acts of mercy and charity.[3] The odds were also stacked against
them because they happened to marry two of the weakest and most incompetent
medieval kings whose disastrous reigns precipitated periods of civil war and their
eventual depositions. The reputations of Isabella of France and Margaret of
Anjou have become tainted by their association with the failures as kings of
Edward II and Henry VI. An understanding of the political context of the lives
of the individual queens is needed in order to explain the hostility expressed
against them and to attempt an impartial assessment of their personalities.

The origins of Margaret of Anjou's reputation as a power-seeker lie in the
period after 1453 when her position as queen consort was suddenly changed
following the total (albeit temporary) physical and mental collapse of her
husband and the birth of her long-awaited son and heir. Finding herself in an
unprecedented and highly vulnerable situation, Margaret was forced by
political necessity and the instinct for survival to intervene personally in
government, seeking to defend her husband's position and her son's future
inheritance. Although her claims to the regency were rejected, in the later
1450s she emerged as the head of the Lancastrian party in the absence of
effective leadership from the king. The eventual triumph of the Yorkists and the
change of dynasty in 1461 produced a strong reaction against the Lancastrian
regime in the following decade which was reflected in many of the partisan
chronicles, the observations of foreign commentators and in political verse.[4] In

---

[3] A. Crawford, 'The King's Burden? – the Consequences of Royal Marriage in Fifteenth-century
England', in *Patronage, the Crown and the Provinces in Later Medieval England*, ed. R.A. Griffiths
(Gloucester, 1981), p. 52.

[4] C.L. Kingsford, *English Historical Literature in the Fifteenth Century* (1913), pp. 122, 129, 166;
Historical Poems of the Fourteenth and Fifteenth Centuries, ed. R.H. Robbins (New York, 1959), pp. 222–6;
V.J. Scattergood, *Politics and Poetry in the Fifteenth Century* (1971), pp. 195–6; P.A. Lee, 'Reflections of
Power: Margaret of Anjou and the Dark Side of Queenship', *Renaissance Quarterly*, XXXIX (1986),
pp. 183–217.

seeking to apportion blame for the disastrous domestic and foreign policies of the previous twenty years, critics vigorously condemned Margaret of Anjou for her unwomanly interference in government and accused her of playing a decisive part in the downfall of the house of Lancaster.

Margaret of Anjou's reputation has been permanently damaged by the insinuations made against her by her political enemies and, as with so many other medieval queens, it is difficult for historians to get behind the myth to find the real person.[5] A start can be made by concentrating on the sources for the early years of her married life from 1445 to 1453. Before 1453 there is very little evidence to suggest that she was anything other than a conventional medieval queen consort who devoted her energies to the support of her husband. During these years there is a distinct lack of adverse comment against her except in connection with her failure in one important area of queenly duty, the production of an heir, which caused curiosity and some anxiety.[6] The survival among the records of the court of King's Bench of an indictment for seditious speech made against the queen in 1447 seems to indicate a feeling of frustration with the incompetence of the Lancastrian government rather than a belief that the queen was directly responsible.[7] This is in marked contrast to the attacks made on her character after 1453 when the wildest libels circulated accusing her of adultery and of plotting to force her husband to abdicate in favour of Prince Edward, using the events of 1327

---

[5] For a discussion of the problem of stereotyping medieval queens, see J.C. Parsons, 'Eleanor of Castile (1241–1290): Legend and Reality through Seven Centuries', in *Eleanor of Castile 1290–1990: Essays to commemorate the 700th Anniversary of her death: 28 November 1290*, ed. D. Parsons (Stamford, 1991), pp. 23–54.

[6] Griffiths, *Reign of King Henry VI*, p. 256. In 1448 it was alleged that a Canterbury man had said that 'oure quene was none abyl to be quene of Inglond, but and he were a pere of, or a lord of this realme he would ne on of thaym that schuld helpe to putte her a downe, for because that sche bereth no child, and because that we have no pryns in this land', *Historical Manuscripts Commission*, V (1876), p. 455, from the dean and chapter of Canterbury Archives, Ch.Ant. C239 (1448).

[7] R.L. Storey, *The End of the House of Lancaster* (1966), p. 46; Griffiths, *Reign of King Henry VI*, p. 255. One indictment made in 1447 concerns Thomas Hunt, a servant of the late duke of Gloucester, who is alleged to have remarked that he would be glad to see the queen drowned because no good had come of her arrival in England, PRO, King's Bench, Ancient Indictments, KB9/256/13.

as a precedent.[8] It is not the purpose of this paper to examine the accuracy of such charges but rather to attempt a reassessment of the role and personality of Margaret of Anjou by using a range of material, including literary and visual evidence, which dates from before 1453 and is not as prejudiced as the work of later critics. The most important sources for the study of the early years of Margaret's married life are a collection of her letters, her household accounts for 1452–3 and five jewel accounts for the period 1445 to 1453.[9] Although these sources have been considered by other historians, they have often been used to reinforce the traditional view of a hard-headed, power-seeking queen rather than treated as independent evidence. Read without regard to Margaret's changed attitude after 1453, these reveal a dutiful wife, a determined and effective distributor of patronage and a woman concerned for the welfare of her household servants.[10]

It is difficult to gain an impression of Margaret's physical appearance. She was considered to be good-looking by contemporaries: the French chronicler, Thomas Basin, described her at the time of her marriage as *filiam specie et formam praestantem, quae tunc 'maturo viro foret et plenis nubilis annis'* ('a good-looking and well-developed girl, who was then "mature and ripe for

---

[8] *An English Chronicle of the Reigns of Richard II, Henry IV, Henry V and Henry VI*, ed. J.S. Davies (Camden Society, old series, LXIV, 1856), p. 75; 'John Benet's Chronicle for the years 1400 to 1462', ed. G.L. and M.A. Harriss, *Camden Miscellany*, XXIV (Camden Society, 4th series, IX, 1972), p. 216; *Calendar of State Papers, Milan, 1385–1618*, I (1919), pp. 27, 55, 58.

[9] *Letters of Queen Margaret of Anjou*, ed. C. Munro (Camden Society, old series, LXXXVI, 1863), contains all but seven of the letters which were copied into a late fifteenth-century commonplace book, BL, Additional MS. 46846; A.R. Myers, 'The Household of Queen Margaret of Anjou, 1452–3', *BJRL*, XL (1957–8), pp. 79–113, 391–431 contains a transcript of the account book of William Cotton, esquire, receiver-general of Queen Margaret for 1452–3, PRO, Duchy of Lancaster, Accounts Various, DL28/5/8; A.R. Myers, 'The Jewels of Queen Margaret of Anjou', *BJRL*, XLII (1959), pp. 113–31, contains a transcript of the account roll of Edward Ellesmere, treasurer of the chamber and master of the jewels of Queen Margaret for 1452–3, PRO, Exchequer, King's Remembrancer, Accounts Various, E101/410/11; other jewel accounts are E101/409/14, 17; 410/2, 8. The two articles by A.R. Myers are reprinted in his collected papers, *Crown, Household and Parliament in Fifteenth-Century England*, ed. C.H. Clough (1985), pp. 135–229.

[10] Tout, *DNB*, p. 1027; Bagley, *Margaret of Anjou*, p. 56; Myers, 'Household of Queen Margaret', pp. 79–99.

marriage"'). In 1458, the Milanese ambassador, writing to Bianca Maria Visconti, duchess of Milan, reported with a measure of diplomacy that she was 'a most handsome woman, though somewhat dark and not so beautiful as your serenity'.[11] At a time when it was conventional to describe all queens as 'beautiful' and before the art of portraiture was fully developed, manuscript illuminations which purport to depict Queen Margaret cannot be used as accurate portraits.[12] They are simply highly stylized and idealistic images of a late medieval queen which take as their model the Queen of Heaven. Although such images cannot be regarded as true likenesses, they do reveal something of a queen's status and dignity. The best-known illustration of Margaret of Anjou is contained in the opening miniature of the book presented to her by John Talbot, earl of Shrewsbury, as a wedding present in 1445.[13] Seated within a richly painted chamber with members of the court, both lords and ladies, looking on from the sides, Margaret is depicted holding her husband's hand. Both monarchs are crowned and both hold sceptres. Talbot kneels in the foreground as he presents his book to the queen, whose personal device, the daisy or marguerite, features prominently in the border decoration of the manuscript. In two other contemporary illustrations Margaret is shown kneeling with an open book before her on a covered table.[14] In each of these she is depicted at different stages of her life: in her prayer roll, as queen consort, suitably robed and bejewelled, wearing her crown with her sceptre resting on top of her book; in the Skinners' Book of the Fraternity of Our Lady's Assumption, as a widow, simply dressed in mourning attire, including a fur-lined cloak and hood (probably of the

[11] Wolffe, *Henry VI*, p. 176n; Basin took the phrase '*maturo viro foret et plenis nubilis annis*' from Virgil's *Aeneid*, Book VII, line 53, where the description is applied to the only daughter of King Latinus. My thanks to Graeme White for this reference. *CSP, Milan*, I, pp. 18–19.

[12] I am grateful to Elizabeth Danbury for her observations on images of medieval queens which have assisted my understanding of depictions of Margaret of Anjou in manuscript illuminations.

[13] BL, Royal MS.15 E.VI, f.2v.

[14] Bodleian Library, Oxford, Jesus College MS.124, Prayer Roll; the Worshipful Company of Skinners, London, Book of the Fraternity of Our Lady's Assumption, f.34v.

Skinners' Fraternity), with both her crown and her sceptre lying on the table next to her book.[15] At one level these images may be regarded as no more than conventional representations of piety and learning but even so they are neglected by historians who prefer to focus on evidence of Margaret's less womanly conduct.[16]

Although still young at the time of her marriage, Margaret may be presumed to have received a conventional education from her mother Isabelle of Lorraine and her grandmother Yolande of Aragon, who was a highly

[15] Compare with the portrait of Lady Margaret Beaufort by Roland Lockey in the hall at St John's College, Cambridge, where she is depicted in sombre dress 'appropriate to the order of widowhood', M.K. Jones and M.G. Underwood, *The King's Mother: Lady Margaret Beaufort, Countess of Richmond and Derby* (Cambridge, 1992), p. 188 and plate 3. In the illustration from the Skinners' Book, she is described as 'the Qween Margaret sumtyme wyff and spowse to kyng Harry the sexthe'. Behind her kneels a lady-in-waiting holding an open book, possibly her faithful servant Dame Katherine Vaux, whose name follows Margaret's own in the list of members of the Fraternity. Katherine Vaux was born in Provence and was granted letters of denization in 1456 (*CPR, 1452–61*, p. 342). She married Sir William Vaux, one of Margaret's loyal supporters who fell fighting for her at the battle of Tewkesbury in 1471. According to one contemporary account, Katherine was with Margaret when she was taken captive by Edward IV after the battle: *A Chronicle of the first thirteen years of the reign of King Edward the Fourth*, by John Warkworth, ed. J.O. Halliwell (Camden Society, old series, X, 1839), p. 19. She must have returned to France with Margaret after the agreement reached by Edward IV and Louis XI under the terms of the treaty of Picquigny, because her name appears amongst the small number of witnesses to Margaret's will drawn up shortly before her death in 1482: A. Lecoy de la Marche, *Le Roi René; sa vie, son administration, ses travaux artistiques et littéraires* (2 vols. Paris, 1875), II, pp. 395–7.

[16] One of the most frequently reproduced illustrations depicting Margaret is in a Flemish painting of *c.* 1500 entitled 'The Marriage of Henry VI and Margaret of Anjou' which once belonged to Horace Walpole and hung at Strawberry Hill, London, but is now in the collection of the Museum of Fine Arts in Toledo, Ohio. The subject of the painting has been disputed and it has been claimed to represent the 'Marriage of the Virgin': R. Strong, *Tudor and Jacobean Portraits*, (1969), p. 148. Other representations of Margaret appear in a drawing by Roger de Gaignières, of a stained-glass window, once in the church of the Cordeliers, at Angers, and on a medal struck by Pietro da Milano in the early 1460s. Although it is possible that Pietro da Milano made a study of Margaret from life, since he was working at her father's court, at Bar-le-Duc, when she was in exile in France, the portrait is highly stylized and lacks any detail of feature; G.F. Hill, *A Corpus of Italian Medals of the Renaissance before Cellini* (2 vols. 1930), I, p. 15; II, plate 13.

educated woman and a patron of the university of Angers.[17] Margaret's father, René of Anjou, took an unusually keen interest in art and literature, collecting and commissioning paintings, manuscripts, medals, jewellery, gold and silver plate, armour, sculpture and tapestries for his palaces.[18] He was himself a writer of both prose and poetry as well as a prodigious book-collector and it seems likely that Margaret would have benefited from this rich educational background and that her literary tastes would have been well developed during her early life.[19] The book presented to her by Talbot in 1445 contains a collection of French texts perhaps originally intended for his own use and likely to have been put together fairly quickly in the ten months between Margaret's betrothal in May 1444 and her arrival in Rouen *en route* for England on 22 March 1445.[20] It has been pointed out that the contents reflect the interests of the great warrior Talbot himself with their emphasis on

[17] Lecoy de la Marche, *Le Roi René*, I, pp. 549–50. There is some disagreement as to Margaret's age at the time of her marriage which arises from a misunderstanding over her date of birth. If it is agreed that she was born on 23 March 1430, she would have been aged fourteen at the time of her betrothal in May 1444 and fifteen at the time of her marriage, in 1445; see C.N.L. Brooke and V. Ortenberg, 'The Birth of Margaret of Anjou', *BIHR*, LXI (1988), pp. 357–8.

[18] Lecoy de la Marche, *Le Roi René*, II, pp. 69–152; R.W. Lightbown, *Secular Goldsmiths' Work in Medieval France: A History* (1978), pp. 106–8. Under the patronage of René of Anjou, Angers became a flourishing centre of the arts in the fifteenth century.

[19] Lecoy de la Marche, *Le Roi René*, II, pp. 153–201. A catalogue of books housed in his library at Angers in the early 1470s lists 202 volumes excluding his own works, his Books of Hours and other gifts too numerous to count. The list includes books written in Hebrew, Arabic, Greek, Latin, French, Italian and German and on subjects as diverse as theology, philosophy, law, history, geography, natural science and astrology. Of his own works, the three best known are the *Livre des tournois*, the *Livre du Cueur d'amours esprit* and a pastoral poem *Regnault et Jeanneton*. His personal involvement in painting and illumination is discussed in J. Harthan, *Books of Hours and Their Owners* (1977), pp. 88–93 and in F. Unterkircher, *King René's Book of Love* (New York, 1980), pp. 8–14.

[20] A.J. Pollard, *John Talbot and the War in France, 1427–1453* (1983), p. 123; C. Reynolds, 'The Shrewsbury Book, British Library, Royal MS. 15 E.VI', in *Medieval Art, Architecture and Archaeology at Rouen*, ed. J. Stratford, British Archaeological Association Conference Transactions, XII (1993), p. 111. Talbot's wife, Margaret Beauchamp, conveniently possessed the same Christian name as the queen so that, had the manuscript been originally intended for Talbot's own use, the inclusion of marguerites in the border decoration would have been equally appropriate.

chivalry and warfare and that they were 'not obvious choices for a young lady turning fifteen, albeit a queen'.[21] However, there was plenty to interest her in the genealogy of the French and English royal descents from St Louis; the three Chansons of Charlemagne, the romances *Quatre fils Aymon*, *Pontus* and *Guy de Warwick*; the *Chroniques de Normandie*; Alain Chartier's *Breviaire de noblesse;* the *Histoire du Chevalier au cygne*; and the Garter Statutes. Two of the most recent writings on the conduct of warfare were also included: Christine de Pisan's *Livre des fais d'armes et de chevalerie* and Honoré Bouvet's *Arbre des batailles*. In his dedicatory poem Talbot expressed his desire that the book should give Margaret pleasure and provide her with some solace as she settled in a foreign country surrounded by unfamiliar people speaking a foreign language.[22] He also used the dedication as a vehicle to deliver a very personal and deep-felt message to the queen reminding her of her dual role as queen of France as well as of England and wishing her a long and glorious reign, triumphing over her enemies and providing heirs to continue the royal line.[23] Apart from this wedding gift, only two other books, both works of John Lydgate, can be firmly identified as belonging to Margaret.[24] It seems likely that she would have spent much of her time during the last lonely seven years of her life back in France seeking consolation in books. She requested Chastellain to compose a treatise for her entitled *Le Temple de Boccace* which included an imaginary dialogue between herself and Boccaccio lamenting the misfortunes of

---

[21] Pollard, *John Talbot*, p. 123; Reynolds, 'The Shrewsbury Book', in *Medieval Art*, p. 111.

[22] BL, Royal MS.15 E.VI, f.2v; Pollard, *John Talbot*, p. 128; Reynolds, 'The Shrewsbury Book', in *Medieval Art*, pp. 109–14.

[23] BL, Royal MS.15 E.VI, f.2v.

[24] Bodl. Lib, MS. Hatton 73, John Lydgate's 'Poems', has a note that it belonged to Queen Margaret; Yale University Library, MS. 281, John Lydgate's 'Life of Our Lady', was presented by a member of the Caraunt family to a queen in the fifteenth century. It is likely that the queen was Margaret of Anjou because of her patronage of Nicholas Caraunt, her secretary from 1445, *Letters of Margaret of Anjou*, pp. 93–4; *Calendar of Papal Registers*, X, *1447–55*, pp. 3, 43, 116; XI, *1455–61*, p. 184; J.J.G. Alexander, 'Painting and Manuscript Illuminations for Royal Patrons in the Later Middle Ages', in *English Court Culture in the Later Middle Ages*, ed. V.J. Scattergood and J.W. Sherborne (1983), pp. 141–62.

contemporary rulers especially the French royal family.[25] Slight as the evidence is for Margaret as a book-owner, there can be no doubt that her family background would have provided her with an education appropriate to a woman of her position.

Margaret appears to have conformed to contemporary expectations of queenly behaviour in other ways. Her love of riding and hunting is evident in some of her letters and from entries in her household accounts. She spent a good deal of her time at the royal palaces outside London and a number of her letters are addressed to the keepers of her parks at Ware, near Hertford castle, Apchild, in the parish of Great Waltham near Pleshy, and Sheen in Surrey, sending them advance notice of her intended visit and instructing them to ensure that the parks were well stocked with game.[26] In a letter addressed to 'W. Chaterley, yeoman of the crown', Margaret chastized the recipient for coming into 'our parke of Aggresley, there distroing our game, where we were disposed to have cherisshed you in your disport in our other places' and forbade him from entering any of her parks in the future.[27] She was in a position to command a Robert Hiberdon whom she had been advised possessed 'the crafte and cunnyng to make blode hondes in the best wyse . . . to make us two blode hondes to oure use' and to instruct John Godwyn to bring a mare and her colt to her.[28] Her household accounts record payments to Sir John Wenlock, her chamberlain, of £23 6s 8d for three palfreys for the use of the queen, and a total of £13 6s 8d was paid to Richard Salisbury 'de Soham' in the county of Kent and to his tenant, John Wright, in compensation for the loss of corn and other stuff in a fire which broke out accidentally at Richard's stables at Newmarket while the queen happened to be staying there. Other payments were made to John Hattecliff, clerk of the queen's stables, for wages to the stable boys and for the cost of purchasing supplies of hay, oats

[25] G. Chastellain, 'Le Temple de Boccace', in *Oeuvres de Chastellain*, ed. Kervyn de Lettenhove (Brussels, 1864), VII, pp. 75–143; Strickland, *Lives*, I, pp. 617–18; Tout, *DNB*, p. 1032.

[26] *Letters of Margaret of Anjou*, pp. 91, 100–1, 106, 137.

[27] Ibid., p. 143.

[28] Ibid., pp. 131, 141.

and other provisions for the stables and to Roger Dyke for the purchase of a horse.[29]

It has been suggested that Margaret was an important influence on English gardening, introducing new ideas learnt from her father, 'the most famous horticulturist of his time', but it is difficult to substantiate this claim fully.[30] There were extensive alterations made to the manor of Plesaunce at Greenwich after it was given to the queen following the death of Humphrey, duke of Gloucester in 1447 and these included the laying out of an enclosed garden with an arbour in which the queen might sit. Similarly, building work at Sheen in 1445 included the construction of a brick wall to enclose the garden. The account of the clerk of the king's works for 1444–7 contains references to the making at Byfleet-by-Sheen of a cloister with a lead cistern in the middle fed by an underground conduit. The cistern, which was probably octagonal, was decorated with eight devices which included the king's and the queen's mottoes, their initials 'H' and 'M' crowned, ostrich feathers, lily-pots and a figure of Saint Christopher.[31] The concept of a 'pleasure garden' was not new in the fifteenth century and it had been customary for queens to have private gardens within the grounds of the royal palaces and castles since at least the thirteenth century, but it seems likely that Margaret would have taken an active interest in the improvement of her places of residence.

In assessing the personality of Margaret of Anjou, her surviving letters provide a useful source of information, although this has not always been recognized by historians. T.F. Tout dismissed the letters as 'of no great value' and yet he was prepared to use them as evidence of her greedy, unscrupulous and reckless nature.[32] He agreed with J.H. Ramsay that 'she was an indefatigable match-maker', but added rather negatively that she 'seldom ceased meddling with the private affairs of the gentry.'[33] J.J. Bagley was no more

---

[29] Myers, 'Household of Queen Margaret', pp. 424, 426.

[30] J. Harvey, *Medieval Gardens* (1981), pp. 114, 135.

[31] *The History of the King's Works*, ed. H.M. Colvin (3 vols. 1963), II, pp. 949, 1001.

[32] Tout, *DNB*, p. 1033.

[33] J.H. Ramsay, *Lancaster and York* (2 vols. Oxford, 1892), II, p. 141; Tout, *DNB*, p. 1027.

impressed, either with the value of these letters or with those aspects of Margaret's personality that they illuminate. 'There is not a single letter of political importance,' he stated, 'but there are several which show that Margaret took an active and officious part in that social life which was a by-product of the political world. She wrote letters to obtain preferments for her friends and dependants, to interfere in impending litigation, and, young though she was, to attempt to arrange suitable marriages between her subjects. Nearly always she acted impetuously. For the moment her enthusiasm consumed her, and without counting the cost or estimating the effect she did what she wished.'[34] This view fails to appreciate the customary practice of queenship which gave to a queen extensive powers of patronage to dispense as she chose. In a more recent and much fairer assessment of Margaret's personality, R.A. Griffiths has concluded that her letters show her to be 'a conscientious patron, eager to cherish loyalty and determined to extend her "good ladyship" to those who merited it'. She was a 'resourceful' and 'persistent' patron and paid 'scrupulous attention' to the interests of her servants as well as her own.[35] Margaret's letters provide clear evidence that she understood the importance of her position as a patron and was prepared to exploit it in order to attract loyalty and support. Similar behaviour observable in other women of noble birth, although not necessarily approved of by contemporaries, has not been condemned so vigorously by historians. An obvious comparison may be made with Lady Margaret Beaufort who wielded enormous power and influence especially after her son was established on the throne. Her recent biographers have revealed her skill as a 'rigorous and highly effective administrator of her estates' whose 'land

---

[34] Bagley, *Margaret of Anjou*, pp. 56–7.

[35] Griffiths, *Reign of King Henry VI*, pp. 257–61. C.L. Kingsford, *English Historical Literature*, p. 223, also disagreed with Ramsay's hostile attitude towards Margaret based on the evidence of her letters: ' . . . Margaret was doing no more than any other person of rank at the time did commonly; there is nothing in the letters to show that her favours were bestowed undeservedly or her influence used unduly; they might be cited with equal force in proof of her solicitude to secure her humble dependants from the oppression of others. At all events Margaret cannot be condemned on their evidence.'

management was founded on a meticulous sense of what was legally due to her'. Her exploitation of her feudal dues may be described as 'harsh and obtrusive' but her reputation as 'the foundress of one of England's greatest ruling dynasties' remains intact.[36]

One of the significant areas of current research is the study of the position of women in medieval society and any reassessment of Margaret of Anjou needs to take into account the development of ideas which have led historians to emphasize the very considerable opportunites for aristocratic women to exercise power despite their inferior status in law. Margaret's actions to longer seem so exceptional when compared with other noble women such as Elizabeth de Burgh, Alice Chaucer, duchess of Suffolk or Elizabeth Talbot, duchess of Norfolk, each of whom played a very active part in the administration of her estates and took a close personal interest in the supervision of her household.[37] Indeed this was what was enjoined upon them by Christine de Pisan writing in the early fifteenth century. In her *Livre des Trois Vertus*, a book addressed to 'all princesses, empresses, queens, duchesses and high-born ladies ruling over the Christian world, and generally to all women', Christine recommended the direct involvement of a queen in the process of government, assisting her husband in his decision-making and acting as a mediator. She should take great care over the selection of her advisers and her household servants, be available to listen to their petitions and requests, set a high moral standard, take a special interest in the welfare of her women and damsels, and, above all, oversee the administration of her estates and the management of her household expenditure.[38]

[36] Jones and Underwood, *The King's Mother*, pp. 106, 259. An interesting comparison between Margaret of Anjou and Margaret Beaufort is made by Jones and Underwood, ibid., pp. 254–5.

[37] J.C. Ward, *English Noblewomen in the Later Middle Ages* (1992); Rowena E. Archer, ' "How ladies . . . who live on their manors ought to manage their households and estates": Women as landholders and administrators in the later middle ages', in *Woman is a Worthy Wight: Women in English Society c. 1200–1500*, ed. P.J.P. Goldberg (Stroud, 1992), pp. 149–81.

[38] Christine de Pisan, *The Treasure of the City of Ladies*, tr. S. Lawson (Harmondsworth, 1985), pp. 35, 50–1, 59–89. The book was dedicated to Marguerite, the oldest daughter of Philip the Bold, duke of Burgundy, who married the dauphin, Louis de Guyenne, in 1405.

Margaret of Anjou's letters are concerned with many of those aspects of administration and personal relationships advocated by Christine de Pisan as proper spheres of activity for a queen: the protection of her servants in disputes over property, wrongful oppression and injury, awards of compensation and dispensation of charity and personal favours, the arrangement of suitable marriages and appointments to offices. Some of her letters reveal personal qualities regarded by contemporaries as being particularly appropriate to a woman, such as compassion for the poor and the needy. In an undated letter to the archbishop of Canterbury, Margaret asks him to expedite the grant of a royal pardon to a 'poore widowe, Alice Marwarth', and desires him to treat her with 'tendernesse and faver that she, upon the socour and trust of oure moene that she putteth in us, may perceive good and brief exploit, to th'accomplissement of my lord's grant in this behalf'.[39] A poignant reminder of one of the common hazards of medieval urban life is provided in the following letter addressed to the master of the leper hospital of St Giles in the Field beside the City of London:

. . . for asmoche as we be enfourmed that oon Robert Uphome, of the age of xvii. yere, late querester [chorister] unto the moost reverende fader in God our beal uncle the cardinal, (whom God assoile,) atte his college at Winchestre, is now by Godd's visitacion become lepour; we desire therfor and praye you, sith he hath noon other socour ne lyvelode to lyve upon, but oonly of aulmesse of cristen peuple, as it is saide, that, at reverence of our blessed Creatour, and in contemplacion of this our prayer, ye will accepte and receive hym into your hospital of Seint Giles, unto such findinge and lyvelode as other personnes ther in suche cas be accustomed to have, as we trust you. In which thinge ye shul not oonly do a right meritorie dede to Godd's pleasir, but deserve also of us right especial thanke, etc . . .[40]

[39] *Letters of Margaret of Anjou*, p. 160.

[40] Ibid., p. 95; The hospital of St Giles, London, was founded in 1117 by Matilda, daughter of Henry I, to provide for forty lepers.

Another letter demonstrating the humane side of Margaret's personality is addressed to the executors of the late Cardinal Beaufort and requests their financial assistance in the form of alms, according to the terms of the cardinal's will, for W. Frutes and Agnes Knoghton, 'poure creatures and of vertuous conversacion, pourposyng to leve under the lawe of God in th'ordre of wedlok . . .'. In making this request, Margaret referred to the clause in the late cardinal's will which offered charity to the poor and needy in return for prayers for his soul.[41]

Many of Margaret's letters were written on behalf of her household servants, as well as those of the king's household, and they clearly indicate that she fully understood the potential power of her position to obtain favours for those whom she chose to assist. In return she could expect loyal service, as in the case of one of her ladies-in-waiting, Margaret Stanlow, on whose behalf she wrote to Edmund Beaufort, duke of Somerset, in the early 1450s asking for his support and favour.[42] The outcome of this request is unknown but Margaret Stanlow's relationship with the queen remained close throughout the period 1445 to 1453, as shown by the inclusion of her name amongst the recipients of gifts of jewels in all five of Margaret's jewel accounts.[43] The queen was also prepared to use her influence with other women of high rank to help her achieve her purposes. One of her letters addressed to the duchess of Somerset seeks the latter's mediation with her husband in the matter of payment of an outstanding debt owed by the duke to 'our wel[beloved] squier', Robert Edmund.[44] Other squires of her household on whose behalf she acted were Thomas Burneby, Edmund Clere, Thomas Sharneborne and Thomas Browne as well as her chaplain, Michael Tregury, her secretary, Nicholas Caraunt, her clerk of the signet, George Ashby, and a yeoman

---

[41] Ibid., pp. 101–2.

[42] Ibid., p. 115. Margaret Stanlow is listed among the queen's ladies-in-waiting in her household accounts, Myers, 'Household of Queen Margaret', p. 405.

[43] Myers, 'Jewels of Queen Margaret', p. 126; PRO, E101/409/14 (1445–6); 409/17 (1446–7); 410/2 (1448–9); 410/8 (1451–2); 410/11 (1452–3). The gifts she received were a silver-gilt belt, a gilt chain, a silver cup 'de opere parys', a silver salt-cellar and a parcel-gilt gadrooned vessel.

[44] *Letters of Margaret of Anjou*, pp. 117–18. The letter probably dates from 1450–4.

of the household, Thomas Mowsherst.[45] She also pressed the cases of some members of the king's household, including the knights, John Montgomery and Robert Wyngfield, and the king's secretary, Robert Osbern.[46]

The close relationship between members of the king's and the queen's household establishments is clear from a comparison of the names of their respective servants for the period 1445 to 1453, and from references to marriages between household servants which appear in Queen Margaret's jewel accounts. These accounts, kept by the treasurer of the chamber and master of the queen's jewels, record the annual purchases of jewels and gold and silver items, listing the names of the recipients of gifts.[47] They are a useful source of information for the personnel of Margaret's household, indicating the identity of those closest to the queen, whether from the ranks of the nobility and gentry or the intimate circle of female 'damsels' who regularly attended the queen. A number of Margaret's personal servants were French and had accompanied the queen to England in 1445, obtaining letters of denization within a few years of their arrival. Settling permanently in their adopted country, they often married members of the king's household.[48] Jamona

[45] Ibid., pp. 91–4, 96–8, 106–9, 119–20, 151–2. Their names appear in the queen's household accounts, Myers, 'Household of Queen Margaret', pp. 406–9. Thomas Burneby, Edmund Clere, Thomas Sharneborne, Thomas Browne and Michael Tregury all received gifts of jewels on at least one occasion between 1445 and 1453.

[46] *Letters of Margaret of Anjou*, pp. 103–4, 155–6. In the letter on behalf of Robert Osbern addressed to the abbess of Barking, Margaret calls upon her to 'be unto hym good and favorable ladye, in his honest desires and resonable offers, and shew unto hym and unto his wif the tendre binevolence of yor good ladyship', revealing her appreciation of the potential influence of another woman of authority. Thomas Montgomery, John's son, described as 'marshall of the hall to the king' in 1447–9, received gifts of gold bracelets in 1451–2 and 1452–3 from the queen, *CPR, 1446–52*, pp. 45, 305; PRO, E101/410/8; Myers, 'Jewels of Queen Margaret', p. 128.

[47] The five surviving accounts of the master of the jewels of Queen Margaret appear to be a unique record for any medieval queen. Although accounts kept by various officers of the queen's household survive for other queens, such as the four for Philippa of Hainault in John Rylands Library, Manchester, Latin MSS.234–7, these latter contain a record of general expenditure on the queen's wardrobe and household and do not list all the jewels purchased each year with the names of the recipients of each jewel.

[48] *CPR, 1446–52*, p. 240.

Cherneys, one of the queen's ladies-in-waiting, was born in Anjou, naturalized in 1449, and married Thomas Sharnebourne, a squire of the queen's household on whose behalf Margaret intervened in a dispute over his title to the manor of Aspeden, Hertfordshire, and to whom she granted £20 yearly from the receipts of the manor of Great Waltham, Essex, in 1449.[49] Thomas was commended for good service to the king and the queen in 1451 and received a gift of £20 from the queen on the occasion of the baptism of his son.[50] His wife also received gifts of jewels from the queen that were recorded in three out of five of the jewel accounts.[51] A pardon granted to Jamona Sharnebourne of Sharnebourne, Norfolk, in 1462 speaks of her as the 'widow of Thomas Sharnebourne esq., late sheriff and executive of his will'.[52] Katherine Gatewyne, another lady-in-waiting, also from Anjou and naturalized in 1449, married Sir Robert Whittingham, usher of the king's chamber, and she received a gift from the queen in each of the years recorded in the jewel accounts.[53] Three further ladies-in-waiting, all of whom had been in the queen's escort which accompanied her to England in 1445, were married to members of the king's household. Rose Merston was the wife of John Merston esquire, treasurer of the king's chamber and master of the king's

[49] *Letters of Margaret of Anjou*, pp. 106–8.

[50] *CPR, 1446–52*, p. 454; PRO, E101/410/8.

[51] PRO, E101/410/2, 8, 11. The gifts were a gold clasp in 1448–9, a silver salt-cellar in 1451–2 and an ornamented gilt vessel in 1452–3.

[52] Myers, 'Household of Queen Margaret', p. 405. In his will, dated 31 January 1459, Thomas requests that the queen be the principal overseer of his last will and testament 'and also to be good and gracious ladie to Jamon my wife and to all myne children'. He leaves bequests to Jamona, to his sons John, Edward and Anthony and to his daughter Margaret: J.C. Wedgwood, *History of Parliament: Biographies of the Members of the Commons House, 1439–1509* (1936), p. 764.

[53] Myers, 'Household of Queen Margaret', p. 405. The gifts received by Katherine were a gold belt in 1445–6, a gold chain in 1446–7, a gold clasp in 1448–9, a silver salt-cellar in 1451–2 and an ornamented gilt vessel in 1452–3. Her husband, Robert, entered the queen's service becoming her keeper of the great wardrobe and also receiver-general of the Prince of Wales's Council, *CPR, 1452–61*, pp. 323, 429. Attainted after the battle of Towton, he went into exile with Margaret, returned with her in 1471 and died fighting for her at Tewkesbury, *RP*, V, p. 479a; VI, p. 27b; Wedgwood, *Biographies*, pp. 943–4.

jewels from before 1445 until Easter 1453.[54] Agnes Parr was the wife of Gilbert Parr esquire, an usher of the king's chamber who had also been in the service of Henry V.[55] Alice Meerbrook married John Noreys, a king's serjeant and usher of the chamber, who rose to become keeper of the king's great wardrobe from October 1444 to October 1446 and treasurer of the queen's chamber and master of her jewels from April 1447 until Michaelmas 1452.[56] Edith Burgh, lady-in-waiting, married Giles Seintlowe, esquire of the king's household and a member of the queen's escort in 1445. He later moved into the service of the queen.[57] A payment of £16 1s 10d was made to Thomas Bateman and John Hardwicke, clerks of the royal household, for providing and ordering all the necessary supplies of food for the marriage of Giles Seintlowe and Edith Burgh in August 1454. In the following year, Giles and Edith were granted an annuity of 20 marks for their service to the king and the queen.[58]

The exchange of New Year's gifts was a well-established practice by the fifteenth century, especially at the French and English courts.[59] Great regard was had to rank

---

[54] Myers, 'Household of Queen Margaret', p. 405. Both Rose and often her husband were regular recipients of gifts from the queen: a silver belt for Rose and a gilt cup for John in 1445–6, a gold chain and a part-gilt cup in 1446–7, a silver cup in 1448–9, two silver-gilt cups in 1451–2 and a silver-gilt cup, a gadrooned parcel-gilt vessel as well as a New Year's present of 13s 4d to Rose Merston's servants in 1452–3.

[55] Myers, 'Household of Queen Margaret', p. 405. Agnes received the following gifts from the queen: a gold belt in 1445–6, a gold chain in 1446–7, a gold clasp in 1448–9, a silver salt-cellar in 1451–2 and an ornamented gilt vessel in 1452–3.

[56] See below, pp. 135–6. Both Alice and John were regular recipients of gifts from the queen: Alice, described as 'capital damisell Regine', received a gold belt and a yard of blood-red fabric in 1445–6, a gold chain in 1446–7, a silver parcel-gilt cup in 1448–9; apart from his annual fee of £20 as treasurer of the chamber and keeper of the queen's jewels, John received a gift of £10 and a silver cup in 1445–6, £10 and a part-gilt cup in 1446–7, £20 in 1451–2 and in 1452–3 when he no longer held the offices mentioned above.

[57] Myers, 'Household of Queen Margaret', pp. 405–6. Giles Seintlowe received a gift of a gold clasp in 1445–6 and in 1452–3.

[58] Ibid., pp. 424–5; *CPR, 1452–61*, p. 243.

[59] Myers, 'Jewels of Queen Margaret', pp. 113–15; R.W. Lightbown, *Mediaeval European Jewellery*, (1992), pp. 71–2. The practice continued into the sixteenth century as is indicated by the survival of a list of New Year's gifts given and received by Queen Elizabeth I in 1559; John Rylands Library, English MS.117. I am grateful to Dorothy Clayton for drawing my attention to this list.

and hierarchy in the choice of these gifts and an examination of the names of those included in Margaret's jewel accounts as recipients provides evidence of the identity of those in favour with the queen between 1445 and 1453. At the head of the list in three of the accounts is the king, who received a pair of silver-gilt bowls *de opere damascino* in 1447, a gold salt-cellar with a large balas ruby in 1449 and a pair of silver-gilt vessels in 1453.[60] Amongst the highest ranks of churchmen who received New Year's gifts from the queen were John Stafford, archbishop of Canterbury, on three occasions, Cardinal Kemp, archbishop of York, in 1452, William Aiscough, bishop of Salisbury, in 1447 and 1449, William Waynflete, bishop of Winchester, in 1449 and 1452, and in one year only Walter Lyhert, bishop of Norwich, William Booth, bishop of Coventry and Lichfield, Adam Moleyns, bishop of Chichester, Marmaduke Lumley, bishop of Carlisle and treasurer of England. Servants of the archbishops of Canterbury and York, the bishops of Winchester, Salisbury and Chichester as well as the abbot of Abingdon also received gifts in some years.[61] These senior churchmen were holders of high government office and regular attenders of meetings of the royal council and therefore it is not surprising that the queen chose to honour them in this personal way. A similarly predictable group of high-ranking noblemen, their wives and servants was rewarded with New Year's presents from the queen in the same period.[62] Many of them had been in the escort which had gone to France in November 1444 to conduct Margaret to England

---

[60] Myers, 'Jewels of Queen Margaret', p. 123. In 1446 Margaret gave her father, described as 'the King of Sicily', a drinking-horn, PRO, E101/409/14. No other gifts to members of her family appear in subsequent accounts.

[61] Myers, 'Jewels of Queen Margaret', pp. 114–15, 119, 124–5; PRO, E101/409/14,17; 410/2, 8, 11.

[62] Ibid. Among the nobles who received New Year's gifts from the queen were: the duke of Gloucester, the duchess of Buckingham, John de la Pole, son of the duke of Suffolk, Margaret Beaufort, daughter of the duke of Somerset, Ralph, Lord Sudeley and Lady Talbot in 1446; Gloucester, Suffolk, his wife and their son, the duchesses of Buckingham, Bedford, Warwick and Exeter, Lords James Fiennes, John Stourton, Thomas Stanley and domino de Talbot, possibly Shrewsbury's younger son, in 1447; Suffolk and his wife, Viscount Beaumont, the duchess of Buckingham, the duke and duchess of Exeter, the countess of Northumberland and Lord Sudeley in 1449; the duke of York, the duchesses of Somerset, Bedford and Exeter and the earl of Wiltshire in 1452; and the duchess of Somerset, the earl of Wiltshire and Lord Lisle in 1453. Uniquely, similar New Year's gifts were given to three unnamed servants of Alice, duchess of Suffolk, in 1446.

following her marriage. Their inclusion in the jewel accounts as recipients of gifts is evidence more of the routine nature of this particular source of patronage than of any direct political involvement by the queen. Amongst those favoured in 1447 was Humphrey, duke of Gloucester, which suggests that Margaret felt no personal antagonism towards this opponent of the peace policy and perhaps indicates that she had distanced herself from any plot by Suffolk and his faction to bring about the duke's death in February that year.[63]

The value of her household accounts as a source for the study of the organization of Margaret of Anjou's household has long been recognized.[64] They serve as a reminder of the independence of late medieval queens who, from the time of Eleanor of Provence, queen consort of Henry III, had their own great and privy wardrobes, chamber, exchequer and council, all staffed with officers and clerks, having their own seals and being allocated special chambers in the palace of Westminster.[65] Although it is unclear how far the queen was directly involved in the day-to-day operation of these offices, Margaret maintained a large staff of professional officials and clerks in addition to her purely domestic servants.[66] The

[63] Contemporaries were unanimous in believing that Gloucester died from natural causes. Suspicion of Suffolk's involvement first appears in *Gregory's Chronicle* but accusations against Margaret do not appear until the sixteenth century: *The Historical Collections of a Citizen of London in the Fifteenth Century*, ed. J. Gairdner (Camden Society, new series, XVII, 1876), p. 189. C.L. Kingsford, *Prejudice and Promise in Fifteenth-Century England* (Oxford, 1925), pp. 163–4; Bagley, *Margaret of Anjou*, pp. 59–60.

[64] Myers, 'Household of Queen Margaret', pp. 79–99; Crawford, 'The King's Burden?', in *Patronage, the Crown and the Provinces*, pp. 47–8.

[65] The earliest studies of the queen's household as an independent organization were those of Hilda Johnstone in T.F. Tout, *Chapters in the Administrative History of Medieval England* (6 vols. Manchester, 1920–33), V, pp. 231–89 and in *The English Government at Work, 1327–1336*, vol. 1, ed. J.F. Willard and W.A. Morris (Cambridge, Mass., 1940), pp. 250–99.

[66] A total of 151 persons were paid wages in 1452–3. It is difficult to make comparisons with other queens because of the lack of detailed records for the queen's household. The accounts of Isabella of France, queen consort of Edward II, indicate that her household establishment numbered 180 persons; Tout, *Administrative History*, V, pp. 241–3. The household ordinances of 1445 attempted to restrict the number of attendants on the queen to 66, but in the 1454 ordinances, a figure of 120 was agreed. In the *Liber Niger*, drawn up for Edward IV in 1472, the problem of the insolvency of the royal household was partly addressed by recommending a reduction in the allowance to the queen for the payment of only 100 servants; A.R. Myers, *The Household of Edward IV* (Manchester, 1959), pp. 92–3.

main task of these professional household men was the administration of her estates and, since the dower assigned to her on her marriage in April 1445 included a significant share of the duchy of Lancaster estates, a number of duchy of Lancaster officials were available to advise her on legal and financial matters.[67] Their names appear in her accounts as recipients of fees and wages in connection with duchy of Lancaster business as well as more general work on behalf of the queen. The accounts for 1452–3 were prepared by William Cotton esquire, receiver-general of the duchy of Lancaster, who rose in the king's service to become keeper of the great wardrobe, treasurer of the queen's household and her receiver-general.[68] In addition to his fee of £50 as receiver-general, Cotton had an allowance of £10 for his London household and he was paid another £10 10*s* for travelling from his home in Suffolk to London to attend to various matters touching the queen and for travelling from Landewade, Cambridgeshire, to Royston, Walsingham, Walden and Windsor on other business.[69] Other duchy officials also employed privately by the queen were John Walsh and Nicholas Sharp, both duchy auditors as well as auditors for the queen; and William Nanseglos, clerk of the receipt for the queen and receiver for the duchy estates in Essex, Hertfordshire, London and Middlesex. In addition to his fee of £5 Nanseglos was paid a total of £3 in expenses for remaining in London during the vacation to attend to the queen's business in the absence of her receiver-general and for hiring a boat to travel from London to Greenwich and from London to Westminster to discuss various matters with the queen.[70]

[67] For a discussion of Margaret's dower, see R. Somerville, *History of the Duchy of Lancaster, vol. I, 1265–1603* (1953), pp. 208–9; Crawford, 'The King's Burden?', in *Patronage, the Crown and the Provinces*, p. 45. Her dower settled by grant of parliament, 19 March 1446, included the duchy honours of Tutbury, Leicester and Kenilworth and lands in Essex, Hertfordshire, Middlesex, Surrey and London, and the 'ancient south parts' of the duchy, comprising lands in Hampshire, Wiltshire, Somerset, Dorset, Devon, Cornwall, Oxfordshire, Herefordshire and Worcestershire, estimated to be worth £2,000.

[68] Somerville, *Duchy of Lancaster*, pp. 398–9; Wedgwood, *Biographies*, pp. 227–8. He died fighting for the Lancastrians at the first battle of St Albans in 1455.

[69] Myers, 'Household of Queen Margaret', pp. 413–14, 422.

[70] Ibid., pp. 414–16, 421. John Walsh and Nicholas Sharp received a gift of a gold clasp from the queen in 1448–9; William Nanseglos received a gold clasp in 1451–2 and 1452–3. Walsh and Sharp also received New Year's gifts of four pounds in 1452–3.

The use of a council of professional financial and legal advisers by noblewomen had become common practice by the fifteenth century.[71] In 1452–3 Margaret drew upon the expertise of a group of experienced men, some of whom she had had close connections with since 1445; they included John, Viscount Beaumont, her chief steward, Sir John Wenlock, her chamberlain, Lawrence Booth, her chancellor, Sir Edward Hall and Sir Andrew Ogard, knights carver, and Edward Ellesmere, treasurer of her chamber.[72] The necessity of employing legal officers to defend and protect her interests was clearly recognized by Margaret who had in her household Robert Tanfield, her attorney-general, as well as ten other attorneys and apprentices-at-law.[73] Service to the queen offered the likelihood of future promotion; Robert Tanfield became Margaret's chamberlain in 1455 and suffered forfeiture of his lands in May 1461 but was pardoned the following year.[74] All five of her apprentices-at-law eventually became judges: Ralph Poole was made a justice of the court of King's Bench in 1452; Robert Danby became chief justice of the court of Common Pleas in 1461; Walter Moyle and John Needham became justices of that court in 1454 and 1457, respectively; and Thomas Billing became chief justice of the court of King's Bench in 1469.[75] As the senior law-officer in the queen's household, Robert Tanfield had the task of prosecuting and defending her interests in the central law courts and in the Exchequer. His fees included payment for attendance in the courts out of the legal term-time to see to matters touching, for example, the queen's manor of Fakenham, the earldom of Pembroke and her right to the customs of Southampton assigned to her as part of her dower. These payments were in addition to his annual fee of £10.[76]

---

[71] Ward, *English Noblewomen*, pp. 114–15; Archer, 'Women as landholders', in *Woman is a Worthy Wight*, p. 169. The effectiveness of Lady Margaret Beaufort's 'unofficial council of the midlands' is discussed in Jones and Underwood, *The King's Mother*, pp. 85–90.

[72] Myers, 'Household of Queen Margaret', pp. 94–7, 412, 427–9.

[73] Ibid., pp. 94–5, 414–15. In comparison, Elizabeth Woodville employed an attorney-general, attorneys in the courts of Common Pleas and King's Bench, a solicitor-general and two apprentices-at-law.

[74] Wedgwood, *Biographies*, pp. 840–1.

[75] Myers, 'Household of Queen Margaret', p. 416.

[76] Ibid., p. 414.

The queen's council met regularly in a special chamber assigned for her use in the palace of Westminster which, according to her accounts, was situated in the 'new tower' next to the king's Exchequer. Not only was this a meeting-place but it was also a place of security for the keeping of the queen's books, documents and personal seals.[77] Roger Morecroft was described as messenger for the council and keeper of the queen's council chamber in the accounts and he was paid for travelling on horseback to various parts of the country on the queen's council business.[78] There were seven ushers of the council chamber, including a William (or John) Randolf, who was granted the keeping of the council chamber within the palace of Westminster and the office of usher of the receipt of the Exchequer for life on 8 February 1448.[79] An indication of the work of the queen's council is provided in two of Margaret's letters concerning the need to protect some of her tenants from attack. John Browne, a tenant of her lordship of Walden, Essex, petitioned her to defend him against a certain Thomas Bawlde, esquire, who was demanding payment of an obligation 'of a greet some not deu, as it is said, putting hym wrongfully to greet trouble, vexation, and losse, likely to be his utter undoing for ever, without summe pourveiance of remedie be the sonner had unto hym in this matter'. The queen proposed that the dispute be put to her council for settlement: 'We, willyng that our said tenant may leve in rest and peax, and in quiet from suche oppression and injurie, and to ministre indifferently to all parties justice as the cas requireth, desire, praye, and exhorte you that ye will, at reverence of us, put th'examination of your said suit to us and to our counseil, where we shall, by good deliberation and advis, see that ye shall have al that rightfully belongeth

---

[77] Ibid., pp. 95, 417. An indication of the quantity of work carried out by the various officers of the queen's council is provided by some of the entries in the accounts for the costs of purchasing parchment, paper, red wax and ink for the drawing up of letters patent, warrants and the writing of memoranda by her chancellor, her receiver-general and her secretary. Other items purchased included boxes for the safe custody of her documents, leather bags, linen cloth, three yards of green cloth for the receiver-general's accounting table and five dozen counters for the accounting office, ibid., pp. 420–1.

[78] Ibid., pp. 417–18.

[79] Ibid., p. 416; *CPR, 1446–52*, p. 149; *CFR, 1445–52*, pp. 208, 253.

unto you in that behalf.'[80] In the second letter, addressed to Henry, Viscount Bourchier, Margaret proposed that, in order to bring the dispute between her tenants of Walden and Nicholas Browne and John Chowne to a conclusion, he agree to an 'arbitrement' to be achieved by a meeting 'with oure counseil, and ther to dispose you t'abide and attende upon the determinacion of all the grevaunces compromitted in maner above reherced, havyng oure seid tenants towards you in suche favor and tendernesse recommended, for oure sake, that they maye fynde, in effecte, that ye be unto theym goode lorde, to th'accomplissement to oure entencion in this mater'.[81] The outcome of this dispute is unknown but the queen was clearly concerned to protect her tenants, who had the advantage of the backing of a powerful administrative and legal machine which secured them the kind of 'good ladyship' that they could reasonably have expected from any landowner.

An examination of the queen's expenditure recorded in her household accounts, especially when compared with the much more restrained spending of her successor, Elizabeth Woodville, has led historians to criticize Margaret for her extravagance and generosity and to blame her for contributing to that poverty of the Lancastrian monarchy which was a major factor in its ultimate demise.[82] While the high level of Queen Margaret's personal expenditure cannot be denied, it could be argued that, on her arrival in England in 1445 as a young and inexperienced queen, she took her lead from her older and more experienced husband and, in maintaining a large court, she was only doing what her background and status demanded. The king's marriage, at a comparatively late age by the standards of the day, necessarily led to an increase in household expenditure but the financial difficulties of the Lancastrian monarchy can be traced back to earlier in Henry VI's reign. The king's complete inability to manage his household was causing concern to the Commons from at least 1440 and led to the presentation of a petition in the form of ordinances for the reform of the household in the parliament of 1445.[83]

---

[80] *Letters of Margaret of Anjou*, p. 154.

[81] Ibid., pp. 122–3.

[82] Myers, 'Household of Queen Margaret', pp. 86–8, 90–1, 98–9; Crawford, 'The King's Burden?', in *Patronage, the Crown and the Provinces*, pp. 48–50, 53.

[83] Griffiths, *Reign of King Henry VI*, pp. 310–17.

These ordinances, which demanded a reduction in the size and costs of the household, clearly demonstrate the parlous state of the royal finances well before Margaret's arrival in England.[84] It was Henry VI's failure to manage his finances and control expenditure, not an over-indulgent queen, which was the real cause of this weakness of the Lancastrian crown.

An example of the unhealthy state of the royal finances is provided by the experiences of one man in the king's service in 1445. In January of that year William Cleve, clerk of the king's works, was instructed to make preparations for the reception of the queen in England by the construction of new buildings at the royal palaces of Sheen, Eltham and Westminster. The country had been without a reigning queen since 1422 and a major overhaul of the royal palaces was needed to provide suitable accommodation for the newcomer. Orders were given to Cleve to make 'in all hast possible' a new hall with a scullery, saucery and serving-place at Eltham, 'honourable for the Queen's loggyng there'. Building work at Westminster included the repair of the Great Chamber, the Queen's Lodging, the Parliament Chamber and the Painted Chamber as well as the construction of a new kitchen at the Tower of London. Cleve experienced great difficulty in securing payment for his work: in July 1445 he was owed £1,000 for wages which he was obliged to pay to various people for their labours in connection with these building works. Things had not improved by the summer of 1447: after the appointment of a new treasurer and new customs officials, Cleve was still complaining about his inability to secure the money due to him against the tallies assigned to him at the exchequer. When his final account was presented to the Exchequer for audit, in 1454, he returned fifty-eight useless tallies to the value of £3,000.[85] The problems faced by Cleve were typical of the experiences of many royal servants in the 1440s and 1450s as the royal finances steadily deteriorated.

It is against this general financial background that the high costs of providing the new queen with a suitable escort for her journey across France to England need to be viewed. Detailed accounts survive for what has been described by R.A.

---

[84] Myers, *Household of Edward IV*, pp. 7–9, 63–75.

[85] Myers, 'Household of Queen Margaret', p. 87; Colvin, *History of the King's Works*, I, p. 198; II, p. 936.

Griffiths as 'the single most expensive enterprise embarked upon by Henry's government after his return from France in 1432', following his coronation in Paris.[86] According to the two clerks in charge of the finances the expedition which left London in November 1444 and returned in April 1445 cost a total of £5,573 17s 5d, far exceeding the original estimate of £3,000 based on a calculation of three months, rather than six, for the length of time required. Payments were made to about 300 people who made up the escort, ranging from the highest-ranking members of the nobility, headed by the duke and duchess of Suffolk, 5 barons and their wives, to lesser personnel including 17 knights and 2 carvers, 65 squires and 204 valets. Another heavy expense was incurred in the provision of fifty-six ships to transport the queen and her household down the River Seine to Rouen and across the channel from Harfleur to Portsmouth. This 'royal household-in-transit' added a heavy burden to the routine household expenditure and the accounts of the great wardrobe for this period show that payments quadrupled during the six months covered by the journey to France compared with its usual annual outlay. The arrival of Margaret of Anjou in England precipitated a crisis in the financial position of the Lancastrian monarchy, resulting in demands for reform.[87] However,

---

[86] Griffiths, *Reign of King Henry VI*, p. 315. The account of John Brekenok and John Everdon, clerks of the king's household, assigned to oversee the finances of the entire enterprise to bring the queen to England, is printed in *Letters and Papers Illustrative of the Wars of the English in France during the reign of Henry VI*, ed. J. Stevenson (RS, 2 vols. in 3, 1864), I, pp. 443–60. They opened their account on 17 July 1444 and it was finally closed on 16 October 1445. Particulars of their account are contained in BL, Add. MS. 23938 which lists the Crown's creditors for the expedition, their daily allowances, wages paid to the sailors for providing passage, the expenses of the wardrobe, kitchen, stables, etc. and the cost of alms given to various churches and paupers by the queen along the route from Mantes through Rouen to Harfleur.

[87] G.L. Harriss, 'Marmaduke Lumley and the Exchequer Crisis of 1446–9', in *Aspects of Late Medieval Government and Society*, ed. J.G. Rowe (Toronto, 1986), p. 148, calculates that the total cost of the marriage embassy was almost £7,000. Myers, *Household of Edward IV*, p. 7: Crawford, 'The King's Burden?', in *Patronage, the Crown and the Provinces*, pp. 48–9. Both Myers and Crawford cite G.L. Harriss, 'The Finance of the Royal Household, 1437–60' (unpub. Oxford D.Phil. thesis, 1953), pp. 235–7. However, G.L. Harriss points out that Margaret experienced considerable difficulty in securing the payment of her annuities in the early years of her marriage because she faced stiff competition from rival claimants for assignments from the exchequer. It appears that she was not in a sufficiently strong position, politically, to press her claims until after 1453 when her growing personal influence assured her greater control over Exchequer revenues: ibid., pp. 237–75.

Margaret cannot be blamed for a situation which existed long before she arrived on the scene, nor can she be held responsible for the scale of the expedition, nor the delays which resulted in much higher levels of expenditure than expected. In fact the evidence indicates that Margaret was accompanied from France by only a very small personal escort of her own Angevin servants, as was the normal custom for foreign princesses.[88] She faced financial embarrassment even before she reached England, necessitating the recycling of silver plate given to her by Henry of Luxembourg, lately chancellor of France, to give presents to people *en route*.[89] The accounts also contain a reference to a payment authorized by Suffolk to John Pole, valet, who was sent from Southampton to London with three horses to fetch Margaret Chamberlayne, 'tyremakere', and to bring her before the queen to attend to various matters.[90] The exact meaning of this entry is obscure but it may refer to the necessity of providing the new queen with suitable attire for her entrance to the city of London on 28 May and her coronation two days later. Further indication that Henry VI appreciated the necessity for his queen to be appropriately decked out for her coronation is provided in some of the entries on the Exchequer's issue rolls for 1445. On 12 January he instructed Adam Moleyns, keeper of the privy seal, to make letters of warrant to be sent to John Merston, treasurer of the chamber and keeper of the king's jewels, ordering him to deliver up certain jewels. These included 'A Ryng of Gold garnished with a fayr rubie, sometyme yeven unto us by our Bel oncle the Cardinal of Englande, with the which we were sacred in the day of our Coronation at Parys, delivered unto

---

[88] The small number of personal servants accompanying the queen from Anjou was commented on by contemporaries, see 'Benet's Chronicle' p. 190, which restricts her Angevin companions to three or four. They are likely to have included some of those ladies-in-waiting named in Margaret's household accounts and naturalized in 1449; and see Myers, 'Household of Queen Margaret', p. 405. Katherine of Valois was in a similar position in 1420: Thomas Walsingham reported that she was accompanied by only three noble ladies-in-waiting and two maid-servants when she came to England following her marriage to Henry V: see C.T. Allmand, *Henry V* (1992), p. 145.

[89] *Letters Illustrative of the Wars in France*, p. 450, records a payment of £2 13*s* 4*d* to John Tybaude, goldsmith of Rouen, for the removal of the arms of Henry of Luxembourg, chancellor of France, from various silver vessels formerly given to the queen.

[90] Ibid., p. 452.

Matthew Philip to Breke and therof to make another ryng for the Queen's wedding ring.'[91] The king also sent the following order to the treasurer of the Exchequer on 18 April:

> We Wol and Charge you that, for such things as oure right entierly Welbeloved Wyf the Queene most necessaryly have for the Solempnitee of hir Coronation, ye Deliver, of oure Tresour, unto oure trusty and welbeloved squier John Merston, Keper of oure Jewell, a Pusan of Golde, called Ilkyngton Coler, Garnished with iv Rubees, iv greet Saphurs, xxxii greet Perles, and liii other Perles. And also a Pectoral of Golde Garnished with Rubees, Perles, and Diamonds, and also with a greet Owche [brooch] Garnished with Diamonds, Rubees, and Perles, sometyme bought of a Marchant of Couleyn [Cologne] for the Price of Two Thousand Marc,
>
> He as wel to deliver the saide Pusan and the said Pectoral unto oure saide Wyf of oure Gyft.[92]

The cost of providing the customary gifts to the queen and members of her entourage in 1445 helps to explain the sharp increase in the king's personal expenditure in the chamber in that year, when assignments of a total of £5,700 were required from the Exchequer, a figure four times the average for the years 1438–44.[93] Clearly Henry was very much aware of the importance of the occasion as an opportunity to display the dignity of the monarchy.

It is hardly surprising that it was among members of the queen's escort who accompanied her to England in 1445, especially her female companions, that Margaret formed the closest friendships. Chief amongst them were Alice, countess of Suffolk, Margaret, countess of Shrewsbury, Beatrice, Lady Talbot, the Portuguese-born sister-in-law of the earl of Shrewsbury, Jacquetta of Luxembourg, the dowager duchess of Bedford, her daughter Lady Elizabeth Grey (the future queen of Edward IV), Emma, Lady Scales and Lady Elizabeth

---

[91] Hookham, *Margaret of Anjou*, I, pp. 417–18; *Foedera*, V, p. 139.

[92] Hookham, *Margaret of Anjou*, I, p. 419; *Foedera*, V, p. 142.

[93] Griffiths, *Reign of King Henry VI*, p. 316.

Hull. They all figure prominently in the queen's household and jewel accounts and gave Margaret loyal service over many years.[94] She formed a particularly close relationship with Suffolk and his wife and this was to have serious consequences for her later reputation, directly linking her with the most unpopular government minister and his disastrous domestic and foreign policies in the period 1445–50. In the sixteenth century she was to be accused of improper relations with Suffolk but the charge is without foundation, the product of later prejudice against both the queen and the duke.[95] In reality Margaret may well have looked upon Suffolk and his wife as surrogate parents, given their respective ages.[96] Suffolk had stood proxy for the king at the betrothal ceremony held at Tours on 24 May 1444 and again at the wedding celebrated at Nancy in February 1445.[97] Suffolk's wife, Alice, was the queen's principal companion on the journey to England and she remained friends with Margaret after Suffolk's death in 1450, continuing to receive gifts of jewels and other favours from the queen. It was into Alice's care that the widowed and, by then, childless Margaret was placed by Edward IV in 1471, and with whom she remained until her eventual return to France under the terms of the treaty of Picquigny of 1475.

A number of Margaret's household servants had strong links with Suffolk and rose to positions of prominence through his influence with the queen. John Wenlock, a member of the king's household by 1441, a frequent envoy to France and in the queen's escort in 1444–5, moved into her service by securing appointment as usher of her chamber by the time of her coronation. By 1448

---

[94] Myers, 'Jewels of Queen Margaret', pp. 124–5; PRO, E101/409/14,17; 410/2, 8.

[95] Kingsford, *Prejudice and Promise*, pp. 174–5; Bagley, *Margaret of Anjou*, pp. 53–5. Shakespeare's portrayal of Suffolk and Margaret as lovers in *Henry VI*, pt. 2, Act III, scene 2, owes much to earlier sixteenth-century popular beliefs which can be traced to Polydore Vergil, Edward Hall and Raphael Holinshed. Hall says of Suffolk that he was 'the Quenes dearlynge' and that Margaret 'entierly loved' him: Edward Hall, *Chronicle*, ed. H. Ellis (1809), pp. 218–19.

[96] Suffolk was nearly fifty in 1445 and his wife was about forty.

[97] The chronology of events from the truce of Tours and the marriage agreement reached on 20–2 May 1444 to the marriage ceremony held at Nancy and the subsequent journey of Margaret through Normandy to England from February to April 1445 are discussed in B.M. Cron, 'The duke of Suffolk, the Angevin marriage, and the ceding of Maine, 1445', *JMH,* XX (1994), pp. 77–99.

Wenlock had become chamberlain of the queen's household; and later, in the service of the Yorkist government, he rose to be chief butler of England and lieutenant of Calais.[98] Another of the king's servants, George Ashby, was appointed clerk of the queen's signet in 1445, a position which he still held in 1453.[99] Both men benefited from the queen's acquisition of the wardship of the young heiress Anne Beauchamp in June 1446, which gave her control of a vast fund of resources to reward her favourites. Wenlock was made constable of Cardiff castle and Ashby steward of Warwick castle, as a result. However, the person to benefit most of all from this inheritance was Suffolk himself who purchased the wardship from the queen in November 1446, thus acquiring control of the richest heiress of Henry VI's reign.[100]

One of the most outstanding of Suffolk's associates to rise to high office and grow rich in the service of the queen was John Noreys, master of her jewels.[101] During the 1440s he was showered with royal favours and gifts from the queen and established himself as a local figure of some influence in west Berkshire, where he held office as sheriff and was elected MP no fewer than seven times. His family, however, did have some tradition of service to English queens and Richard le Noreys, 'the queen's cook', had been granted 'a purpresture within the forest of Windsor called Ocholt' (Ockwells, near Bray in east Berkshire) on 8 February 1268.[102] Thanks to a profitable marriage to Alice Meerbrook, daughter and heiress of Richard Meerbrook of Yattendon, Berkshire, John Noreys inherited the manor of Yattendon which became his principal residence. In 1445 he turned his attention to the rebuilding of the manor of Ockwells,

---

[98] Wedgwood, *Biographies,* pp. 931–2; J.S. Roskell, *The Commons and Their Speakers in English Parliaments, 1376–1523* (Manchester, 1965), pp. 258–62. Wenlock laid the foundation stone of Queen's College, Cambridge, on 15 April 1448.

[99] A.J. Otway-Ruthven, *The King's Secretary and the Signet Office in the XV Century* (Cambridge, 1939), pp. 135, 139, 142, 158, 185; Wedgwood, *Biographies,* pp. 21–2.

[100] Griffiths, *Reign of King Henry VI,* pp. 363–4; C. Carpenter, *Locality and Polity: a Study of Warwickshire Landed Society, 1401–1499* (Cambridge, 1992), pp. 421–2.

[101] Wedgwood, *Biographies,* pp. 637–9; C. Silk, 'The lifestyle of the gentry in the later middle ages, with special reference to John Norreys of Ockwells Manor, Berkshire' (unpub. Southampton B.A. dissertation, 1989), pp. 10–23.

[102] *CPR, 1266–72,* p. 190.

conveniently sited near the royal castle of Windsor, and, by the time of his death in 1466, his family possessed what Nicholas Pevsner has described as 'the most refined and the most sophisticated timber-framed mansion in England'.[103] In the stained-glass oriel window at the east end of the great hall are displayed the heraldic arms of John Noreys, by then a knight, alongside those of Henry VI, Margaret of Anjou, Henry Beauchamp, duke of Warwick, Edmund Beaufort, duke of Somerset, John de la Pole, duke of Suffolk and other prominent Lancastrians. The plain surrounding glass bears the motto of John Noreys, 'Feyth fully serve', and his badge of office as keeper of the great wardrobe, three golden distaffs banded with a gold tasselled ribbon.[104] Noreys has been described by R.A. Griffiths as 'a prototype among Suffolk's household associates' and he was identified as such by contemporary critics of the government in 1450, attracting popular odium and denunciation from Cade's followers.[105] He survived the political crisis of 1449–50 which destroyed Suffolk and he was specifically exempted from the act of resumption of 1450, possibly thanks to the protection of the queen. But, by linking herself so closely to unpopular figures such as Noreys, Margaret ran the risk of severe criticism even if she was not directly connected with their policies.

The influence of Suffolk with the queen can also be found in the promotion of some senior churchmen. This can be most obviously demonstrated in the case of Walter Lyhert, Suffolk's chaplain, who was in the embassy to France in

---

[103] N. Pevsner, *The Buildings of England: Berkshire* (Harmondsworth, 1966), pp. 187–9.

[104] Silk, 'The lifestyle of the gentry', pp. 52–4; C. Platt, *The Architecture of Medieval Britain* (Yale, 1990), pp. 257–8. Other prominent Lancastrians with close connections with the queen whose arms are displayed in the windows are James Butler, earl of Wiltshire, Richard Beauchamp, bishop of Salisbury, Sir John Wenlock, Sir Richard Nanfan and Richard Bulstrode, a nephew of Noreys and executor of his will. Bulstrode became keeper of the queen's wardrobe: see Wedgwood, *Biographies*, pp. 130–1; Myers, 'Household of Queen Margaret', p. 422. I am grateful to Anne Curry for drawing my attention to the stained-glass at Ockwells.

[105] Griffiths, *Reign of King Henry VI*, p. 303. He was attacked, along with so many members of the royal household, in the political verse of 1449–50 directed against those members of the government held responsible for the loss of English lands in France, *Political Poems and Songs relating to English History*, ed. T. Wright (RS, 2 vols. 1859–61), II, pp. 221–3, 'On the popular discontent at the disasters in France'.

1444–5 and thence moved into the service of the queen as her confessor. In January 1446 he was elevated to the see of Norwich at Suffolk's express request, possibly in preference to the king's own recommendation for the vacancy, John Stanbury, his confessor.[106] Whether or not Lyhert's appointment indicates some conflict within the royal household, the significant point is that Suffolk's protégé was successful. Similarly, the appointment of William Booth, the queen's chancellor, as bishop of Coventry and Lichfield in 1447 was due to the advocacy of Suffolk, but this time with the support of both the king and queen who petitioned the pope for his appointment. William Booth was another victim of the satirical verse written at the expense of Suffolk and his associates in 1449 and 1450, which may imply a widely held belief that his promotion to the bench of bishops had been achieved by irregular means.[107] Other notable royal servants and high churchmen closely connected with Suffolk and favoured by the queen were Adam Moleyns, keeper of the privy seal, who was promoted to the see of Chichester in September 1445, and William Aiscough, the king's confessor and bishop of Salisbury from 1438. The latter had married the royal couple at Titchfield abbey on 22 April 1445 and received regular gifts of jewels from the queen. Their long association with the unpopular government of the 1440s ultimately led to their murders, that of Moleyns at Portsmouth on 9 January 1450 and Aiscough at Edington on 29 June 1450.[108] It is difficult to

[106] Griffiths, *Reign of King Henry VI*, pp. 348, 645. He was the recipient of gifts from the queen, as recorded in her jewel accounts in 1445–6 and 1446–7. For the influence of Suffolk on appointments of bishops, see R.J. Knecht, 'The episcopate and the Wars of the Roses', *University of Birmingham Historical Journal*, VI (1957–8), pp. 110–11.

[107] Griffiths, *Reign of King Henry VI*, pp. 348–50; A. Compton Reeves, 'William Booth, Bishop of Coventry and Lichfield, 1447–52', *Midland History*, III (1975), pp. 11–29. For attacks made on Booth, see Kingsford, *English Historical Literature*, pp. 242–3, and Wright, *Political Poems*, II, pp. 225–9, which contains the poem 'On Bishop Boothe', discussed in Scattergood, *Politics and Poetry*, pp. 168–9.

[108] Griffiths, *Reign of King Henry VI*, pp. 281–2, 347–8, 639–40; Wright, *Political Poems*, II, pp. 232–4. Griffiths emphasizes that no obvious hostility was shown to the queen in 1450 but hostility was focused on a group of eleven bishops, most of whom had been royal chaplains, councillors and former confessors to the king and many of whose appointments to sees had taken place since 1443, during Suffolk's ascendancy.

know exactly what impact the influence of Suffolk over the queen had in the long term and to what extent her close friendship with this highly unpopular minister affected her reputation as she declined in public esteem after 1453. The truth is that her name became linked with a number of people regarded as being responsible for the loss of the English possessions in France and the growing bankruptcy and weakness of the government, and this resulted in long-lasting damage to her own reputation.

It is hard to find much evidence before 1453 of the queen seeking power for herself or of pushing her own interests independently of the king. Her letters indicate that Margaret did use her prerogative as queen to promote those whom she favoured but it is generally impossible to tell with whom the initiative lay in recommending a royal servant or cleric for promotion. There are only very occasional references in the patent rolls to grants being made 'at the queen's request' and these are usually to her female servants.[109] It is more common to find a royal servant being rewarded 'for good service to the king and the queen', such as the grant to John Bere, yeoman of the chandelry, of the office of porter of Rochester castle on 13 December 1451, 'for good service to Henry V, the king and queen Margaret'.[110] In the year following her arrival in England a series of grants was made to members of her household including her grooms of the chamber, William Burton and Thomas Eyre, her pages of the chamber, John Thlude, Roger Everdon and Richard Frebody, as well as to Master Francis Panizonus of Alexandria, master of medicine.[111] These were all rewarded for domestic service to the queen of one kind or another and were the sort of routine grants which any royal household servant might expect. Margaret did take a personal interest in securing the promotion of her chaplain, Michael Tregury, who was in her escort in 1445 and on whose behalf she wrote to the abbess of Shaftesbury in 1447, requesting her support in her recommendation for his appointment to the bishopric of Lisieux. Her petition was unsuccessful

---

[109] For example, a grant of 10 marks per annum from a subsidy and aulnage on the sale of cloth was made to Margaret Fastolf and Alice Bertelot on 1 February 1447 'for good service to the queen': *CPR, 1446–52*, p. 59.

[110] Ibid., p. 509.

[111] Ibid., *1441–6*, pp. 394, 406, 433.

but in 1449 Tregury was appointed to the archbishopric of Dublin.[112] Margaret also gave her support and protection to Nicholas Caraunt, her secretary in 1446–7, when his election to the deanery of Wells was challenged. She wrote to Thomas Forest, executor of John Forest, late dean of Wells, pressing for the appointment of Caraunt against a rival candidate, a dispute which she eventually won.[113] Likewise, Margaret was able to help her chaplain, John Hals, to become archdeacon of Norwich in 1453. Both Caraunt and Hals continued to benefit from the queen's patronage in the later 1450s.[114] These examples show that Margaret was capable of taking action to support her servants when she chose, but this need not be regarded as anything other than normal behaviour for a queen.

Another strong influence on Margaret in these early years was exerted by Andrew Doket, principal of St Bernard's College, Cambridge, who played a major role in her foundation of Queen's College, Cambridge, in 1448.[115] There is no reason to believe that, in petitioning the king for permission to found her own college, she was seeking to outdo her husband whose foundation of King's

[112] *Letters of Margaret of Anjou*, pp. 91–3; *CPR, 1446–52*, pp. 304, 310, 325. Tregury received gifts of a set of gold *paternosters* in 1445–6, a parcel-gilt paxbread in 1446–7 and a silver salt cellar in 1448–9 from the queen, PRO, E101/409/14,17; 410/2.

[113] *Letters of Margaret of Anjou*, pp. 93–4; *C. Pap. Reg.*, X, *1447–55*, pp. 3, 43, 116; XI, *1455–61*, p. 184. He received gifts of a set of gold *paternosters* in 1445–6 and a silver-gilt paxbread in 1446–7 from the queen, PRO, E101/409/14,17.

[114] Griffiths, *Reign of King Henry VI*, p. 258. Hals was one of the few members of the queen's household to receive gifts from the queen in every year covered by her surviving jewel accounts. In addition, in 1452–3, there is a record of gifts of two gold rings to the duke of Somerset and the earl of Wiltshire, *ut in signis eiusdem missis per dictam Reginam pro promocione magistri Johannis Hals*: Myers, 'Jewels of Queen Margaret', p. 129.

[115] The important role of Andrew Doket in the foundation of Queen's College has long been recognized: see Tout, *DNB*, p. 1027; Bagley, *Margaret of Anjou*, p. 57; W.G. Searle, *The History of Queen's College of St Margaret and St Bernard in the University of Cambridge, 1446–1560* (Cambridge, 1867), pp. 15–65; A. Crawford, 'The piety of late Medieval English Queens' in *The Church in Pre-Reformation Society: Essays in Honour of F.R.H. DuBoulay*, ed. C.M. Barron and C. Harper-Bill (Woodbridge, 1985), p. 49; J. Twigg, *A History of Queen's College, Cambridge, 1448–1986* (Woodbridge, 1987), p. 6.

College and Eton preceded the queen's by several years.[116] A number of reasons for the foundation are given in the petition: the lack of a college founded by a queen, the inspiration provided by other women foundresses, particularly the countesses of Clare and Pembroke, as well as the king's own example. The two most important reasons for Margaret's action were perhaps her desire for the 'conservacion of oure feith and augmentacion of pure clergie' and 'to laud and honneure of sexe femenine'.[117] Whatever the queen's motives, the guiding hand behind the foundation was that of Doket who wanted to enlarge and upgrade his college of St Bernard and worked through the queen to achieve his own aims. He was a substantial property owner in the area of Cambridge where the college was built. He made endowments to both King's and Queen's Colleges, was influential in persuading others to do so, and became the first president, a position he held until his death in 1484. It was Doket who ensured the survival of Queen's College after the collapse of the Lancastrian government by involving Elizabeth Woodville in the foundation and later still her successor as queen, Anne Neville. There is no record of any direct monetary gifts by Margaret nor were any statutes issued during Henry VI's reign.[118] The overall impression is of an unfinished project that fell victim to the deterioration of the political situation. Margaret's support for Queen's College was in name only and she never seems to have taken the sort of close personal interest in the details of the planning of the buildings which was such a major preoccupation of her husband at King's.

It was, above all, Margaret's involvement in politics which turned popular opinion against her and made her name synonymous with the worst qualities associated with a power-seeker. However, it is wrong to assume that from the

---

[116] According to the seventeenth-century historian Thomas Fuller, Margaret was prompted to found a college because 'beholding her husband's bounty in building King's College was restless in herself with holy emulation, until she had produced something of the like nature, a strife wherein wives without breach of duty may contend with their husbands which should exceed in pious performances'. T. Fuller, *The History of the University of Cambridge*, ed. J. Nichols (1840), p. 120.

[117] Searle, *History of Queen's College*, pp. 15–16; Twigg, *History of Queen's College*, pp. 2–3.

[118] Searle, *History of Queen's College*, pp. 62–3; Twigg, *History of Queen's College*, pp. 7–11. Some of the queen's closest associates were among the benefactors, including her chamberlain, Sir John Wenlock, her chief steward, Viscount Beaumont, and Marmaduke Lumley, bishop of Carlisle.

moment she arrived in England, following her marriage, she sought power for herself and that she took a leading part in the politics of the 1440s and early 1450s. The evidence simply does not support that view. There are very few instances when it could be argued that she was directly involved in affairs of state and her actions were usually determined by other people of influence in government. The occasion most often cited by historians as evidence of Margaret's power to influence the king and thus determine the course of politics relates to the agreement made by Henry in December 1445 to surrender Maine and Anjou to Charles VII as a preliminary to a peace settlement between England and France.[119] The exact sequence of events which led to the agreement that proved to be the undoing of the English position in France is confusing. It seems likely that Charles VII saw the marriage of his wife's niece to the king of England as a means of achieving a satisfactory resolution to the long-standing conflict between the two countries. As a young bride, Margaret was in a good position to put pressure on her husband to do what the French wanted. In support of this view, there survives a letter, signed by Margaret and addressed to her uncle, Charles VII, king of France, dated 17 December 1445, in which she acknowledged receipt of letters from Guillaume Cousinot, master of requests of Charles's household and Jehan Havart esquire, his carver, and agreed to do her best to assist the peace process by the deliverance of the county of Maine.[120] This letter was quickly followed by another, dated 22 December 1445 from Henry VI to Charles VII, agreeing to the surrender of Maine because of his desire for peace and 'favouring also our most dear and well-beloved companion the queen, who has requested us to do this many times, and out of regard to our said father and uncle, for whom it is most reasonable that we should do more than for others who are not so nearly connected with us'.[121] It is impossible to calculate how far Henry VI was influenced by his wife's

---

[119] Wolffe, *Henry VI*, pp. 169–89; Griffiths, *Reign of King Henry VI*, pp. 255, 482–95.

[120] *Letters Illustrative of the Wars in France*, I, pp. 164–7.

[121] Ibid., II, pt. ii, pp. 639–42. The respective roles of Suffolk and Margaret in the negotiations for the surrender of Maine are discussed in Cron, 'The duke of Suffolk, the Angevin marriage, and the ceding of Maine, 1445', pp. 77–99.

supplication in coming to this decision. His lack of interest in warfare and his general inclination towards a peace settlement with France were evident earlier in his reign and the idea of the surrender of Maine as an essential prerequisite for peace may well have been suggested to the English embassy led by Suffolk to negotiate a French marriage for the king of England in the spring of 1444. Although there is no evidence to support the later charge levelled against Suffolk that he had agreed to the surrender of Maine during these marriage negotiations, Charles VII and René of Anjou are likely to have had the idea in their minds at that time. It was one of the requests made by the French embassy in London in July 1445 and it was later asserted by the French that Henry had given an oral undertaking to surrender Maine by 1 October 1445.[122] The young queen may well have been regarded as a useful agent in the furtherance of his plans by Charles VII and she had little option but to do what she was told by her uncle. Although she may have played some part in influencing the king's decision, it is likely that Henry was pursuing his own natural inclinations in his strong desire for peace and it is hard to imagine that he would be dictated to by a fifteen-year-old girl however much he may have loved her.[123]

The other major political event in which it has been argued that Queen Margaret played an important part was Cade's rebellion in the summer of 1450.[124] At the height of the rebellion the king withdrew from the capital to the safety of the royal castles of Berkhamsted and Kenilworth, leaving his wife behind at Greenwich as the rebels ran riot in the city of London. On 6 and 7 July the two archbishops of Canterbury and York and the bishop of Winchester succeeded in negotiating a general pardon with Cade and his followers on condition that they withdrew from London. The evidence for Margaret's involvement comes from the enrolment of the general pardon which was said to

[122] Wolffe, *Henry VI*, p. 172.

[123] A sceptical view of the significance of the part played by Margaret in the negotiations for the surrender of Maine and Anjou is provided by Gillingham, *Wars of the Roses*, pp. 58–9.

[124] Griffiths, *Reign of King Henry VI*, pp. 262, 616, 640. The most recent historian of Cade's rebellion makes no mention at all of the queen's role: I.M.W. Harvey, *Jack Cade's Rebellion of 1450* (Oxford, 1991).

have been granted at the request of the queen.[125] Did Margaret instigate the issue of a general pardon to the rebels? It seems more likely that the initiative for peace came from members of the government and the city authorities who may have appealed to the queen to use her name as the guarantor of the general pardon, in the absence of the king. According to a letter written by John Payn, who had been forced to join the rebels against his will, he was arrested and committed to the Marshalsea prison 'by the Quenes commaundment'.[126] However, this letter was written to John Paston I in 1465 fifteen years after the event and long after Margaret had indeed become a political figure. The lapse of time and the very different political circumstances must make its reliability as a source highly questionable. This is the full sum of the evidence for Margaret's involvement in Cade's rebellion and it hardly adds up to conclusive proof that she played a significant role in determining the eventual outcome.

Past studies of Margaret of Anjou have often failed to draw a distinction between two quite separate phases in her life, divided by the illness of her husband and the birth of her son in 1453. The resulting dramatic change in her position pushed Margaret to the forefront of politics in the absence of effective leadership from the king. From then on her main aim was to ensure that her son would one day inherit the throne and continue the Lancastrian line in fulfilment of the wish made by the earl of Shrewsbury when he offered his wedding gift to the queen in 1445. The mature woman who emerged from the changed political circumstances of 1453 was of a very different character from the young girl who arrived in England in 1445 with such high expectations of her new life as queen of England and France. In seeking to reassess the personality and role of Margaret of Anjou, her actions before 1453 deserve to be judged as those of a dutiful young wife and effective distributor of patronage rather than of an imperious and passionate power-seeker.

[125] *CPR, 1446–52*, p. 338.
[126] *Paston L&P*, II, p. 315.

6

PATRONAGE, VIOLENCE AND REVOLT IN THE REIGN OF HENRY VII

Dominic Luckett

When he ascended the throne in August 1485, Henry Tudor was a man burdened by debt. While in exile and on the Bosworth campaign he had enjoyed no regular income and had been living, effectively, on credit. His supporters had afforded him service of all kinds, in return for which they can have received little material recompense from the landless pretender. Only with the victory at Bosworth did Henry at last acquire the resources with which to reward them.

It was not just a vague sense of moral obligation which prompted Henry's early rewards. For a long time after his accession he remained politically vulnerable, and his chances of holding on to power and consolidating his fragile position were fundamentally dependent on his success in securing the continued assistance of his early supporters. At the same time he was also under pressure to broaden his base of support. Richard III's demise provided a clear illustration of the potential danger of too narrow a patronage policy, as he allowed his predominantly northern affinity to exert an ever tighter grip on patronage.[1] Clearly, if Henry was to succeed in re-uniting the political nation he had to prevent the development of a similar situation, in which his southern supporters monopolized favour at the expense of men from the north and others who had not backed him from the start. The basic problem, as always, was one of reconciling finite resources with insatiable demand. However many grants Henry made, there would always be men seeking more. Indeed, excessive royal

---

[1] R.E. Horrox, *Richard III: A Study of Service* (Cambridge, 1989), p. 316 *et passim*.

open-handedness no doubt merely encouraged petitioners to try their luck, thus further fuelling the appetite for patronage. All the king could hope to do was strike acceptable balances, first between the twin necessities of rewarding his subjects and maintaining the crown's solvency, and secondly between satisfying his existing supporters and attracting new men into his service. For every petition which led successfully to a grant, there would be others which failed. The art of kingship lay in choosing which to grant, and in persuading those who failed that it was worth trying again.

This brief survey aims to illustrate how, in the early years of the reign, Henry's patronage policy worked in practice, and to suggest some ways in which that policy was deficient. Limitations of space make it impossible to survey the whole country, and so a sample area has been selected, covering the counties of Berkshire, Oxfordshire, Dorset, Hampshire, Somerset and Wiltshire. It should at once be realized, however, that any conclusions reached for these shires are not necessarily valid for other parts of the country. For, if this study suggests anything, it is that in the early years of his rule, the young and inexperienced King Henry distributed his *largesse* in an extremely *ad hoc* way. Indeed, it could hardly be otherwise given the fact that the support which he enjoyed at the beginning of the reign was far from evenly spread.

It is well known that there was a north–south divide in 1485: the north had been Richard's heartland, while the south had always been reluctant to embrace the Yorkist usurper. What is perhaps less readily appreciated is that even quite small areas were capable of exhibiting distinct political sympathies. Thus, within the six south-western shires studied here, there was a discernible difference between Somerset, Dorset, Wiltshire and Hampshire, whence came many of Henry's staunchest supporters, and Oxfordshire and Berkshire, where support for him was less pronounced. This was largely a legacy of the 1483 revolt against King Richard. As most of Henry's active support had initially come from those rebels dispossessed after the collapse of the uprising, many of whom subsequently joined him in exile, it was consequently greatest in areas where the revolt had been most successful. The 1484 Act of Attainder identified two centres of the revolt within these six shires, Salisbury (Wilts.) and Newbury (Berks.), emphasizing the fact that both the Thames valley and the shires further to the south and west were implicated in the rising.[2] Yet, whilst not all the rebels were attainted, analysis of those who were strongly suggests that fewer men from the former area had been party to the uprising.[3] Not only were thirty-three men named in the Salisbury sector compared with only fourteen in the Newbury, but most of the former actually came from Wiltshire, Dorset, Somerset and Hampshire, whereas relatively few of those named in the Newbury sector were from Oxfordshire and Berkshire. Of the 'Newbury' rebels, William Berkeley was from Beverston (Glos.), Roger Tocotes and his stepson, Richard Beauchamp, were of Bromham (Wilts.), William Uvedale lived at Wickham (Hants.), and Amyas Paulet at Hinton St George (Soms.). Edmund Hampden, although he had Oxfordshire connections through his kinship with the Stonor family, was the younger son of Thomas Hampden of Hampden (Bucks.) and was described in the Act as 'late of Fisherton' (Wilts.). Roger Kelsall, Walter Williams and William Overy were all noted in the Act as Southampton men, and Sir Richard Woodville was described as late of London. Thus the only Oxfordshire and Berkshire men attainted in the Newbury sector were Sir William Stonor of Stonor (Oxon.), Sir William Norreys of Yattendon (Berks.), Sir Thomas Delamare of Aldermaston (Berks.) and John Harcourt, esquire, of Stanton Harcourt (Oxon.). All were important local figures, representing four of the area's most distinguished houses, but the clear impression is that these shires were less generally committed to the rebellion than those to the south and west. Indeed, Buckingham even had trouble in bringing his own clients in the Thames valley into revolt. John Isbury of Lambourn (Berks.), who as recently as 23 August 1483 had been granted a buck from one of the duke's parks, failed to join the rebellion.[4] The result of all this was that when Tudor landed in Wales in August 1485 he knew personally a substantial and influential section of the gentry communities of Wiltshire, Dorset, Somerset and Hampshire but only a few men from Oxfordshire and Berkshire. This fact was to have a profound effect upon Henry's distribution of patronage within these shires, and thus upon how successfully he established his rule in each.

---

[2] *RP*, VI, pp. 244–9.

[3] Horrox, *Richard III*, p. 160.

[4] PRO, Special Collections, Ancient Correspondence, SC1/44/75.

One of Henry's priorities in the autumn of 1485 was to minimize the hostility which his victory was likely to arouse amongst supporters of the old regime. Thus the continuator of the Croyland chronicle considered that his treatment of Richard III's supporters bespoke 'far greater moderation than was ever witnessed under similar circumstances in the time of king Richard or king Edward', a moderation reflected in the large number of exemption clauses appended to his Acts of Resumption.[5] There were still, of course, losers, notably those who had made big gains, especially of forfeit land and office, as a result of Richard's increasingly desperate search for political friends. But as most of these men were northerners, reflecting the geographical imbalance of Richard's support, few men native to the south-west suffered heavy deprivation in the post-Bosworth settlement.

There is, consequently, little evidence to suggest that the redistribution of grants which accompanied Henry's victory fostered much immediate resentment in the south-west. Where it did, and the aggrieved party felt compelled to act, the object of his aggression tended to be the beneficiary of the redistribution rather than the crown. Thus, for example, the king's attempt to establish Edmund Hampden, a Buckinghamshire younger son, as a crown agent in Oxfordshire, where the king had relatively few reliable supporters in the early part of the reign, evidently caused some anger among Hampden's new neighbours. This came to a head in June 1494 when Edmund was alleged to have assembled twenty armed men near his home at Woodstock, with whose assistance he attacked John Horne of Sarsden, Richard Croft of Chipping Norton and Robert Harcourt of Stanton Harcourt.[6] There is reason for

---

[5] *Ingulph's Chronicle of the Abbey of Croyland*, ed. and trans. H.T. Riley (1854), p. 511.

[6] PRO, King's Bench, Ancient Indictments, KB9/404, m.7r. This was not the first time since coming to Oxfordshire that Hampden had been accused of lawlessness. It was alleged in King's Bench that as early as July 1487 he had harboured a murderer. Later, in 1491, the University of Oxford complained that its students were liable to be assaulted by Hampden's men if they went about the city. Hampden was duly reprimanded by the king, and he was subsequently replaced as steward by Reginald Bray: PRO, King's Bench, Coram Rege Rolls, KB27/907, Justice rot. 65d; KB27/908, Justice rot. 73r; *Epistolae Academicae Oxon.*, ed. H. Anstey, Oxford Historical Society (2 vols. Oxford, 1898), II, pp. 607–10.

believing, however, that Hampden was not solely to blame for these disorders. In the first place, the indictment against him may have taken a jaundiced view of events, as his adversaries were all JPs and Croft presided over the quarter sessions at which the indictment was made. Secondly, all the attacks were alleged to have taken place at Woodstock, suggesting that the victims had approached Hampden and not *vice versa*. Finally, at least one of them had every reason to resent Edmund's presence in the shire. Richard Croft's family had dominated office holding in the area around Woodstock since Edward IV's reign. In February 1465 Richard, a staunch Yorkist and later a Ricardian esquire for the body, and his brother Thomas had been appointed parkers and keepers of the manor of Woodstock, in which offices they were confirmed in 1484. In 1467 Thomas Croft received the stewardship of the manor, his grant later being confirmed by Richard III.[7] Both Richard and Thomas secured clauses of exemption for these grants in Henry's first Act of Resumption, but this did not prevent Hampden from acquiring them shortly afterwards.[8] Richard Croft had also been receiver of the manors of Woodstock, Handborough, Wootton and Stonesfield under the Yorkists, and in February 1486 converted his receivership into a farm for seven years.[9] On the expiry of this lease Hampden was given custody of the lands, which is likely to have further antagonized Croft.[10] The clash at Woodstock may also have had still deeper roots, being the last chapter in a saga which highlights the legacy of rivalry and hostility left by the factionalism of the mid-fifteenth century. In 1461 Edmund's grandfather, another Edmund Hampden, one of Henry VI's household esquires, was attainted by the triumphant Yorkists and the Crofts

---

[7] E. Marshall, *The Early History of Woodstock Manor and its Environs* (Oxford, 1873), pp. 131–2; *CPR, 1467–1477*, pp. 17, 117; *CPR, 1476–1485*, pp. 432, 75; W.E. Hampton, *Memorials of the Wars of the Roses: A Biographical Guide* (Gloucester, 1979), p. 150; *VCH, Oxfordshire*, XII, p. 434. In 1482 Richard Croft was further appointed ranger of the 'new forest' in the forest of Wychwood adjoining the park of Woodstock: *CPR, 1476–1485*, p. 253.

[8] *RP*, VI, p. 342.

[9] *VCH, Oxfordshire*, XII, p. 432; *Materials for a History of the Reign of Henry VII*, ed. W. Campbell (RS, 2 vols. 1873–7), I, p. 310; B.P. Wolffe, *The Royal Demesne in English History* (1971), p. 206 and n.

[10] *CPR, 1494–1509*, p. 57; *CFR, 1485–1509*, p. 232.

were granted custody of his forfeit lands.[11] Nearly a decade after Henry's accession, the complex local effects of dynastic turmoil were evidently still capable of fostering violence.

Similar disputes within the south-western political community over the redistribution of patronage towards Henry's men continued to arise periodically throughout the reign. In August 1502, for instance, there were armed clashes at Chute (Wilts.) between the followers of the knight for the body, William Sandes of the Vyne, near Basingstoke, and John Lisle of Chute.[12] The immediate cause of the trouble appears to have been the king's grant to Sandes of the rangership of Chute forest in September 1501.[13] The Lisle family had dominated office holding here since the reign of Edward I, and Sandes's grant was a clear challenge to their traditional local position.[14] And in this case, their violent reaction seems to have paid off, prompting a royal re-think: in January 1505 John Lisle was granted the rangership after Sandes had 'surrendered' his patent.[15]

These purely localized clashes can have caused the crown little real concern, and for those denied or deprived of patronage, such attacks on more fortunate neighbours offered a relatively safe way of giving vent to resentment. A far more dangerous course for those who felt excluded from favour was to attack the crown itself. The dangers inherent in such activities, coupled with the high level of support which Henry initially enjoyed in most parts of the south-west, no doubt account for the scarcity of such incidents within this region in the period immediately after Bosworth. In Somerset, Dorset, Hampshire and Wiltshire there are no signs of opposition in the early part of the reign, as might be expected from traditionally Lancastrian shires which had furnished much of the gentry support for Henry's usurpation. Only in Oxfordshire is there any evidence of conspiracy. Even here, however, gentry opposition tended to come

---

[11] *CPR, 1436–1441*, p. 66; *1461–1467*, p. 108; *History of Parliament: I, Biographies of the Members of the Commons House, 1436–1509*, ed. J.C. Wedgwood (1936), pp. 413–15, 238.

[12] PRO, KB9/429 m.57r.

[13] *CPR, 1494–1509*, p. 265.

[14] PRO, SC1/19/19; *CPR, 1494–1509*, p. 219.

[15] Ibid., p. 425.

not from local men but from outsiders, drawn to the area primarily through the personal influence of Francis, Viscount Lovell, one of Richard III's staunchest noble supporters.

Besides being the head of an important northern family, Lovell also inherited extensive interests in the Thames valley, which made his support especially valuable to King Richard.[16] Among Lovell's southern associations, his links with the town of Abingdon and its influential Fraternity of the Holy Cross, which is said to have given Richard III assistance at Bosworth, have a special significance.[17] For it appears to be this Lovell connection which explains Humphrey Stafford's decision to seek sanctuary at Culham, near Abingdon, in 1486 after the collapse of the rebellion which he had launched with Lovell. Stafford may also have enjoyed the sympathy of John Sant, abbot of Abingdon since 1468. Sant had been favoured by Edward IV, for whom he served as an Oxfordshire JP and as a diplomat.[18] He was less successful under Richard III, from whom he received no official appointments, and it is therefore difficult to see why he should have been so hostile to Henry VII. Nevertheless, when on 13 May 1486 Sir John Savage and others intruded into the sanctuary at Culham and seized Stafford, whom they handed over to the king, Sant immediately challenged the arrest. At Stafford's trial in the King's Bench, he argued that the prisoner should be restored to sanctuary, the privilege of which should be recognized for the future.[19] The royal council effectively determined the issue, and its decision that sanctuary did not extend to traitors was followed by Stafford's conviction at common law and his execution at Tyburn.[20]

---

[16] P.A. Johnson, *Duke Richard of York, 1411–1460* (Oxford, 1988), p. 64; J. Sherwood and N. Pevsner, *The Buildings of England: Oxfordshire* (Harmondsworth, 1974), p. 706.

[17] J. Townsend, *A History of Abingdon* (1910; republished Wakefield, 1970), p. 56. In February 1484 Lovell, the bishop of Lincoln and the duke of Suffolk were granted a royal charter permitting them to re-found the fraternity with increased powers: *CPR, 1476–1485*, p. 386.

[18] Ibid., *1467–1477*, p. 115.

[19] PRO, KB27/900, Rex rot. 8r–9d.

[20] *Select Cases in the Council of Henry VII*, ed. C.G. Bayne and W.H. Dunham (Selden Society, LXXV, 1958), pp. 8, 13; C.H. Williams, 'The Rebellion of Humphrey Stafford in 1486', *EHR*, XLIV (1928), pp. 186–7.

Sant was, of course, defending an abbatial privilege. But on 21 May 1486, just eight days after Stafford's seizure, he was bound to the king in 2,000 marks conditional on the payment of £800 in two instalments. This strongly suggests that he was at least suspected of having some sympathy with Stafford.[21] Moreover, by the beginning of 1487 Sant was, according to a subsequent Act of Attainder, 'falsly and traiterously compassyng, conspiryng and ymaginyng the destruction of the Kyng'.[22] It is impossible to say whether this was because of a deep commitment to the Yorkist cause or the alienating effect of his treatment over the Stafford incident. What is clear, however, is that Sant's chief co-conspirators, Edward Franke, Henry Davy and Christopher Swanne, all had close links with Lord Lovell. Franke was originally from Knighton in Richmondshire. He had served in Lovell's retinue since 1482 and after Buckingham's revolt Richard III moved him down to Oxfordshire, Lovell's secondary sphere of influence.[23] After Bosworth he fled to Furness Fells (Cumb.), where he joined a group of Ricardians with strong Lovell connections. He fought at Stoke and was subsequently reported to be in the north searching for Lovell, which suggests a marked degree of personal loyalty.[24] Davy, another northern gentleman who had served as King Richard's sergeant-tailor, had been Lovell's deputy as chief butler of England in the ports of Ipswich and Chichester.[25] Swanne was not a northerner, being a yeoman from Abingdon, but his connections with Lovell are suggested by his position as mainpernor in February 1484 when the Berkshire manors of Cookham and Bray were

---

[21] The entry in the *Calendar of Close Rolls* incorrectly states that Sant was bound to pay £80 in instalments: PRO, Chancery, Close Rolls, C54/346 m.15d; *CCR, 1485–1500*, p. 27.

[22] *RP*, VI, p. 436.

[23] Horrox, *Richard III*, p. 221; *Materials*, I, p. 237; *List of Sheriffs for England and Wales from the Earliest Times to A.D. 1831* (PRO Lists and Indexes, IX, 1963 reprint), p. 108.

[24] S. O'Connor, 'Francis Lovell and the Rebels of Furness Fells', *The Ricardian*, VII, no. 96 (March 1987), pp. 366–7; *RP*, VI, pp. 397–8; D. Baldwin, 'What Happened to Lord Lovell?', *The Ricardian*, VII, no. 89 (June 1985); *Paston L&P*, II, p. 456.

[25] *CPR, 1476–1485*, p. 408; Horrox, *Richard III*, p. 141; *British Library Harleian MS 433*, ed. R.E. Horrox and P.W. Hammond (4 vols. 1979–83), I, p. 78.

committed to Franke and other Lovell associates. Lovell himself was steward there by January 1485.[26]

After the discovery of this conspiracy in 1491, Franke and Davy were both executed, and with their demise the Lovell connection ceased to exist as a political force. There is, moreover, no evidence to suggest that Henry was again troubled by any serious opposition within the Oxfordshire/Berkshire region. He may well, therefore, have felt satisfied that he had established his rule in the south-west with very little trauma: what little open hostility there had been was both limited in extent and motivated largely by malcontent outsiders who managed to attract little significant native support. Having weathered this early, and most dangerous, part of the reign, the king must have looked forward to a more comfortable future for his rule in the south-west.

With hindsight it is, of course, clear that the situation within the south-west was not as healthy as it may have seemed in the early 1490s. Before the decade was out, the region had provided Henry with one of the most serious challenges to his rule in the form of the popular rebellion which erupted in 1497. Quite apart from the very size of the uprising, the nature and extent of the revolt must have been especially worrying to the king. For one thing, it did not involve shires such as Oxfordshire and Berkshire which had shown only marginal enthusiasm for the Tudor cause, but erupted and spread in precisely those shires whence had come the greatest support for Henry's usurpation. Moreover, the movement was not orchestrated by fanatical anti-Tudor outsiders, but involved a spontaneous outburst of hostility from men whose support Henry must have taken for granted.[27]

Why was it that in the late 1490s, shires such as Dorset, Somerset and Hampshire, which had posed Henry no problems in the first decade of the reign, were now looking dangerously volatile, whereas counties where he had

---

[26] *CFR, 1471–1485*, pp. 273–4; *CPR, 1476–1485*, p. 508.

[27] For the best published account of the rising, see I. Arthurson, 'The Rising of 1497: A revolt of the Peasantry?', in *People, Politics and Community in the Later Middle Ages*, ed. J. Rosenthal and C. Richmond (Gloucester, 1987). I am most grateful to Dr Arthurson for sharing many of his thoughts on the rising with me.

initially experienced difficulties appeared to have been pacified? The principal reason seems to have been the way in which Henry had distributed his patronage. Crucial to this was the king's realization that favour could not simply be spread on the basis of who deserved what by dint of past service. Of course that was important, and the biggest winners were invariably men who had done most to secure Henry's accession. For those members of the gentry whose contribution to his victory had been more modest, however, the correlation between past service and reward was more tenuous. The main reward open to such men was office, and to be of real value to them such offices had to be near their homes and existing spheres of influence. Thus an important factor in determining whether a deserving individual got a grant was the level of competition from within his own shire. Hence, in counties where there was a particularly high number of deserving candidates for favour, it was inevitable that some would be disappointed. In shires where there were fewer such individuals, by contrast, the king would not only be able to reward those who had done him service, but could also seek to patronize others, thus broadening his base of support. There was, in other words, greater scope for disappointment in areas where the initial level of support for Tudor had been high than in those which had been more lukewarm.

From the start of his reign, Henry had employed a variety of means in an attempt to compensate for his lack of support in Oxfordshire and Berkshire. In the short term he bolstered his position by importing allies, including Edmund Hampden. More important, he sought in the long term to win over the political community through a relatively broad spread of favour, patronizing men who had not previously supported him. Thus, while his existing supporters here, such as the household knights William Stonor and William Norreys, were rewarded for their exertions, offices were also given to leading local figures such as the Fettiplace brothers who had not assisted the king's usurpation.[28] The result of this apparent royal liberality was that, after initial misgivings, Oxfordshire and Berkshire had settled down, by the mid-1490s, to quiet and passive obedience.

---

[28] *CPR, 1485–1494*, pp. 205, 273, 157, 229, 7, 36, 137.

Things were rather different in the shires further to the south and west. With many of his closest political allies living here, Henry felt little need to win over fresh supporters. Thus in distributing rewards here, he ignored all but his closest friends.[29] This was most clearly seen in Somerset and Dorset, where the king's former companion in exile, Sir Giles Daubeney of South Petherton, acquired almost all the available offices. A similar situation prevailed in Wiltshire, where the important positions were initially divided between two more of Henry's long-standing supporters, Sir Roger Tocotes of Bromham (Wilts.) and Sir Robert Willoughby of Broke (Wilts.). After Tocotes's death in 1492 the subsequent redistribution of office left Willoughby and Sir Walter Hungerford of Heytesbury (Wilts.), another rebel of 1483, as the dominant office holders. In Hampshire office was spread a little more broadly, but was again monopolized by men from Henry's original following. Daubeney was appointed steward of the duchy of Lancaster estates, while Sir John Cheyne acquired several senior positions, including the constableships of Southampton and Christchurch castles and the stewardship of Christchurch and Ringwood. John and Nicholas Gaynesford, both attainted by Richard III, were appointed to the constable's office at Odiham. David Owen, who had been knighted by Henry at Bosworth and subsequently appointed a king's knight, was installed as constable of Winchester castle.

This concentration of patronage in the hands of a few of Henry's long-standing supporters was quite understandable: he could hardly escape the necessity of providing his leading allies with suitable rewards. But with so many deserving candidates for favour living here, there were bound to be difficulties in satisfying them all. Faced with competition for office and authority from men such as Daubeney, Cheyne, Tocotes and Willoughby, those south-westerners who had failed to show Henry conspicuous support before his accession stood little chance. Even those who had given only limited or indirect assistance found it extremely difficult to engineer advancement. The problem was most acute in

---

[29] What follows is based upon the more detailed account in D.A. Luckett, 'Crown Patronage and Local Administration in Berkshire, Dorset, Hampshire, Oxfordshire, Somerset and Wiltshire, 1485–1509' (unpub. Oxford D.Phil. thesis, 1992), ch. 2.

Somerset and Dorset. These shires had probably the highest concentration of Tudor loyalists, but also the narrowest spread of grants, with Daubeney absorbing almost all the available offices. An inevitable consequence was that even men with good claims on the king's gratitude had difficulty in securing tangible reward. Thus Amyas Paulet of Hinton St George, an able man who had early allied himself to Henry's cause, had to wait well over a decade before his service attracted material recognition.[30] Others with equally good claims failed to win any preferment at all. Nicholas Latimer of Duntish (Dors.) had had a long, and largely unhappy, experience of fifteenth-century politics and after Bosworth he must have had high hopes of advancement. Yet while Henry reversed the attainder passed against him in the wake of Buckingham's revolt and placed him on the Dorset bench, Latimer received only one other commission, to assess the value of the king's possessions at Calais, and no grants.[31] Nicholas no doubt believed that after fighting for Henry VI and rebelling with Buckingham he was owed rather more by the new king. The same must have been true of Hugh Luttrell, a man whose ancestral connections with the Lancastrian cause were untainted by complicity with the Yorkists. Sir Hugh did not serve either of the Yorkist kings, joined Buckingham's revolt and after Bosworth secured a reversal of the attainder passed against his staunchly Lancastrian father. He was a Somerset JP from May 1487 and sheriff of Somerset and Dorset between 1488 and 1489, but received no other commissions before the 1497 revolt and won no crown grants.[32]

Both Latimer and Luttrell must have felt, after they and their families had endured the hardships of dispossession and attainder, incurred, ostensibly, in the name of the Lancastrian cause, that Henry's failure to go further than restoration of their ancestral estates smacked of ingratitude. Indeed, in a very real sense their restoration was incomplete, for both recovered their estates but not the role in local, let alone national, affairs which their forefathers had enjoyed. Vergil's observation that some men considered themselves 'ill-rewarded

---

[30] Wedgwood, *Biographies*, pp. 667–8; Hampton, *Memorials*, p. 158; *CPR, 1494–1509*, p. 349.

[31] *RP*, VI, p. 273; *CPR, 1485–1494*, p. 485; *1494–1509*, p. 637; *Materials*, II, p. 67.

[32] Horrox, *Richard III*, p. 169; *CPR, 1485–1494*, p. 499; *List of Sheriffs*, p. 124.

by King Henry for the services they had zealously rendered on his behalf' doubtless applied to them.[33] By 1497 their positions showed no signs of improvement and the king was actually making demands upon them and their neighbours for a war to safeguard his regime. The political tradition in which they had been nurtured suggested only one way to make their grievance heard: by recourse to arms. The outbreak of revolt amongst the lower orders in 1497 gave them their opportunity.

This gentry involvement in the 1497 revolt demonstrates that in the shires where the rebellion took hold Henry had not just failed to enlarge his base of support since Bosworth, he had actually succeeded in limiting it by alienating men who had initially been uncommitted or even sympathetic towards him. This was obviously true with men such as Latimer and Luttrell who felt cheated out of their just rewards. It was also the case at the top of the south-western political community, where the effect of Henry's patronage was to supplant the established aristocracy with another of his own making. The creation and empowerment of Lords Cheyne, Daubeney and Willoughby of Broke of necessity marginalized the region's older baronial families and thus it was that two of the region's peers showed more or less active signs of opposition in 1497, a reaction against a régime which effectively sought to deny them the influence which they must have seen as their birthright. James, Lord Audley actually came out in open rebellion in 1497. His family had played an important part in both local and national affairs over previous decades, but on succeeding his father in 1491 he was largely ignored by the crown.[34] He served on the Hampshire bench between 1488 and 1493 and on the Somerset commission from July 1491, but received no other commissions and no grants.[35] This denial of authority and influence was not merely a personal humiliation. It would also have robbed him of the capacity to act as 'good lord' to those who were, or would be, members of his affinity. This can hardly have failed to be a source of

[33] Polydore Vergil, *The Anglica Historia of Polydore Vergil*, ed. and trans. D. Hay (Camden Society, third series, LXXIV, 1950), p. 33.

[34] Hampton, *Memorials*, p. 179; *GEC*, I, pp. 341–2.

[35] *CPR, 1485–1494*, pp. 499, 500; *1494–1509*, p. 656.

frustration, and even before the first stirrings of the 1497 revolt Audley was evidently under some suspicion. In August 1497 Heron noted that Sir Walter Hungerford had forfeited a recognizance made on his behalf.[36] The terms of the bond are unknown, but the timing of its forfeiture suggests that it was dependent on Audley's good behaviour or allegiance.

Lord Stourton's immediate predecessors had enjoyed a less prominent role in national affairs than had the Audleys, although John, first Baron Stourton, who died in 1462, had been treasurer of Henry VI's household and had served for a time as governor of Calais.[37] The family had, however, become extremely powerful in the south-west during the 1470s,[38] something reflected in the extensive local commissions received by William, Lord Stourton (d. 1478).[39] Under Richard III the family's influence waned somewhat, at least partly due to connections with dissidents.[40] William inherited the barony in February 1487 when he was about thirty.[41] Yet despite his entry to the peerage, his official involvement in local affairs was small. After a brief appearance as a Wiltshire JP in November 1485 he did not return to the bench until November 1499, and, except for one commission in 1486, received no other official employment prior to the 1497 revolt.[42] He was, in short, effectively excluded from any official part in the running of affairs in his 'country'. In 1497 Stourton did not, apparently, take up arms at any point, either for or against the king. He does, however,

---

[36] PRO, Exchequer, King's Remembrancer, Accounts Various, E101/414/16, f.88r.

[37] *GEC*, XII, part 1, pp. 301–2.

[38] Wedgwood, *Biographies*, p. 819.

[39] *CPR, 1452–1461*, pp. 58, 62, 346, 408, 490, 492, 495, 558, 653, 657, 665; *1461–1467*, pp. 37, 98, 101, 202. All the above came before inheriting his title. He was commissioned as an arbitrator in January 1463, but received no more commissions until July 1466 when he was appointed a justice of *oyer et terminer* in the south-west: ibid., pp. 234, 529. Thereafter his career resumed, lasting until 1475 when he received his last commission: ibid., *1467–1476*, pp. 126, 128, 196, 220, 284, 350, 351, 522, 573. He was a JP for Dorset, Somerset, Wiltshire and Hampshire: ibid., *1461–1467*, pp. 563, 571, 575; ibid., *1467–1477*, pp. 613, 628, 629, 635.

[40] Horrox, *Richard III*, pp. 142–3, 172, 274; *GEC*, XII, part 1, p. 303.

[41] *CIPM, Henry VII*, I, pp. 2–3, 6, 9, 123–4, 141–2, 477–82; *GEC*, XII, part 1, pp. 303–4; *CCR, 1485–1500*, p. 229; *CFR, 1485–1509*, pp. 216–18.

[42] *Materials*, II, pp. 55–6; *CPR, 1485–1494*, p. 504; *1494–1509*, pp. 637, 657, 665, 487.

appear to have sympathized with the rebels, for in 1501 John Heron entered a memorandum of 'the deteccon ageinst the lorde Sturton for treason'. The matter was then allowed to rest until Easter 1505 when the Council Learned's entry book records that he was to appear before the king and council in the following term to answer the charge that he 'received ii of his s[er]v[a]unts being at Blakhethe'. In the following November he submitted a bond for the payment of 1,500 marks at the rate of £200 per annum, with a further 500 marks respited during the king's pleasure.[43]

A final consequence of Henry's narrow spread of patronage in the area of the revolt was that there were too few men there who had benefited from the régime sufficiently to want to defend it. This situation was only exacerbated by the king's own conception of the relationship between the crown and those enjoying its patronage. From early in the reign a series of statutes and other official pronouncements indicate that he recognized his security to lie chiefly in the hands of those receiving crown grants. The earliest of these statutes, 3 Henry VII c. 15 of 1487, made it clear that the tenure of crown offices was dependent on continued service: any crown stewards, constables, bailiffs or other officials who, without reasonable cause, failed to come to the king's aid 'in tyme of troble or werre' were to forfeit their offices.[44] Eight years later, the statute 11 Henry VII c. 18, whilst noting the general duty of the subject to serve the king when required, went on to claim that this duty was especially incumbent on those who had received any grants of office, fee or annuity from the crown. Such men were particularly bound to come to the king's defence and failure to do so, except with good reason or by royal licence, was to be punished by deprivation of grants.[45] Henry was, effectively, acknowledging that it was not vague ties of loyalty or gratitude that secured service. Rather, men were prompted to serve by nothing more lofty than material self-interest. Thus he made it manifest to them that to keep existing favours, let alone acquire new ones, fresh efforts were constantly required on his behalf.

---

[43] BL., Additional MS. 21480, f.181r; PRO, Duchy of Lancaster, Entry Books of Decrees and Orders, DL5/4, f.52r; Exchequer, Treasury of Receipt, Miscellaneous Books, E36/214, f.237v.

[44] *SR*, II, pp. 522–3.

[45] Ibid., II, p. 582.

Such an approach was fine in areas such as Oxfordshire and Berkshire where the king's initial lack of firm support had led him to spread patronage amongst a significant proportion of the gentry. The wisdom of such a policy was less apparent in a shire such as Somerset where only a few men had received grants from the king. Thus in 1497 the rebels met no serious opposition as they passed through Somerset towards London. This, then, is the crucial point in understanding the revolt's success in these shires. Too few men here had a stake in Henry's régime to wish to support it, and when heavy taxes were imposed in 1497 and the lower orders began to rise in the south-west, a large part of the area's gentry and nobility, depending on the strength of their grievance, either rose up, or sympathized with the movement, or let it pass by unopposed.

Ironically, therefore, the geographical spread of Henry's support made resentment most likely in areas where that support appeared greatest. The more secure the king felt in a particular county, the narrower his spread of patronage and thus the greater the scope for disappointment among those who were omitted. The message of the 1497 revolt was clear: in areas where Henry had hitherto been most confident of his security, he was in fact relying on a dangerously narrow base of support. Yet there is little evidence that he did anything to change his patronage policy as a result of the uprising. Most notably, and despite allegations of his reluctance to engage the rebels in 1497, Daubeney's domination of office-holding in the region continued and was even extended. In 1499 he was granted a number of Dorset offices formerly held by John Cheyne, and in 1504 he was confirmed as steward of Queen Elizabeth's lands in Somerset and Dorset.[46] The one change which did occur in the wake of the revolt was in the king's method of governance: a move away from favour to coercion, and a more aggressive statecraft.

---

[46] *CPR, 1494–1509*, pp. 188, 346.

7

THE TAILORS OF LONDON: CORPORATE CHARITY IN THE LATE MEDIEVAL TOWN

Matthew Davies

Thomas Parker, citizen and tailor of London, made his will in 1470 'knowyng that no thing is more certaine than deth nor no thing is more uncertayn than is the houre of the comyng of hitt'.[1] Such trepidation was doubtless appropriate in an era when plague was a recurrent presence in the lives of Londoners, yet an untimely death was by no means the only cause of anxiety in the late medieval town.[2] The highly specialized nature of the urban economy of London produced its casualties, even among the most successful merchants and craftsmen; the financial viability of many businesses balanced on a knife edge, dependent as they were upon the complexities and fluctuations of the productive and distributive processes. Credit loomed large in these processes: on the one hand it served to ensure the smooth completion of transactions, particularly when there was a shortage of hard currency, yet on the other it involved many town dwellers in a perpetual struggle to remain solvent.[3] Some were successful, often through diversification: ale brewing, for instance,

---

[1] PRO, Prerogative Court of Canterbury, Register of Wills, Prob. 11/5, ff.243–243v. I am grateful to Gervase Rosser and to Caroline Barron for their comments upon earlier drafts of this paper.

[2] For the London plagues see J.M.W. Bean, 'Plague, Population and Economic Decline in England in the Later Middle Ages', *EcHR*, 2nd ser., XV (1963), pp. 427–31. The results of a study of property holding in Cheapside support the view that London's population may have continued to decline in the early fifteenth century: D. Keene, 'A new study of London before the Great Fire', *Urban History Yearbook* (1984), esp. pp. 18–19.

[3] See M.M. Postan, 'Credit in Medieval Trade', *EcHR*, I (1928–9), pp. 234–61.

became a 'safe and profitable sideline' to the activities of many families, which
brought in badly needed cash.[4] Yet many more failed to keep their heads above
water, and as a result became dependent upon whatever sources of assistance
they could find. The lack of municipal systems of poor relief in late medieval
London, and indeed in most towns and cities in Europe, has focused attention
upon the efforts of individuals and institutions in the provision of charitable
support. The resulting studies have emphasized that the mechanisms set up
were primarily the product of pious motives and as such were not intended to
solve the problem of poverty but to ameliorate it and thereby benefit the souls of
the departed benefactors.[5] The Europe-wide growth of lay fraternities in the
fourteenth and fifteenth centuries owed much to the principle of *caritas* which
emphasized mutual assistance through the prayers offered for the souls of the
dead and charity provided for the living. Such solutions were essentially 'local'
in character: even the confraternities of Venice, founded specifically to care for
the poor and sick, were limited in scope, providing help primarily for their own
members.[6] Yet despite the fact that such institutions never formed part of wider
schemes to help the urban poor, particularly those who could not afford to join
fraternities, it is important not to dismiss their efforts which were often
pragmatic and effective in their own way. As one historian has pointed out,

---

[4] S.L. Thrupp, *The Merchant Class of Medieval London* (Ann Arbor, 1948), p. 8.

[5] W.K. Jordan, *The Charities of London, 1480–1660* (1960); J.A.F. Thomson, 'Piety and Charity in
Late Medieval London', *Journal of Ecclesiastical History*, XVI (1965), pp. 178–96; C. Rawcliffe, 'The
Hospitals of Medieval London', *Medical History*, XXVIII (1984), pp. 1–21. Regional studies include
M. Rubin, *Charity and Community in Medieval Cambridge* (Cambridge, 1987); G. Rosser, *Medieval
Westminster, 1200–1540* (Oxford, 1989), pp. 294–325; P. Heath, 'Urban Piety in the later Middle
Ages: the evidence of Hull wills', in *The Church, Politics and Patronage in the Fifteenth Century*, ed. R.B.
Dobson (Gloucester, 1984), pp. 209–34; P.W. Fleming, 'Charity, Faith and the Gentry of Kent,
1422–1509', in *Property and Politics: Essays in Later Medieval English History*, ed. A.J. Pollard (Gloucester,
1984), pp. 36–58; P.H. Cullum, '"And Hir Name was Charite": Charity by and for Women in Late
Medieval Yorkshire', in *Woman is a Worthy Wight: Women in English Society, c. 1200–1500*, ed. P.J.P.
Goldberg (Stroud, 1992), pp. 182–211.

[6] See B. Pullan, *Rich and Poor in Renaissance Venice: the Social Institutions of a Catholic State, to 1620*
(Oxford, 1971), pp. 63–77, and R. Mackenney, *Tradesmen and Traders: The World of the Guilds in Venice
and Europe, c. 1250–c. 1650* (1987), p. 62.

successful mechanisms for poor relief were created in urban society despite the fact that the inner, selfish motivations of donors seeking an eternal reward were 'not conducive to the efficient systematization of social care'.[7] Recently, for instance, Dr Cullum has charted the growing number of foundations of small almshouses or *maisonsdieu* in the century after 1350 which exploited often limited resources to provide flexible assistance for the poor and sick in towns. Most such foundations arose out of the *post-mortem* arrangements made by testators, but many individuals also contributed during their lifetimes to the variety of charitable assistance available in the medieval town: in her will of 1512 Thomasine Percyvale, widow of a former mayor of London, mentioned three boys and two girls in her household 'which I have brought up of almes'.[8]

The efforts of craft guilds in the area of poor relief have often been underplayed owing to a widely held, but somewhat inaccurate, assumption that the religious and social functions of craft associations, though prominent, were incidental to their main purpose and thereby inferior to the facilities provided by parishes or parish fraternities.[9] In England the parish, it is true, became the basic unit for poor relief through the sixteenth-century poor laws and contributed in no small way to the lack of success of large-scale foundations such as municipal workhouses and hospitals before 1700, as compared with their continental counterparts.[10] This development was certainly testimony to the durability of the ties of locality and neighbourhood which had earlier found their expression in the late medieval parish. On the other hand, a concentration upon the vitality of the late medieval parish can result in a distorted and over-

---

[7] Rosser, *Medieval Westminster*, p. 294.

[8] P.H. Cullum, '"For Pore People Harberles": What was the Function of the Maisonsdieu?', in *Trade, Devotion and Governance: Papers in Later Medieval History*, ed. D.J. Clayton, R.G. Davies and P. McNiven (Stroud, 1994), pp. 36–54; Matthew Davies, 'Dame Thomasine Percyvale, 'The Maid of Week' (d. 1512)', in *Medieval London Widows, 1300–1500*, ed. C.M. Barron and A.F. Sutton (1994), p. 202.

[9] See, for instance, H. Swanson, 'The Illusion of Economic Structure: Craft Guilds in Late Medieval English Towns', *Past and Present*, CXXI (1988), pp. 29–49; Rubin, *Charity and Community*, p. 250; J.J. Scarisbrick, *The Reformation and the English People* (Oxford, 1984), p. 20.

[10] P. Slack, *Poverty and Policy in Tudor and Stuart England* (1988), pp. 131, 206.

simplified view of urban society in general, and mechanisms for poor relief in particular. Citizens of towns and cities displayed allegiances to a variety of overlapping historical communities of which the parish was just one. A London citizen making a will in the fifteenth century would normally identify himself as a member of a craft or 'mistery', besides indicating his loyalty to a particular parish. At the head of most of the trades and occupations in the capital was a guild, often dedicated to a patron saint, which represented the needs and aspirations of the mistery in the wider urban community and was responsible for the supervision of the craft through the enforcement of ordinances concerning apprenticeship, standards of workmanship and so on.[11] The relative dearth of detailed studies of crafts and their guilds in European towns has, unfortunately, led to an over-reliance upon the records of municipal authorities, to the exclusion of discussion of the internal lives of the guilds themselves.[12] Documents such as the *Livre des Métiers* compiled in the thirteenth century by the royal prévôt in Paris, or the charters granted to the London craft guilds in the fourteenth and fifteenth centuries, are generally used by historians to emphasize the control exercised by the state, rather than the fraternal aspects of craft associations which are often also present in these sources.[13] Dr Swanson, for example, asserts that the guilds of late medieval York principally acted as the policing agents of the city authorities and possessed little or no independence of their own.[14]

Recently, however, historians have begun to peer beneath the 'rhetoric of directive legislation' in order to reassess the roles played by craft organizations

[11] For the development of the London merchant and craft guilds see G. Unwin, *The Gilds and Companies of London* (1908).

[12] These issues are touched on by R. Holt and G. Rosser in *The Medieval Town, 1200–1540*, ed. R. Holt and G. Rosser (1990), pp. 9–11.

[13] G.-B. Depping, *Réglemens sur les Arts et Métiers de Paris . . . connus sous le nom du Livre de Métiers d'Étienne Boileau* (Paris, 1837), pp. 7–8. A more sophisticated analysis of the structure of the Parisian crafts can be found in B. Geremek, *Le Salariat dans l'Artisanat Parisien au xiiie–xve Siècles* (Paris, 1982).

[14] Swanson, 'The Illusion of Economic Structure', pp. 29–49. Swanson does however emphasize the extent of the unregulated sphere of the urban economy, and hence the practical limitations to the authority of guild and municipal governments alike.

in urban society.[15] As Dr Veale has shown in an important contribution to the debate, craft guilds often sprang from the same roots and impulses as parish fraternities, traditionally seen as distinct from their occupational siblings.[16] In London and elsewhere, the thirteenth and fourteenth centuries saw an extraordinary growth in the number of fraternities of all kinds, initially attached to parish churches, which drew their strength from notions of the community of the living and the dead and the coincidence of individual action with the collective needs of members. Such associations became the natural organizing units for men and women who were not blood relatives but who wished to use the analogy of brotherhood in order to achieve corporate aims.[17] Some were occupationally based at an early stage: the saddlers of London were described as a *congregatio* as early as 1180 when they entered into an agreement with the canons of St Martin le Grand.[18] Likewise the Skinners' fraternity, dedicated to the feast of Corpus Christi, had moved out of a parish church (St John Walbrook) and acquired a hall of its own by the early fourteenth century. Royal charters, granted to both the Saddlers and the Skinners in the fourteenth century, formalized their authority over their respective crafts, yet also emphasized their continued social and religious

---

[15] G. Rosser, 'Crafts, Guilds and the Organization of Work in the Medieval Town', p. 6. I am grateful to Dr Rosser for allowing me to consult this unpublished paper. For examples of the revisionist approach, see Geremek, *Le salariat*; J-P. Sosson, 'La Structure Sociale de la Corporation Médiévale: l'exemple des Tonneliers de Bruges de 1350 à 1500', *Revue Belge de Philologie et d'Histoire*, XLIV (i) (1966), pp. 457–78; idem, *Les Travaux Publics de la Ville de Bruges xiv*–*xv* Siècles (Brussels, 1977). The most substantial single survey of crafts and their guilds in medieval Europe remains S.L. Thrupp, 'The Gilds', in *Cambridge Economic History of Europe* (8 vols. Cambridge, 1941–91), III, pp. 230–79. For discussion of these issues in the context of the London crafts see M.P. Davies, 'The Tailors of London and their Guild, *c.* 1300–1500' (unpub. Oxford D.Phil. thesis, 1994), esp. pp. viii–xxiv, 87–134, 163–80.

[16] E.M. Veale, 'The "Great Twelve": Mistery and Fraternity in Thirteenth Century London', *Historical Research*, LXIV (1991), pp. 237–63.

[17] S. Reynolds, *Kingdoms and Communities in Western Europe 900–1300* (Oxford, 1984), pp. 67–75.

[18] G. Martin, 'The Early History of the London Saddlers' Guild', *BJRL*, LXXII (1990), pp. 147–52.

[19] E.M. Veale, *The English Fur Trade in the Later Middle Ages* (Oxford, 1966), pp. 101–31. In Venice too, despite the separation of the *arti* and the *scuoli*, the devotional activities of the former were inseparable from their political and administrative functions, see Mackenney, *Tradesmen and Traders*, p. 44.

functions.[19] On the other hand, the development of a fraternity did not always follow this pattern: some associations, like the fraternity of the Holy Trinity, St Fabian and St Sebastian in St Botolph's Aldersgate, remained parish fraternities despite drawing a large number of members from one particular occupation.[20]

Evidence for collective action on the part of the London tailors before 1300 is rare. Corporate spirit was certainly demonstrated in 1267 when running battles took place with a group of goldsmiths through the streets of London.[21] However, the first indication that there was a ruling body for the craft occurs in a will of 1278 in which Robert de Mounpeillers bequeathed a quit rent on a shop and solar, belonging to the Tailors, to his sons.[22] By 1320, if not before, a fraternity, dedicated to St John the Baptist, was clearly identified as the governing body of the craft. Interestingly the master was, for a time, known as the *peregrinus* of the mistery, reflecting contemporary interest in pilgrimage which found expression in fraternities of 'palmers' such as at Ludlow.[23] By 1400 the fraternity of London tailors was among the most important in the capital: it had acquired two royal charters, a hall with a chapel attached, a second chapel in St Paul's, letters of confraternity with several religious foundations in and around London and extensive property holdings in the city.[24] As a consequence of these institutional developments and the perceived social and spiritual benefits of affiliation, the fifteenth century saw the acquisition of a large and influential non-tailor membership. Indeed, between 1398 and 1470 over 1,200 non-tailors joined on

---

[20] P. Basing, *Parish Fraternity Register: the Fraternity of the Holy Trinity and SS Fabian and Sebastian in the Parish of St. Botolph without Aldersgate* (London Record Society, XIX 1982), pp. xxii–iii. Although 40 occupations were represented, few had more than three members. Of those that did, the 25 brewers stand out from the 7 grocers, 7 tailors, 7 goldsmiths, 6 carpenters and 4 representatives each of the butchers, dyers, maltmen and smiths.

[21] *De Antiquis Legibus Liber*, ed. T. Stapleton (Camden Society, orig. ser., XXXIV, 1846), p. 99.

[22] *Calendar of the Wills proved and enrolled in the Court of Hustings, London, A.D. 1258–1688*, ed. R.R. Sharpe (2 vols. 1889–90), I, p. 38 (hereafter *CWCH*, I, II etc.).

[23] M(erchant) T(aylors') Co(mpany), Ancient MS. Books (hereafter Anc. MS. Bks.), vol. IX, f.12. The records of the company are on microfilm at Guildhall Library; *English Gilds*, ed. T. Smith (EETS, XL, 1870), pp. 193–9.

[24] Davies, 'The Tailors of London', pp. 1–86; C.M. Clode, *The Early History of the Guild of Merchant Taylors of the Fraternity of St. John the Baptist, London, with Notices of the Lives of Some of its Eminent Members* (2 vols. 1888), I, pp. 33–59, 82–126.

payment of 20 shillings, compared with the 600 London tailors who were admitted to what was now known as the 'livery' of the craft, after the livery suit which members were required to wear on official occasions (see Table 1). Members included the king and queen of the day, prominent courtiers, nobility and gentry, as well as members of other London crafts. Participation in the activities of the fraternity varied, as did the reasons behind their affiliation to it. Some individuals were perceived as important patrons by the master and wardens of the craft: Humphrey, duke of Gloucester, became an important ally for the Tailors during their bitter dispute with the London Drapers in the 1430s and 1440s, and another illustrious member, Henry VII, granted the guild the title of *Merchant* Taylors in 1503, much to the annoyance of the other companies.[25] Others, such as the Pastons, were customers and friends of London tailors, particularly the wealthier members of the craft such as John Lee, who became master of the craft in 1483.[26] Moreover, many successful tailors lived and worked in Fleet Street, close to the inns of court, the legal training ground for the sons of the gentry, as well as the town houses of prominent clergy, gentry and nobility, many of whom forged links, whether formal or informal, with the Tailors' fraternity.[27]

[25] C.M. Barron, 'Ralph Holland and the London Radicals, 1438–1444', in *The Medieval Town*, ed. Holt and Rosser, p. 167 and n. 37; H. Miller, 'London and Parliament in the reign of Henry VIII', *BIHR*, XXXV (1962), pp. 130–43; Davies, 'The Tailors of London', pp. 120–34.

[26] Sir John Paston was admitted to the tailors' fraternity in 1466–7: MTCo., Accounts, vol. II, f.296 (hereafter MTA, I, II etc.). Paston, like his younger brother John III, was friendly with John Lee and his wife, referring to them on one occasion as 'my ryght trusty frendys': *Paston L&P*, I, pp. 590, 617–18; MTA, III, f.169. For other letters from the Pastons which mention Lee see *Paston L&P*, I, pp. 592, 615.

[27] Two bishops of Salisbury, Robert Neville and Richard Beauchamp, were admitted in 1436–7 and 1458–9 respectively, with two bishops of Exeter, George Neville and John Booth, becoming members in 1459–60 and 1469–70: MTA, I, f.280; II, ff.152, 173; and III, f.6. For the location of their mansions see *The British Atlas of Historic Towns, III: The City of London from Pre-historic Times to c. 1520*, ed. M.D. Lobel (Oxford, 1989), maps 1–2. Although tailors were not generally concentrated in any one geographical area of London, the parishes of St Dunstan in the West and St Bride Fleet Street appear to have attracted some of the most successful members of the craft. Sixty-nine out of 412 London tailors whose wills were proved between 1388 and 1512 chose to be buried in the parishes of St Dunstan or St Bride, with forty-three preferring the former. References to tenements, membership of fraternities and other inhabitants indicate that the attachment was a very real one. PRO, Prob.11/1–11; London G(uildhall) L(ibrary), MS. 9171/1–9 (Commissary Court); 9051/1 (Archdeaconry Court); and *CWCH*, II, *passim*.

Table 1

ADMISSIONS TO THE FRATERNITY OF ST JOHN THE BAPTIST, 1398–1473

Years	Tailors	Non-tailors	Total
1398–1445	487 (10.36 per annum)	1031 (21.93)	1518 (32.29)
1453–73	168 (8.4)	197 (9.85)	365 (18.25)
Total	655 (9.78)	1228 (18.33)	1883 (28.10)

Though unusual in the size and scope of its membership and in the wealth that it was able to draw upon for its activities, the Tailors' fraternity affords a rare opportunity to see, in the context of a craft guild, the operation of the principles of community and mutual support which underpinned the existence of all lay fraternities, large and small.[28] The returns made by scores of guilds to the governmental enquiry of 1388–9 are dominated by descriptions of mechanisms established to provide help for poor or infirm brothers and sisters, whether in the form of cash hand-outs, accommodation or food. The provision of funerals was also a common clause in the ordinances of fraternities.[29] It is illuminating to note that in an early fourteenth-century grant, the wardens of the Tailors' fraternity were described as *collectores elemosinam*, a phrase which helps to emphasize that the officials of craft guilds were not solely concerned with the supervision of the craft but were also responsible for the social and religious services which were typically provided by fraternities in the late medieval period.[30] Alms,

---

[28] See B. McRee, 'Charity and Gild Solidarity in Late Medieval England', *Journal of British Studies*, XXXII (1993), pp. 195–225; G. Rosser, 'Going to the Fraternity Feast: Commensality and Social Relations in Late Medieval England', *Journal of British Studies*, XXXIII (1994), pp. 430–46.

[29] For those returns in English, see Smith, *English Gilds*, pp. 1–122. For the activities of the London parish fraternities, see C.M. Barron, 'The Parish Fraternities of Medieval London', in *The Church in Pre-Reformation Society: Essays in Honour of F.R.H. Du Boulay*, ed. C.M. Barron and C. Harper-Bill (Woodbridge, 1985), pp. 13–37.

[30] MTCo., Anc. MS. Bks., vol. IX, f.12. John Stow, writing at the close of the sixteenth century, was evidently well informed about his company's history when he stated that until 1388 'the foure wardens were then called Purveyors of almes (now called quarterage) of the said fraternitie'. *A Survey of London* (1603), ed. C.L. Kingsford (2 vols. 1908), I, p. 181.

collected on each quarter-day during the year by the wardens and entered in a book, provided the Tailors with the bulk of the revenue they needed to satisfy the needs of the poor among them. Each brother and sister of the fraternity, both tailors and non-tailors, was required to contribute one shilling per annum.[31] The large and heterogeneous membership made the task of collecting the alms money a difficult one, particularly from those who were unlikely to spend much time at Tailors' Hall. Robert Fitzhugh, bishop of London from 1431 until his death in 1436, failed to pay any alms at all during his time as a brother. His executors, perhaps mindful of the good relations which the fraternity enjoyed with the see of London, were more forthcoming and handed over 19s *pur sa almoigne arere par xix ans* in 1435–6.[32]

At no time, however, did the fraternity lose its association with the craft of tailoring in the capital. All the officers and members of the court of assistants were tailors and, it will be shown, virtually all the recipients of charitable assistance were members of the craft. A distinction was even drawn after 1453 between alms received *de confratribus huius mistere* and *de fratribus et sororum extra artem cissorem*.[33] Yet despite the decline in the level of non-tailor admissions to the fraternity in the later fifteenth century (in Table 1), they continued to outnumber the tailor membership, a fact which was reflected in the amount given in alms by the two groups. In 1463–4, for instance, a total of £14 15s was raised, £9 of it from non-tailors with the remaining £5 15s given by tailors.[34]

---

[31] In 1406–7, 2s 8d was paid *pur xii pelles et un sourpel de parchemyn pur entier faire un livre pur almoigne*: MTA, I, f.32.

[32] Ibid., I, f.265v. In 1417–18 'maister Robert ffithugh clerk' had been admitted as a 'confrere', ibid., I, f.101v. Four other bishops of London, Nicholas Bubwith, John Kemp, William Gray and Robert Gilbert, became brethren of the fraternity which, by the late fourteenth century, had the use of a chapel by the north door of the cathedral, dedicated to St John the Baptist, in which the chantries and obits of benefactors were celebrated: Davies, 'The Tailors of London', pp. 13, 18–20, 56–7.

[33] MTA, II, f.228v (1462–3).

[34] Ibid., II, f.278v.

Table 2

AVERAGE ANNUAL ALMS COLLECTIONS AND DISTRIBUTIONS, 1400–75[35]

Years	Alms collected			Alms paid out			Recipients
	£	s	d	£	s	d	
1400–10	16	14	0	30	1	5	15.2
1410–20	15	12	2	32	7	1	14.3
1420–30	16	18	2	30	0	2	13.8
1430–40	14	17	8	25	1	6	12.5
1440–5	15	9	11	35	3	2	13.4
1453–60	17	7	10	26	10	5	12.0
1460–70	14	7	2	17	16	2	7.3
1470–5	13	5	0	19	17	6	8.5

Although the fraternity was normally able to raise at least £15 every year from alms collections, the actual payments made to almsmen almost always totalled far more than was raised through the regular alms collections alone. This is shown in Table 2. It was only in the early 1460s, when the number of almsmen being supported consistently numbered fewer than ten, that the income from official collections exceeded expenditure upon the needy.[36] Work on the parish fraternities of London has drawn attention to a similar imbalance in income and expenditure on poor members, but it is important to remember that craft associations, particularly the most successful ones, had a variety of sources of income which could be tapped in order to meet demand.[37] For instance, in addition to their quarterly alms donations, new members admitted to the Tailors' fraternity each had to pay 20*s* to the common box on entry. With an average of twenty-eight new members admitted each year, this constituted a

[35] Figures calculated from the yearly entries in the Tailors' accounts: ibid., I–III. The account years 1445/6 to 1452/3 are missing.

[36] Between 1460 and 1465 an average of £14 9*d* was collected, with distributions to fewer than seven recipients averaging £14 0*s* 7*d*: ibid., II, *passim*.

[37] Barron, 'Parish Fraternities', in *The Church in Pre-Reformation Society*, ed. Barron and Harper-Bill, p. 27.

valuable source of income in the fifteenth century. Testamentary bequests were received from many quarters and were a constant ratification of the bonds of fraternity and of the duties of the master and wardens towards the membership. In 1433–4, for example, a total of £18 13s 4d was bequeathed by five individuals, including William Crowmer, a prominent draper and alderman, who left 100s to the common box.[38] Bequests such as these normally took the form of general donations, without specifying the relief of poverty, but this was in keeping with the nature of the organization – funds donated to the common box could thus be used for a variety of purposes connected with the aims of a lay confraternity, of which help for poor members was but one. Many testators were more specific, however: in 1397 John Levendale, senior, left 6s 8d to the fraternity as a whole and another 6s 8d to the alms box, and another tailor, John Dadyngton, whose bequest of 40s was recorded in the accounts for 1407–8, was clear that it should be spent exclusively on the almsmen of the fraternity.[39]

These were, of course, relatively small sums compared with the total annual income of the fraternity which doubled from £110 in 1400 to more than £220 by 1453. Normally about 60 per cent of the revenue was derived from properties left to the fraternity by benefactors who wished to establish chantries and obits to be administered by the master and wardens. The first half of the fifteenth century saw the rapid accumulation of property by the fraternity and the foundation, in eight London churches, of five perpetual chantries and twelve obits before 1460. The properties concerned generated more than enough income to pay for the services, salaries and lights specified by the donors, as well as any repairs to tenements, leaving a 'profit' which the fraternity could use to fund its other activities, including assistance for the almsmen and women.[40] In some cases donors of lands and tenements were

---

[38] MTA, I, f.244v; Crowmer was admitted to the livery of the fraternity in 1404–5: ibid., I, f.22v. For his civic career, see Thrupp, *Merchant Class*, Appendix A, p. 336.

[39] For the wills, see GL, MS. 9051/1, ff.62, 177v–78; MTA, I, f.38v.

[40] MTA, I–III. By 1545, immediately prior to the promulgation of the first Chantries Act, the Merchant Taylors' Company was paying the salaries of thirteen priests and funding twenty-seven obits at a total cost of just over £130. In the same year the company's income from property stood at £229 12s 6d: ibid., IV, ff.9–12, 25v.

quite specific about the use to which income generated over and above charges for chantries and obits should be put. Thomas Sutton and Ralph Holland, both of whom were former masters of the fraternity, left property in several parts of London, the income from which was to be used by the master and wardens to increase the weekly amount paid to almsmen and women in the almshouse near the hall, by 2*d* and 1*d* respectively.[41] To put it another way, charitable provision to the poor and sick of the fraternity was not determined solely by the amount of money given in alms and could be augmented by the 'comon chatell' as the need arose. Income from all sources was, in theory, available for pious uses: there was no 'earmarking' of revenues in the accounts for 'religious' or 'economic' purposes; the master and wardens merely had to ensure that the craft was being supervised and that the fraternity was able to carry out its duties to its members both living and dead.

Before looking in detail at the range of services that could be provided by the fraternity as a result of both almsgiving and bequests, it is important to examine the social composition of those who benefited from them. The fifteenth-century accounts of the Tailors of London provide an unusually detailed record of those who were in receipt of alms because of their impoverished circumstances. As an organization for the liveried members of the craft, as well as for non-tailors of a similar standing, the fraternity was not in the business of helping poor tailors in general but those who had generally enjoyed successful careers and had since fallen upon hard times, whether through poverty or sickness. This was a common pattern among the craft guilds of London, the aim being to maintain the status and dignity of liverymen, and their wives, rather than attempting the difficult task of helping all poor members of the mistery. The Skinners, for instance, stipulated in an ordinance of 1472 that recipients of alms had to have been liverymen for at least seven years.[42] This was an implicit recognition of the status which came with membership of a fraternity, of the importance of both

---

[41] Sutton left lands, tenements and a wharf in the Vintry to the fraternity, GL, MS. 9171/3, f.381v, and Holland lands and tenements in several parishes, including Basset's Inn in the parish of St Mary Aldermary: *CWCH*, II, pp. 525–6.

[42] J.J. Lambert, *The Records of the Skinners of London* (1933), p. 90.

the horizontal bonds created between brethren and sisters and also of the vertical bonds inherent in such hierarchical and, indeed, gerontocratic organizations. Age and experience were valued in the context of the livery company: ordinances were typically ratified not just by the master and wardens, but also by the 'courts of assistants' which were composed of former masters and wardens, who would keep an eye on their young successors. In return, these elder statesmen could be assured of maintaining their sense of dignity even in the most straitened of circumstances through the help provided by their guilds. Nicholas Preest, a London grocer who represented the borough of Southwark in the parliament of 1433, had been a liveryman of his craft for over thirty years when he began receiving 12*d* a week in alms from the guild in October 1456, probably following the failure of his business. He died in the early spring of 1462, still dependent on the charity of his fellow grocers.[43]

The maintenance of status, and hence the preservation, often in difficult circumstances, of a sense of solidarity among guild members, were key principles behind the setting up of mechanisms for poor relief. The financial help given to almsmen and women was itself only one element in this process. In 1430, for instance, a goldsmith, John Hille, provided for thirteen black gowns to be given to thirteen poor goldsmiths 'in those years that the livery customarily have new clothing'; a year later Andrew Hunt, a girdler, left two chambers near the entrance of Girdlers' Hall to be inhabited by two 'decayed persons of the livery' who were each to have 7*d* a week and a hood of livery at the time of the granting of liveries, ensuring that they continued to participate in the guild's annual rituals and ceremonies.[44] Recipients of charitable aid were not only required to be liverymen. An emphasis upon the moral character of the poor was very much a feature of guild charity: one tailor, Hugh Cavendish, specified that the recipients of his charity were to be 'such who may have been honourable and discreet men of the mysterie and afterwards by the visitation of

---

[43] GL, MS. 11,571/1 (Grocers' Company Accounts), ff.55v, 110v; 2, f.14.

[44] *8th Report of the Charity Commissioners* (HMSO, 1823), p. 320; *6th Report of the Charity Commissioners* (HMSO, 1822), p. 258.

God come to poverty'.[45] The ordinances of Richard Whittington's almshouse, founded on his death in 1424, echo these sentiments: the thirteen 'pore folke' were to be 'hable in conversacion and honest in lyvyng', wearing a livery 'of esy prised cloth according to their degre' and at meals to 'absteyne thaime fro veyn and ydil wordes'.[46]

Hugh Cavendish's sentiments certainly seem to be borne out by the evidence for the careers of those tailors receiving alms, indicating that poverty could strike even the most successful. Several indeed were former masters of the guild: William atte Rule, master in 1384, received £6 a year for the eight and a half years that he remained an almsman from 1405–6.[47] Another distinguished tailor and former warden, Geoffrey de Kent, was already a senior member of the fraternity when he went on the 'crusade' led by Bishop Despenser in 1385. Fifteen years later he appears in the Tailors' accounts as an almsman and received £3 a year until his death in 1401–2.[48] Three more former masters of the Tailors' fraternity are numbered among the seven almsmen whose wills survive, suggesting that dependence upon the fraternity was perhaps only partial in some cases. All seven were still in receipt of alms at the time of their deaths and one of them, John de Ese, described himself in the preamble to his will as 'citizen and tailor of London and poor man of the craft of tailors'. For five of the seven, dependence upon the fraternity was only a reality for the last two or three years of their lives.[49] On the other hand, Robert Fenescales, master in 1420–1, was an almsman for six and a half years along with his wife Christian, who survived him as an almswoman for another eleven years, probably indicating more long-term economic or physical

---

[45] Clode, *Early History*, I, p. 121.

[46] J. Imray, *The Charity of Richard Whittington: a History of the Trust Administered by the Mercers' Company, 1424–1966* (1968), Appendix I, pp. 111, 116.

[47] MTA, I, f.29.

[48] PRO, Chancery, Treaty Rolls, C76/67, m.18 (I am grateful to Colin Paine for this reference); MTA, I, f.6v (1399–1400) and f.13v.

[49] GL, MS. 9171/3, f.272v (de Ese); 9171/2, f.228v (Robert Ascowe, d. 1412); 9051/1, f.292v (John Hamerton, 1413); 9171/3, f.156 (Simon Leef, 1426); and 9171/3, f.271v (Robert Crokehorn, 1430).

difficulties.[50] Fenescales, along with two other former masters, did, however, possess sufficient resources to provide for a funeral, but it may be significant that all three asked to be buried in the Great Churchyard of St Paul's, rather than in their own parish church or cemetery. This was undoubtedly a lowering of expectations on their part: not one of the parishes to which they belonged was without a churchyard of its own and as senior members of a prominent craft guild they could normally expect burial within the parish church itself.[51]

The emphasis upon respectability was also a factor in the legitimizing of the fraternal and convivial activities of the 'yeoman' or 'bachelor' fraternities in late medieval London. These were organizations which, in the late fourteenth century, gained a reputation for subversion because of the attempts by journeymen of the Saddlers, Cordwainers and other crafts to push wages up through collective action.[52] By the fifteenth century, however, some of these fraternities were well on the way to becoming integral parts of what would later be known as the livery companies, acting as organizations for freemen outside the livery, some of whom would go on to join the senior fraternity.[53] By 1400, for instance, those London skinners who were not members of the Corpus Christi fraternity had their own fraternity dedicated to the feast of the Assumption of the Virgin.[54] The yeomen tailors in 1415, like the saddlers and cordwainers before them, became involved in a dispute with the senior fraternity. However, in this case the actions of a rebellious few seem merely to have tarnished the reputation of an established organization for freemen outside the livery of the craft: two years later the senior fraternity paid all the expenses incurred by the yeomen when they petitioned the mayor and aldermen to be allowed to celebrate their feast, the Decollation of St John the Baptist, in St

---

[50] Ibid., 9171/4, ff.221v, 222v; MTA, I, f.332 (1440–1); and II, f.16v (1453–4).

[51] GL, MS. 9051/1, f.92v (Hamerton); 9171/3, f.156 (Leef).

[52] H.T. Riley, *Memorials of London and London Life in the XIIIth, XIVth and XVth Centuries* (1868), pp. 250–1 (shearmen, 1350), 495–6 (cordwainers, 1387), 542–4 (saddlers, 1396).

[53] By the close of the fifteenth century most, if not all, of the 'Great Twelve' companies were divided into a 'livery' and a 'yeomanry': Unwin, *Gilds and Companies*, p. 224.

[54] Veale, *Fur Trade*, pp. 112–15.

John's Church, Clerkenwell.[55] Bequests to the fraternity of Yeomen Tailors indicate the extent to which the Yeomen built up their religious and charitable activities, alongside those of the senior fraternity. Several successful tailors even made bequests to both fraternities, as if remembering the stages in their careers. Thomas Parker, left 'my best standyng maser' to the 'maister taillours' and 'also I biqueth unto the felawship of the yemen my standyng maser next the best', and Robert Colwich in 1480 left 'ii basyns of sylver with myn armes in the bothom' to the Tailors' fraternity and 66s 8d 'to the felaship called the yemanry of the same craft'.[56] Another tailor, Stephen Trappys, was more specific when he left 20s 'to the pore almesmen of the yomen taillours', in 1485.[57] It is probable also that alms were collected periodically as was the case with the senior fraternity, and the potential for corporate action to alleviate the poverty of members seems clear, although given that the fraternity does not seem to have possessed income-generating properties, the scope for action was doubtless limited.[58]

Although women were active in many of the trades and occupations of medieval London, their position within the livery companies normally depended upon the status of their husbands. Apart from wealthy and influential women from outside the craft, only the wives of masters of the Tailors' fraternity were admitted as members with any regularity. Occasionally the widows of liverymen were admitted, indicating both the status enjoyed by their late husbands and the extent to which women were involved in continuing to

---

[55] *Calendar of the Letter Books Preserved Among the Archives of the Corporation of the City of London*, ed. R.R. Sharpe (11 vols. A–L, 1899–1912), Letter Book I, pp. 136, 187–8; MTA, I, f.212: *Espens faits pur defence faire envers les vadlets de lour supplicacion direct as Mair et aldermanis*. The City turned down the request of the yeomen, which led Unwin and other historians to assume that their fraternity (and hence others) was still 'illegal', a view which is negated by other references in the tailors' records and by a bequest of 20s to the alms of the *valect cissorum* made in 1414 by John Creek, a prominent member of the senior fraternity: GL, MS. 9051/1, ff.308–9v.

[56] PRO, Prob. 11/5, ff.243–43v; 11/7, ff.6–7v.

[57] GL, MS. 9171/7, f.33v.

[58] For discussion of the role played by yeomen fraternities in late medieval London see Davies, 'The Tailors of London', pp. 147–56.

run their husbands' businesses.[59] Female members appear to have enjoyed the same rights as men: 'sustren' are mentioned along with 'brethren' in many of the fraternity's ordinances and in the oaths sworn by new members. They could, for instance, attend the annual feast when garlands of roses were ordered for the 'maisters et maistreses' of the fraternity.[60] Status within the guilds of London was transferable: an ordinance of 1490 recognized that tailors who married the widows of former masters and wardens were entitled to be admitted to the fraternity at any time, not just at the annual feast. The same applied to any other tailor who was 'promoted by maryage of eny other woman oute of the felaship'.[61] The distribution of alms to women is an important aspect of the charitable provision made by the fraternity. In 1398–9, the first year for which the fraternity's accounts survive, Christian Wycham and Sarah Lunt are listed as almswomen, the latter being the widow of Roger Lunt, a fairly wealthy tailor who died in 1388. It is not clear how soon after his death Sarah became in need of assistance but she continued to receive help for another eleven years, her funeral being paid for by the fraternity in 1410–11.[62] The usual pattern seems to have been for the husband to be the named recipient of the alms money but, occasionally, husband and wife are named together in the accounts, as in the case of John and Julian Whoton who both began receiving alms from 1420–1. John died in 1428–9 while Julian continued to receive alms for another five years.[63]

In addition to tailors and their wives, the fraternity sometimes aided its non-tailor membership and even brethren from outside the city. The numbers are small, which is no surprise given the services of a similar nature which would

---

[59] See K.E. Lacey, 'Women and Work in Fourteenth and Fifteenth Century London', in *Women and Work in Pre-Industrial England*, ed. L. Charles and L. Duffin (1985), pp. 24–82; and *Medieval London Widows, 1300–1500*, ed. Barron and Sutton, *passim*.

[60] MTA, I, f.6 (1399–1400).

[61] MTCo., Court Minutes, II, f.21v (hereafter MTM, I, II etc.).

[62] MTA, I, f.3; Roger Lunt's will was enrolled in the hustings court: *CWCH*, II, p. 265 and in the commissary court: GL, MS. 9171/1, f.158; 6*s* 8*d* was paid for the funeral and 15*d* for a 'windyngcloth': MTA, I, f.57.

[63] Ibid., I, ff.119v, 196, 248.

have been provided by other craft and parish guilds in London and elsewhere. It is probable too that the Tailors were keen to give members of the craft priority over other brothers and sisters, though such preference was never made explicit. On the other hand, the fact that individuals such as Nicholas Cook, a dyer, and Richard Reynold, a vintner (both from London), did receive alms from the fraternity is certainly an indication of the importance attached by members of other crafts to membership of a larger and more successful fraternity than their own.[64] Plurality in the allegiances of town-dwellers is perhaps an under-emphasized aspect of urban life in this period, and in London this applied as much to the fraternities established by the crafts as to parish guilds. Indeed, more than 400 members of other London crafts joined the Tailors' fraternity between 1398 and 1480. William Gregory, the prominent skinner and alderman, left sums of money in his will to the Tailors' fraternity and to the fraternity of the Name of Jesus in St Paul's, in addition to his substantial bequests to the two fraternities founded by the skinners themselves.[65]

Although over fifty craftsmen from other towns and cities were admitted to the fraternity (twenty-four of whom were tailors), it is almost certain that most of those who fell upon hard times would seek help in their home towns. The fact that two such craftsmen, John Bridgesthorn of St Albans and John Staveley, a tailor from Salisbury, became almsmen of the London Tailors, the former in 1416–17 and the latter by 1453, is therefore both a significant indication of the standing of the fraternity as compared with provincial guilds and a pointer to the extent to which the *foci* of people's lives could shift during a career.[66] The career of Staveley is of particular interest as he seems to have enjoyed stronger links with the fraternity than most. His admission as a brother in 1434–5 is not unusual but the admission of his wife Christian two years later is a unique occurrence and suggests a strengthening connection with the London fraternity, made all the more likely by subsequent events in the West Country.[67] Staveley

---

[64] Cook received alms in 1416–17 and Reynold from 1423–4: MTA, I, ff. 96v, 135.

[65] PRO, Prob. 11/5, f.123v (proved 6 Nov. 1465). Gregory was admitted as a brother of the tailors' fraternity in 1436–7: MTA, I, f.280.

[66] Ibid., I, f.96v; II, f.16v.

[67] Ibid., I, ff.258, 280v.

had evidently enjoyed a conventional and successful career as a member of the guild of Salisbury tailors and is listed as one of the two wardens of the guild in 1441. Between 1447 and 1449, however, his loyalties to his parish, St Thomas's, brought him into conflict with his craft when a chantry, originally based in St Thomas's, was moved to St Edmund's church. He and Stephen Hendy were accused of withholding vestments and of trying to 'destroye the sayd chaunterie'.[68] It cannot be proved that Staveley then transferred his loyalties to the London Tailors but it is likely that by the time he was in need of financial assistance his relations with the London Tailors were a good deal more cordial than those with his brethren in Salisbury.

The London Tailors provided a variety of services for the poor brethren of the fraternity and their wives, the payment of a fixed annual rate being the main item of expenditure. Some bequests to the fraternity, particularly those made by prominent tailors, are of special interest to the historian as they help to shed light on the nature of this financial provision and of distinctions made between different groups of almsmen and women. As already indicated, both Thomas Sutton and Ralph Holland made bequests which enabled the master and wardens to increase the weekly amount paid to the almsmen and women by $2d$ and $1d$ respectively.[69] This raised the maximum amount paid out to poor members to $17d$ a week or £3 $13s$ $8d$ a year, with $14d$ of it coming *de antiqua elemosina*.[70] This sets the Tailors' fraternity apart from most of the other craft fraternities of London which, like the girdlers and salters, generally had to rely upon individual benefactions for the entirety of their provision. In 1431 Andrew Hunt provided $7d$ a week for two girdlers and in 1454 Thomas Beaumond allowed the same for six salters dwelling in houses built by him.[71] Only the

[68] Wiltshire RO, MS. G23/1/1, ledger A, f.125v (I am grateful to Dr Andrew Brown for this reference); Andrew D. Brown, *Popular Piety in Late Medieval England: the Diocese of Salisbury, 1250–1550* (Oxford, 1995), pp. 156–7.

[69] Sutton left lands, tenements and a wharf in the Vintry, GL, MS. 9171/3, f.381v, and Holland lands and tenements in several parishes, including Basset's Inn in the parish of St Mary Aldermary: *CWCH*, II, pp. 525–6.

[70] MTA, II, f.72v (1455–6).

[71] 6th Report of the Charity Commissioners, pp. 258, 325.

charity of wealthy members of the greater companies could result in rates of 2*d* a day or better: two foundations by goldsmiths in the 1450s, for example, provided 14*d* a week for a total of nine poor goldsmiths.[72] Whittington's charity, administered by the Mercers, allowed for the payment of 14*s* a week to those in his almshouse, out of the revenues of his impressive estate.[73] The Tailors were able to adopt a generous and flexible approach to charitable provision which was constrained not by the wealth or wishes of testators but by the more substantial resources of the fraternity itself. The absence of a poor rate or any other city-wide system of charitable assistance means that the actions of parishes and craft fraternities take on a new significance, despite their limited scope. In his analysis of standards of living in the middle ages, Professor Dyer concluded that a sum of 1*d* per day, close to the average guild stipend in this period, would allow the beneficiary 'a decent but sparse living with meat and ale to go with the bread'. Housing would require an additional 5*s* per annum.[74] Indeed, the provision made by the London Tailors for their almsmen in the fifteenth century compares very favourably with the sums spent by the Grocers and Clothworkers in the mid-1590s, figures employed by Dr Ian Archer to demonstrate the contribution made by the livery companies in a period of population growth.[75] The maximum of 17*d* a week paid by the Tailors compares well with the 12*d* paid by the Goldsmiths in the later sixteenth century and the parish rate of 6*d* a week. What is perhaps striking about the later sixteenth

[72] 8th Report of the Charity Commissioners, p. 321. John Patteslie in 1450 left lands and tenements in St Mildred Poultry to pay 1*s* 2*d* a week to five almsmen, and William Walton in 1458 the same amount to four goldsmiths with four yards of woollen cloth *blodii coloris* at 2*s* a yard.

[73] Imray, *The Charity of Richard Whittington*, Appendix I, p. 118.

[74] C. Dyer, *Standards of Living in the Later Middle Ages: Social Change in England, 1200–1520* (Cambridge, 1989), pp. 208, 253. For an analysis of the stipends paid by parish guilds see McRee, 'Charity and Gild Solidarity', pp. 195–225.

[75] I.W. Archer, *The Pursuit of Stability: Social Relations in Elizabethan London* (Cambridge, 1991), pp. 120–4. In 1595 the clothworkers spent £12 7*s* 6*d* and the grocers £12 11*s* 4*d* on their almsmen, ibid., Table 4.1, p. 124. These amounts were, however, increased more than six-fold by the payment of pensions to the elderly, £48 17*s* 6*d* and £62 5*s* 6*d* respectively, a relatively unusual occurrence in the fifteenth century.

century is the volume and scope of charitable activity, made possible partly by
the diversion of funds previously used for chantries and obits, rather than the
principles of brotherhood and indeed pious duty which were a continuous
feature of the development of craft and merchant guilds.[76]

Another indication of the developed and flexible nature of the mechanisms for
poor relief set up by the London Tailors may be the fact that not all almsmen
and women were paid the same amounts each year. Before 1450 this took the
form of step-by-step increases in the amount received in alms each year,
probably based on the seniority of the recipient as an almsman or woman. The
career of John Martin, almsman from 1424 until his death in 1430, was typical:
he received 40s a year for the first three years before benefiting from two
successive increases of 10s, taking him to the then top rate of £3 per annum.
Some, such as John Speke, started on the 'top rate' of £3, while others, including
John Staveley, failed to get there despite at least five years as an almsman.[77] In
the first half of the century most people eventually received the full amount,
perhaps as their dependence upon the fraternity grew. After 1453, however, the
almsmen and women seem to have been more permanently divided into income
groups with two or three receiving the full 73s 8d a year, another group getting
44s 4d and a third group 31s. There were exceptions to these categories but their
introduction and, more importantly, the lack of mobility between them are
indicative of a new system of alms distribution and a more rigid categorization of
recipients according to need, status or a combination of the two.

The need for affordable accommodation on the part of the poor was
obviously a pressing one and was answered by the foundation of almshouses
and hospitals of all kinds, by lay institutions and individuals, with increasing
frequency in the fourteenth and fifteenth centuries.[78] These aimed to care as
much for the spiritual as for the physical needs of inmates who were often seen
as deserving of individual attention because of their status and bearing. In the

[76] Ibid., pp. 120–1.

[77] MTA, I, ff.153, 185, 196 (Martin); I, f.143v (Speke); II, ff.16v, 40, 73, 109, 135v (Staveley).

[78] See, for instance, Cullum, '"For Pore People Harberles"', in *Trade Devotion and Governance*, ed.
Clayton, Davies and McNiven, pp. 36–54.

early years of the fifteenth century, some attempt was made by the Tailors to help those guild members who could not afford a place to live, as in the case of Flora Cornewaille who survived her husband Nicholas for one term in 1403–4 and received 20*d pur son hostel pur un terme*.[79] The opportunity for the establishment of more permanent arrangements came in 1405 when a prominent grocer and alderman, John Churchman, granted four messuages and seventeen shops in the parish of St Martin Outwich to the fraternity, as well as the advowson of the parish church itself. Churchman had enjoyed a long and successful relationship with the Tailors which can be traced back to at least 1388, when he helped solve a dispute over a plot of land near Tailors' Hall in Broad Street.[80] The master and wardens evidently valued the grant of 1405 because they were prepared to pay £40 for the licence to grant in mortmain and to commit themselves and their successors to the funding of Churchman's perpetual chantry in St Martin's.[81] The grant was made, according to the chronicler John Stow, 'in perpetuall almes, to bee employed on the poore brethren and sisters' and included a plot of land lying between Tailors' Hall in Broad Street and St Martin's, 'wherupon adioyning unto the West end of the parish church, the said maister and wardens builded about a proper quadrant or squared court, seaven almeshouses . . .'.[82] The building work did not in fact begin until 1413, the year of Churchman's death, which suggests that an agreement had been entered into in 1405 in which the Tailors undertook to erect the almshouses at their own expense as a memorial to their benefactor. Despite the delay, the Tailors' almshouse pre-dated Whittington's almshouse as well as that of the Brewers' Company, founded in 1423, and is thus of some importance in marking the start of a series of foundations of almshouses by the London guilds in the fifteenth and early sixteenth centuries.[83]

---

[79] MTA, I, f.19v.

[80] H.L. Hopkinson, *The History of Merchant Taylors' Hall* (1931), pp. 53–4.

[81] *CPR, 1405–8*, p. 56; Churchman's obit was celebrated from 1413–14: MTA, I, f.78.

[82] Stow, *Survey*, I, p. 181.

[83] Imray, *The Charity of Richard Whittington*, Appendix I, p. 111; M. Ball, *The Worshipfull Company of Brewers* (1977), pp. 46–9. For other foundations see Stow, *Survey, passim* and *The British Atlas of Historic Towns, III: The City of London*, ed. Lobel, pp. 63–99.

That preparations were underway in 1413–14 is clear from the accounts which record some of the preliminary steps taken to clear the site and pull down existing structures. Expenses amounting to £32 3s 7d are recorded, most of which was spent on work done by a mason and a carpenter. It is interesting to note too that the almshouse was referred to as the *maison dieux*, a term which was used for foundations of various kinds, from Whittington's own 'goddeshous' to many much smaller, unendowed foundations.[84] Other payments included parchment for the indentures entered into by the company with the craftsmen as well as *ii pell de parchemyn pur patrons* (the plans of the building), drink and, significantly, *pain et vin al evesq de Norwich*.[85] The bishop, Richard Courtenay, also headed a list of donors who contributed £19 13s 4d to the *novel overage* that year.[86] It is likely that the bishop was chosen because of John Churchman's strong links with Norfolk: he was born in Necton, had a house in Norwich and founded a perpetual chantry in Heylesdon.[87] The Tailors' actions in enlisting the support of the bishop is highly suggestive of an attempt to recall Churchman's dual allegiances to Norfolk and London and, through the services offered for his soul in perpetuity, enshrine further the debt owed to him in the collective memory of the fraternity. A year later the building work proper got under way and to help pay for the initial outlay £51 16s 6d was raised from the membership. Forty-seven liverymen contributed to the levy, Thomas Bridlyngton and Thomas Whitingham giving £15 and £20 respectively. All but one of the contributors were tailors, following the pattern set at earlier levels in 1406–7 and 1408–9.[88] This once again highlights the difference between the obligations placed on the tailor and non-tailor sections of the membership and is consistent with the fraternity's concentration upon the craftsmen for its

---

[84] MTA, I, f.78v; Imray, *The Charity of Richard Whittington*, Appendix I, p. 111; Cullum, '"For Pore People Harberles"', in *Trade Devotion and Governance*, ed. Clayton, Davies and McNiven, p. 36.

[85] MTA, I, f.78v.

[86] Ibid., I, f.74. Richard Courtenay was consecrated bishop of Norwich on 17 September 1413 but had been a brother of the fraternity since 1411–12: ibid., I, f.61v.

[87] Thrupp, *Merchant Class*, p. 332.

[88] MTA, I, f.82. Sir John Doyly, one of the chaplains to the fraternity, was the only exception: ibid., I, ff.33v, 44.

charitable provision. The cost of the building work carried out that year came to an impressive £96 16s 2d, and the very detailed entries for the work done by 'maister Nicholl', the carpenter, and Walter Holty, the stonemason, and other craftsmen give a few clues to the construction and appearance of the almshouse. Holty, for instance, was paid £8 13s 4d *de paver le aley et le yerd ove hewen ragge* as well as for work carried out on *le cloistre . . . chimeneis et le fonteigne*, features which help to bring Stow's description of 'a proper quadrant or squared court' to life.[89] By the middle of 1415 the work was largely completed and the next year saw the finishing touches put to the latest and most significant work of piety and charity carried out by a London fraternity to date.[90] The construction of the almshouse enabled the Tailors to house the most indigent of their almsmen and women but, as the accounts testify, the fraternity continued to provide financial assistance to those living in their own houses or in the houses of friends and relatives. Several testators recognized the particular needs of poor householders: Hugh Cavendish, for example, provided not only for the annual distribution of 36 quarters of coals to the poor and needy in the almshouse, but also help for those poor members who were 'receiving alms in houses or dwellings and not at the hall'. In similar vein another tailor, Stephen Trappys, left £5 to be distributed among poor householders of the fraternity in 1485.[91]

The absence of surviving ordinances for the Tailors' almshouse means that the rules and regulations by which its inmates had to live can only be inferred from scattered references in the fraternity's accounts and other sources. Those rules which can be reconstructed seem to be similar in tone and content to those

---

[89] Ibid., I, f.86v; Stow, *Survey*, I, p. 181. For the popularity of this design, see W.H. Godfrey, *The English Almshouse* (1955), pp. 45–75.

[90] These included *viii boltes de ferre* for the windows and 22d for a labourer to *netter les maisons*: MTA, I, f.93. It was not until 1435–6 that any more expenditure of significance was necessary with regard to the almshouse, this taking the form of £6 11d spent primarily upon re-tiling the roof but, despite this, efforts to raise funds continued, starting with £8 3s 10d collected in 1415–16: ibid., I, ff.273, 89v. A further 6s 8d was received in 1416–17, £3 13s 4d in 1417–18, and 37s 6d in 1418–19: ibid., I, ff.95v, 101, 108.

[91] Ibid., II, f.247; 17th Report of the Charity Commissioners (HMSO, 1826–7), p. 460. Trappys's will is in GL, MS. 9171/7, f.33v.

which Whittington drew up for his foundation a decade later. Although no direct influence can be proved, the early date of the Tailors' almshouse means that by 1420 it was still the only one of its kind in London, possibly acting as an exemplar for subsequent founders. For example, one of the requirements of Whittington's ordinances was that inmates should be 'destitut of all temporell goodes in othir places by the whiche he might competently lyve al be hit he were none of ye noumbre of ye seide almeshous', and it may have been that a similar stipulation prompted one tailor, William White, to divest himself of many of his worldly goods including a 'fedderbed', six candlesticks and two pewter pots in 1464–5, the year in which he began to receive alms from the fraternity.[92] Other evidence, however, suggests that almsmen were allowed to keep at least some of their goods. Throughout the fifteenth century, the company sold off the goods of deceased almsmen, the proceeds often being specifically allocated for the funeral. The amounts raised were generally small but some almsmen had evidently kept some quite valuable items: the sale of *les biens de William Herford* yielded £13 14*s* 9½*d* in 1412–13 and in 1473–4 the fraternity raised £6 2*s* 9*d* from the sale of Henry Ketelwell's possessions.[93]

An illuminating example of the ways in which the fraternity helped its poor members occurs in the accounts for 1406–7, before the foundation of the almshouse. In that year the last illness and death of Simon Gairdner led the fraternity to pay 3*s* 4*d* for the rent on his house and, significantly, the same amount to *une feme qui lui garda en sa infirmite*.[94] This was probably an informal arrangement and does not imply that any formalized system of nursing care was in operation. A more likely scenario, perhaps, particularly after the construction of the almshouse, is described in Whittington's ordinances which required 'thei that ar myghty and hole of the body of the seid Almeshous and specially

---

[92] Imray, *The Charity of Richard Whittington*, Appendix I, p. 114; MTA, II, f.253. White gave the bulk of these goods *ad opus eiusdem fraternitatem*, while other items including towels and a tablecloth were sold.

[93] Ibid., I, f.68; III, f.58v; Ketelwell had himself given a silver vessel weighing 13.75 ounces (troy) to the fraternity in 1466, the year of his admission as an almsman: ibid., II, f.292.

[94] Ibid., I, f.37v. Gairdner had been an almsman since 1402–3: ibid., I, f.16.

wommen if ther by eny ther Inne helpe and ministre unto ye felawes of the seid hous that ar seke and feble'.[95] The absence of any subsequent references to the hiring of nurses makes it a reasonable assumption that the running of the Tailors' almshouse made use of similar principles of mutual assistance and community. After all, the charitable activities of Londoners were not solely confined to the provisions of their wills: one tailor, William Mawere, was discharged from jury service in 1436 because of his 'constant attention to the poor mad inmates of the Hospital of St. Mary de Bedlam without Bisshopesgate'.[96]

The daily religious activities of the almsmen and women in the almshouse are less easy to trace but there seems little doubt that inmates were expected to pray regularly for their benefactors. One of the ordinances drawn up by the Tailors after the acquisition of their fifth charter in 1503 stipulated that all almsmen should be 'personally present' at St Martin's, in order to attend weekly services 'serving God and all his seintes' and pray daily for the king, queen, and all members of the fraternity, living and dead.[97] The close relationship between the Tailors and St Martin's, and the role of John Churchman in founding the almshouse, make it almost inconceivable that the latter was not remembered at these services and in the daily prayers of the inmates. Thomas Sutton, whose bequest helped to increase the weekly rate paid to almsmen, required them to 'pray devoutly' for his soul, and it is likely that Churchman, Sutton and Ralph Holland headed the list of those benefactors to be prayed for on a regular basis.[98] No mention is made in the accounts of a chapel attached to the almshouse, which is perhaps not surprising given the proximity of St Martin's, the strong links it had with the Tailors and, in addition, the existence of a chapel in Tailors' Hall itself.[99] It is almost certain that daily services were conducted in one of these two places by one of the three chaplains employed by the fraternity.

---

[95] Imray, *The Charity of Richard Whittington*, Appendix I, p. 117.

[96] *Calendar of Letter Books*, ed. Sharpe, Letter Book K, p. 194.

[97] C.M. Clode, *Memorials of the Merchant Taylors' Company* (1875), p. 48.

[98] GL, MS. 9171/3, f.381v (1434).

[99] For the hall see Hopkinson, *Merchant Taylors' Hall, passim*; J. Schofield, *The Building of London from the Conquest to the Great Fire* (1984), pp. 117–19; and *Royal Commission on Historical Monuments: London* (5 vols. 1924–30), IV, pp. 34–7.

The picture of poor relief in the fifteenth century was not static. It shifted in response to social and economic change as well as the changing needs and preoccupations of citizens and the institutions to which they belonged. The extent and nature of the charitable provision made by the fraternity of St John the Baptist changed in key areas, the first of which was the actual number of people who received alms in any one year. Before the late 1450s an average of fourteen people a year were receiving financial assistance from the fraternity. After this date, as Table 2 shows, a significant decline in numbers occurred, whereby the average fell to eight. Subsequent entries in the minutes of the court of assistants show that the downward trend continued and in the mid-sixteenth century recipients numbered only about five each year.[100] It is possible that this was the result of a more selective admissions policy when tailors were for the first time beginning to achieve prominent positions in the city in the quarter century prior to the granting of the title of 'Merchant Taylors' by Henry VII in 1503. As an essentially artisan craft, the Tailors might have felt under pressure to make the fraternity more exclusively mercantile in order to be able to compete with the Mercers, Grocers and Drapers for offices.[101] An ordinance of 1490 seems to support this by suggesting that men admitted to the fraternity 'have bene in substaunce of goods as it hath bene supposed whereby they have lytely fallen into the almes of this fraternity to the grete charge of this fraternyte'.[102] This certainly indicates a concern among the elders of the craft that those admitted should be men of means, yet the rhetoric of such ordinances is not reflected in the trend in admissions for the twenty years after 1450, when the numbers of almsmen on the fraternity's books experienced such a dramatic decline. As Table 1 indicates, although annual admissions to the fraternity as a whole declined by nearly 50 per cent in the second half of the fifteenth century, the drop in numbers was almost exclusively confined to the non-tailors, who rarely benefited from the fraternity's charity. The number of tailors admitted to

[100] MTM, I, f.3v (1486–7); MTA, IV, ff.4, 85, 164 (1545–7).

[101] See Barron, 'Ralph Holland', in *The Medieval Town*, ed. Holt and Rosser, pp. 160–83, and Miller, 'London and Parliament', pp. 130–43.

[102] MTM, II, f.21v (Quarter-day held on 5 May 1490).

the livery of the craft, though declining, did not do so anywhere near as rapidly as the numbers who received alms payments.

An alternative explanation for the reduced numbers of almsmen and women receiving assistance from the Tailors is suggested by the change which occurred in one particular area of charitable provision made by the fraternity. Perhaps one of the most important services provided by lay fraternities in the late medieval period was the burial of deceased almsmen and women. Lacking the resources to found an obit of any kind, or even pay for a rudimentary funeral themselves, the poor were dependent upon relatives, friends and the extended family of the fraternity for the maintenance of a degree of dignity in death and the prospect of the prayers of fellow liverymen. As Table 3 shows, the Tailors' fraternity was particularly active in the provision of funerals for deceased almsmen and women in the early decades of the fifteenth century. The picture changed, however, as the century progressed and a decline occurred in the proportion of funerals paid for by the fraternity, such that after 1430 only four out of sixty-six almsmen and women were buried at the fraternity's expense. In one or two cases it is clear that relatives were taking on the burden themselves but these cases are too few to account for such a dramatic change, and they date with one exception from the first half of the fifteenth century.

Table 3

FUNERALS OF ALMSMEN 1398–1475

Years	Deceased almsmen	No. of funerals	Percentage
1398–1430	79	43	54.4
1430–75	66	4	9.1
Total	145	47	32.4

A possible explanation for these changes takes into account shifts in the pattern of bequests in late fifteenth-century London and a consequent change in the range of services offered by lay fraternities of all kinds. It has already been shown, by Dr Thomson, that Londoners were increasingly reluctant to found perpetual chantries as the fifteenth century wore on: the tailors' fraternity itself administered no new perpetual chantries between 1425 and 1500, tailors preferring instead to establish temporary arrangements.[103] Preliminary research into the testamentary provisions of parishioners of two London parishes not only confirms this, but suggests that testators were increasingly inclined to channel the resources freed as a result into charity and poor relief on a parish level, often specifying the funerals of poor parishioners.[104] The focus of the charitable bequests made by the gentry of Kent would also appear to have shifted in the later fifteenth century towards poor relief on a parish level.[105] This shift towards individual, parish-centred charitable work is likely to have been related to a decline in the importance of the funerary dimension to the work of lay fraternities in general. This has been noted by Dr Barron in relation to the parish fraternities of London, where she suggests that the Black Death gave an impetus to the emphasis on funerals in the ordinances of the fourteenth-century fraternities, whereas 'by the late fifteenth century the concern for a decent burial had shrunk simply to one clause in twenty or thirty'.[106] This was but one of the changes in emphasis which took place during the fifteenth century as the preoccupations and social needs of fraternity members evolved.

This apparent shift away from fraternities towards parish-centred poor relief may well have been a factor in the later fifteenth-century decline in the charitable activities of the Tailors' fraternity, both in terms of the actual numbers in receipt of alms and in the proportion of almsmen and women whose funerals were paid for by the guild. No longer was the fraternity seen as the obvious source of charitable assistance; instead the parishes began to develop their own mechanisms which may have been all the more attractive because they were local. Certainly, the evidence from the records of the Tailors' fraternity suggests that the hey-day of the fraternity as a provider of charitable assistance was in

[103] Thomson, 'Piety and Charity', pp. 191–2.

[104] I owe this possible explanation to the comments of Dr C.R. Burgess, arising out of his preliminary work on the parishes of St Mary at Hill and St Andrew Hubbard in London.

[105] Fleming, 'Charity, Faith and the Gentry of Kent', in *Property and Politics*, ed. Pollard, pp. 45–6.

[106] Barron, 'Parish Fraternities', in *The Church in Pre-Reformation Society*, ed. Barron and Harper-Bill, pp. 25–8.

the first half of the fifteenth century. That period saw between twelve and sixteen almsmen and women on the fraternity's books at any one point, the provision of funerals for at least two-thirds of them and, finally, the foundation of a well-endowed almshouse. By the 1480s, by contrast, there were not even enough almsmen to fill these houses. This is not to suggest that the fraternity as a whole was in decline, or that it was in some way losing its original identity as a focus for the spiritual as much as the occupational loyalties of craftsmen, merely that it was reflecting a more general shift in the focus of charitable provision in London before the Reformation.

Corporate charity is a surprisingly neglected aspect of late medieval piety. Concentration upon the efforts of individuals, particularly through studies of testamentary provisions, only reveals half the picture. For a fuller picture of the nature and extent of charitable assistance to emerge it is important to study the interaction between individuals and the variety of historical communities to which they belonged. Until relatively recently craft guilds have received little attention from historians of lay piety, let alone from those looking at charity in the late medieval town. Yet to suggest, for example, that 'religious and charitable undertakings were adopted in occupational gilds' is to underplay the extent to which these undertakings underpinned the very existence of a large number of these institutions in London and elsewhere.[107] Robert FitzRobert, a London grocer, made provision in his will for distributions to be made to the poor of the *artificiorum aurifabrorum grocerum et cissorum* in the city, a specific bequest to three guilds which, from their inception, had articulated not only craft identities and loyalties, but also the popular enthusiasm for institutions where individual salvation could be sought through collective devotion and mutual assistance.[108]

[107] Rubin, *Charity and Community*, p. 250.

[108] *The Register of Henry Chichele, Archbishop of Canterbury*, ed. E.F. Jacob and H.C. Johnson, Canterbury and York Society (4 vols. Oxford, 1937–47), II, pp. 510–11 (dated 27 October 1434, enrolled 1445–6).

8

THE ALEWIVES OF LATER MEDIEVAL CHESTER

Jane Laughton

In March 1295 a letter reached Chester from Edward I, currently based in his castle at Conway and running alarmingly short of supplies. In it the king commanded his clerk, William Hamilton, to enlist the help of the mayor and bailiffs of Chester and to hastily assemble all the brewsters (*totes les braceresses*) of the city and order them to brew good ale for the king and his army. Arrangements were then to be made to ship these supplies to Conway as quickly as possible.[1] Edward evidently assumed that many – if not all – the producers of ale in Chester were female, as was apparently the case in towns and villages elsewhere in his realm. Current research is proving his assumption correct and is revealing that women were actively involved in the brewing and selling of ale in both rural and urban communities throughout the medieval period.[2]

This study of the Chester alewives is intended to show how the brewing business was organized and conducted in one city in the later middle ages. The

---

[1] PRO, Special Collections, Ancient Correspondence, SC 1/45/71.

[2] See D.J. Keene, *Survey of Medieval Winchester* (2 vols. Oxford, 1985), I, p. 265; J.M. Bennett, 'The Village Alewife: Women and Brewing in Fourteenth-Century England', in *Women and Work in pre-Industrial Europe*, ed. B.A. Hanawalt (Bloomington, 1986), pp. 20–36; M. Kowaleski, 'Women's Work in a Market Town', in ibid., p. 151; J.M. Bennett, *Women in the Medieval English Countryside: Gender and Household in Brigstock Before the Plague* (Oxford, 1987), p. 212; H. Graham, '"A Woman's Work . . .".: Labour and gender in the Late Medieval Countryside', in *Woman is a Worthy Wight: Women in English Society, c. 1200–1500*, ed. P.J.P. Goldberg (Stroud, 1992), pp. 136–44. J.M. Bennett's forthcoming study of alewives is eagerly awaited.

women of Chester had perhaps engaged in the trade since the eleventh century, if not earlier, although no sex-specific term was used in the Domesday entry for the city which noted the penalties imposed on those who used false measures or who brewed bad ale.[3] The practice of English common law whereby the legal identity of a woman merged with that of her husband on marriage has tended to obscure much female activity in the medieval period.[4] The documentary sources for Chester, in particular the judicial records, do, however, reveal something of the townswomen's involvement in the ale trade. In 1383, for example, a male defendant was named as owing 8s for malt but the court entry added that it was his wife who had actually made the purchase.[5] And in 1450, when two male litigants disputed the delivery of twenty quarters of malt, the clerk noted that the plaintiff's wife had made the agreement and that the malt was to be handed over to her.[6] Thefts of ale commonly involved women, as in 1399 when a sextary and a half of ale was taken by a woman from the home of John de Bebington, against his wishes and also against the wishes of his wife.[7] Such evidence is plentiful and suggests that Chester's wives played a significant role in the ale trade.

In 1295 the city's brewsters had responded (successfully one hopes) to a wartime emergency but it is likely that their peacetime production was always substantial. Throughout the medieval period ale, with its cereal base, provided a vital source of nutrition, forming a staple of the diet of young and old, rich and poor.[8] The amount consumed each day by an individual adult is not known

---

[3] *VCH, Cheshire,* (1987), I. p. 343. Both men and women were mentioned in connection with the use of false measures.

[4] C.M. Barron, 'The "Golden Age" of Women in Medieval London', *Reading Medieval Studies,* XV (1989), pp. 35–7.

[5] Chester C(ity) RO, SR 97/1d.

[6] Chester CRO, SR 287/1d.

[7] Chester CRO, MB 1, f.57.

[8] C. Dyer, *Standards of Living in the Later Middle Ages: Social Change in England, c. 1200–1520* (Cambridge, 1989), p. 57; J.M. Bennett, 'Misogyny, Popular Culture and Women's Work', *History Workshop Journal,* XXXI (1991), p. 176.

with any certainty but possibly approached a gallon.[9] Demand would thus have remained high in the fifteenth-century city even though by this date Chester's earlier prosperity and importance had certainly declined. Nevertheless, it was still a large town by medieval standards, with perhaps some 3,500 inhabitants.[10] Moreover, these numbers were regularly increased: twice a week by neighbouring communities coming to market, twice a year by even larger crowds flocking to the great fairs at Midsummer and Michaelmas. People from the adjacent March of Wales were said to purchase their daily bread and ale in Chester and there may well have been some foundation for this claim, judging from the anguished cries which arose when trade routes were disrupted during Glyn Dŵr's rebellion.[11] Other regular visitors to the later medieval city included government officials on palatinate business, gentry suitors to the county court, and sailors and traders using the port. The commercial opportunities were, therefore, considerable and many townspeople responded; aldermanic households brewed on a large scale, while less affluent families merely supplemented their income by the occasional sales of surplus production. At all levels of society it seems that the contribution of the womenfolk was indispensable.

A considerable amount of skill and care was essential in the brewing business. Ale was produced by steeping grain in water for several days, draining it and allowing it to germinate. The resulting malt was then kiln-dried and taken to the mill to be ground. Next came the process of fermentation, achieved by

[9] Bennett, 'Village Alewife', in *Women and Work*, ed. Hanawalt, p. 31, n.7; Dyer, *Standards of Living*, p. 64. The daily allowance for each 'poor and feeble' inmate of St John's Hospital in Chester included half a gallon of ale and it would seem likely that a healthy adult would consume more than this: *VCH, Cheshire*, III, p. 180.

[10] C.V. Phythian-Adams, *Desolation of a City: Coventry and the Urban Crisis of the Late Middle Ages* (Cambridge, 1979), p. 12; *VCH, Cheshire*, V (forthcoming).

[11] Chester CRO, CH/28; CH/30; *Calendar of Recognizance Rolls of the Palatinate of Chester from Earliest Times to the End of the Reign of Henry IV, Report of the Deputy Keeper of the Public Records*, XXXVI, Appendix II (1875), pp. 60, 211, 225, 230, 247, 373, 475, 544. In 1406, although the immediate Welsh threat had receded, orders to the dossers to give priority to the sacks of the *braciatorices* at the malt mills apparently remained in force (PRO, Palatinate of Chester, Indictment Rolls, CHES 25/10, m.22).

adding hot water. Finally, the wort was drained from this mixture and, after the optional addition of a sprinkling of herbs, the ale was ready to drink. The process was labour-intensive and time-consuming; the product soured within days. Domestic brewing may, therefore, have been seen as a task ideally suited to the female members of the household, who were constantly on hand to oversee production. In wealthy homes female servants brewed under the supervision of the mistress. In humbler establishments wives did the brewing, possibly when tied to the house by the demands of small children; this could explain the occasional nature of their brewing activity. At other times such households perhaps chose to purchase ale.

Surviving accounts of Chester's Dee mills indicate the varieties of malt handled there in the later medieval period. Large quantities were recorded each year, made from oats, barley and wheat.[12] All three crops were grown in the neighbouring hinterland, with oats perhaps the major regional crop.[13] Additional supplies were obtained from Wales and, until the 1420s, also from Ireland.[14] Ale produced from barley malt was the preferred choice of medieval England, but ale made from oat malt was common in the bleaker agricultural areas.[15] The Dee mills' accounts reveal that until the 1440s half the malt

[12] The earliest detailed account dates from 1354–5 (PRO, Special Collections, Ministers' and Receivers' Accounts, SC6/784/5, m.3). Accounts survive for most years 1378–1485 (SC6/787/9–801/2) and list five types of malt: wheat malt, oat malt (both milled and unmilled), barley malt and 'fee' malt. The amounts of unmilled oat malt were invariably the largest, suggesting that a significant percentage of the mills' profits came from tolls levied on malt passing through the city rather than from the milling process.

[13] For the crops grown on the demesne lands of nearby Frodsham, see P.W.H. Booth and J.P. Dodd, 'The Manor and Fields of Frodsham, 1315–74', *Transactions of the Historic Society of Lancashire and Cheshire*, CXXVIII (1979 for 1978), pp. 40–5, 54–7.

[14] Grain from Wales (Chester CRO, SR 135/1d; SR 136/1; SR 155/1d; SR 196/1d); grain from Ireland (ibid., CHB/2; MB 2, ff.40v, 41, 42, 51). For Ireland becoming an importer of wheat by the 1430s and for the prohibition of exports, see E.M. Carus-Wilson, 'The Overseas Trade of Bristol', in *Studies in English Trade in the Fifteenth Century*, ed. E. Power and M.M. Postan (1933), p. 199; K. Down, 'Colonial Society and Economy in the High Middle Ages', in *A New History of Ireland, II: Medieval Ireland, 1169–1534*, ed. A Cosgrove (Oxford, 1987), p. 485.

[15] Dyer, *Standards of Living*, p. 57.

handled there was oat malt, wheat and barley accounting for the remainder. Thereafter, wheat malt dwindled away to nothing, to be replaced by barley malt; in the 1480s almost 75 per cent of the malt was barley malt, possibly to the relief of visiting ale-drinkers, who perhaps considered an oat-based brew inferior.[16]

It seems likely that Chester's wealthiest citizens controlled supplies of the necessary ingredients. Some of the grain used to produce malt was grown on their land, stored in their barns and sold by them to other townspeople.[17] These rich men also owned the malt-kilns in which the malt was dried; these kilns were found throughout the city and were not infrequently sited in the gardens of their homes.[18] They employed bailiffs to oversee production.[19] In the fifteenth century leading townsmen regularly exported quantities of malt to Wales, even though this represented an infringement of civic ordinances.[20]

These wealthy individuals were also able to invest in the equipment needed to brew on a large scale. In 1423, for example, the assemblage of two furnaces, three 'aleledes', 'brulede' and a vat valued at £20 were owned by an alderman.[21] Some thirty years later a prominent city weaver entrusted a 'breweledde, a massh combe, a trogh, six turnels and a wetyng combe' to a

---

[16] Visitors to Devon in the sixteenth century found the local ale brewed from oats likely to induce vomiting: H.S.A. Fox, 'Devon and Cornwall', in *The Agrarian History of England and Wales, III, 1348–1500*, ed. E. Miller (Cambridge, 1991), p. 304. Much of the oat malt recorded in the Dee mills' accounts passed through the city and was not processed there.

[17] E.g. Chester CRO, SR 208/1; SR 240/1; SR 285/1; SR 300/1d; SR 355/1; SR 402/1; SR 423/1; SR 461/1d.

[18] E.g. in Northgate Street in 1354–5 (PRO, SC 6/784/5, m. 5d); in a garden in Lower Bridge Street in 1415 (Chester CRO, MR 77/1); in Commonhall Lane in 1422 (BL, Harleian MS. 2063, f.122).

[19] E.g. Chester CRO, SR 285/1d.

[20] Chester CRO, SB 2, ff.24v–25, 27v; SB 3, ff.25v, 69v, 94, 96v. In 1536 it was ordered that malt was henceforth not to be sold outside the city since 'couetose and gredye persons' with regard only for their own 'aduantages, singular profutes and lucre' had regrated and engrossed the market in barley and caused the price of malt to rise substantially (ibid., AB 1, ff.65–6).

[21] Chester CRO, SR 152/1d.

bailiff who had to account for production.[22] It was possible, however, to produce ale with more limited equipment, much of which – wooden containers and tubs for example – would have been found in any middling household. Evidently the term 'comb' was used locally in Chester for a brewing tub. In 1477 one such comb together with other assorted treenware was valued at 6s 8d, and in the 1490s the price of a comb varied from 10s when new to 3s secondhand.[23] In 1423 an incident involving a comb filled with hot wort led to an alewife taking to court the woman who had overturned it.[24] These brewing tubs could be large; in 1293 one woman fell into a vessel of hot water called a 'mascomb' and drowned.[25] Almost four centuries later, in 1636, another city brewster was found dead in her brewing pan, 'with her heels upwards'.[26]

These unfortunate accidents hint at female participation in ale production in the thirteenth and seventeenth centuries, and it would seem likely that women brewsters worked in the city in the intervening years. The later medieval documents do indeed indicate the involvement of women, an involvement which evidently began when the malt was taken to the mills to be ground. The records of the court of Dee mills imply that this was a task normally carried out

[22] Chester CRO, SR 285/1d. An indication of the equipment needed to brew on a substantial scale is perhaps provided by that which was found in the Franciscan friary at the Dissolution: a great lead to steep 20 bushels of malt in the kitchen, a great furnace, a mashing comb, an ale vat, a stone trough, an 'hayer' to dry malt and two ale barrels in the brewhouse: L(etters and) P(apers), Foreign and Domestic, Henry VIII, ed. J.S. Brewer, J. Gairdner and R.H. Brodie (23 vols. 1862–1932), XIII, pt. 1, no. 1298.

[23] Lancashire and Cheshire Wills and Inventories at Chester, with an Abstract of Wills now Lost or Destroyed; Transcribed by the late Revd G.J. Piccope, ed. J.P. Earwaker (Chetham Society, new series, III, 1884), pp. 1–4; Chester CRO, SR 418/1; SR 429/1d. In 1477 the cost of the accompanying lead cistern was 18s.

[24] Chester CRO, SR 151/1.

[25] Calendar of County Court, City Court and Eyre Rolls of Chester, 1259–1297, ed. R. Stewart-Brown (Chetham Society, new series, LXXXIV, 1925), p. 180. This thirteenth-century reference to a comb, together with the references in the fifteenth-century court rolls, perhaps invalidate the suggestion that the use of the term in the Cooks' play in Chester's Mystery Cycle points to an early sixteenth-century date for the text: The Chester Mystery Cycle: Essays and Documents, ed. R.M. Lumiansky and A.D. Mills (Chapel Hill, 1983), pp. 46–7.

[26] Chester CRO, QCR C/1/10.

by women; victims of the millers' extortions in the corn mills were invariably male, victims in the malt mills exclusively female. Only a handful of individual plaintiffs were named each time, but they were always women of high status and typically included the wives of the serving sheriffs plus one or two wives of aldermen.[27] These worshipful wives were apparently chosen to represent the full complement of Chester's brewsters, great and small, all of whom doubtless resented the millers' extortions: the demands for excessive multure, the insistence on extra monetary payments, the refusal to let them pick up grain which had fallen to the floor.

The subsequent stages of ale production took place in the home. Chester's records suggest that in middling craft households brewing was largely done by the family's womenfolk and that in wealthy establishments the task was consigned to female servants who worked under their mistresses' supervision. Evidently no social stigma attached to élite wives who engaged in such activities.[28] Alice le Armerer, wife of the man who held the mayoralty six times in the 1380s and 1390s and herself a member of the prestigious Trinity guild of Coventry, possibly controlled a sizeable staff.[29] Nine female servants (among them Magota Brouster) were named in her husband's will in 1396, and Alice was still sending malt to be milled twenty years later and employing servants in her own right.[30] Cecily Wotton, married to the mayor of 1433–4, also supervised the household's ale production. During his lifetime Thomas Wotton took to court those townspeople (often female) indebted to his wife for ale and after his death she herself acted as plaintiff.[31]

---

[27] E.g. PRO, CHES 25/11, m.8d; CHES 25/12, mm.4, 18d.

[28] For similar involvement by the élite wives of Colchester, see R.H. Britnell, *Growth and Decline in Colchester, 1300–1525* (Cambridge, 1986), pp. 89–90. Margery Kempe of Norwich, daughter of a former mayor, became one of that city's greatest brewers because she wished 'to maynten hir pride' and have fine clothes: *The Book of Margery Kempe*, ed. S.B. Meech and H.E. Allen (EETS, o.s., CCXII, 1940), pp. 9–10.

[29] *The Register of the Guild of the Holy Trinity, St. Mary, St. John the Baptist and St. Katherine of Coventry*, ed. M.D. Harris (Dugdale Society, XIII, 1935), p. 5.

[30] PRO, Principality of Wales, Ancient Deeds, Series F, WALE 29/291 (possibly not all nine servants were still in his employ); CHES 25/11, m.8d; Chester CRO, SR 140/1d.

[31] E.g. Chester CRO, SR 150/1d; SR 219/1; SR 248/1d; SR 249/1; SR 268/1; SR 312/1.

Thomas and Cecily Wotton employed female servants who evidently assisted in the household's brewing activities. In 1439 one of these girls herself pursued a debt for ale in the Pentice court.[32] Other prominent families similarly engaged female labour.[33] There is no medieval evidence for the training given to these girls, but an early seventeenth-century abstract of the indentures whereby a weaver's daughter was bound as an apprentice for seven years to the mayor's wife may mirror earlier practice. Grace Turner was to be instructed in all trades used by Mistress Bavand, especially that of malting.[34] The fact that female servants of the later medieval period are occasionally attested pursuing an independent career in the ale trade in later life suggests that they had perhaps received similar instruction.[35]

Throughout England the trade was regulated by the assize of ale, which linked the price of ale to the price of grain and which ordained public checks on the quality of the brew. The measures by which ale was sold were outside the scope of the assize but they were carefully monitored and borough courts dealt severely with any irregularities.[36] Separate lists naming those who brewed and sold ale against the assize or who used false measures begin to survive among Chester's sources only in the last quarter of the fifteenth century. In earlier years townspeople who paid an annual fine to sell ale were listed among those who were amerced for offences such as regrating victuals, evading custom or failing to keep watch on the walls.[37]

Evidence of female involvement in the brewing business is by no means straightforward. The late fifteenth-century lists imply that the city's brewers

[32] Chester CRO, SR 239/3.

[33] E.g. Chester CRO, MB 3, f.79; MB 4, f.40v; SB 3, ff.21v, 66; SR 218/1; SR 259/1; SR 351/1d.

[34] BL, Harl. MS. 2020, f.469.

[35] See the career of Alice Duy below.

[36] Britnell, *Colchester*, p. 89 and n. 20.

[37] For those fined in the first half of the fifteenth century, see e.g. Chester CRO, MB 2, ff.26v–28v, 58v–59v, 92v; MB 3 ff.45–45v, 65–65v; SB 1, ff.64v–66v. There does survive one separate list of those who brought their measures to be sealed in *c.* 1408; thirty of the sixty or so names are legible (MB 2, f.57). For lists from the last quarter of the fifteenth century, see e.g. MB 6, ff.166v, 167v–168, 169v–170v; SB 3, ff.64v, 91v–92v, 93–93v; SB 4, ff.32, 49v–50, 74v, 91v, 94–94v, 110v–111.

were predominantly male. Of the fifty-seven individuals who brought their measures to be sealed by the mayor in November 1487, for example, forty-nine were men.[38] Among these brewers were several aldermen and leading citizens who later served as sheriff.[39] Other brewers were master craftsmen, a number of whom had held guild office: the baker Stephen Baxter, for instance, and John Pampton, steward of the painters and glaziers. None appear to have been humble artisans. Eight brewsters were named in the list, of whom only one was described as a wife. At least one was a widow and three others may also have been widows. At first glance, therefore, it would seem that in November 1487 the townsmen dominated the brewing industry. Analysis of a list of 1476–7 suggests, however, that this masculine dominance was more apparent than real.[40] This earlier list named those *braciatorices* who had broken the assize: thirty-one in total, of whom twenty-five were wives, one or perhaps two were widows and four were possibly single women. Seven of the wives were married to men named as brewers in 1487; one had been widowed by that date and now brewed in her own name.

It would seem probable that among the aldermanic brewers of 1487 were men who employed female servants to brew, as had long been customary. In 1398, for example, Joanna del Heth had worked as *receptrix et brasiatrix* for one such man, from whom she received weekly supplies amounting to 20s, for which she had to render account.[41] Prominent citizens named in the late fifteenth-century lists of brewers were unlikely to have done the brewing themselves and were doubtless named as the heads of the households in which brewing took place. The civic authorities were perhaps concerned only with those who brewed regularly. This could explain the absence from the records of the poorer families who engaged in brewing on an occasional and insignificant basis.

Always more numerous than the brewsters of later medieval Chester were the women who sold ale. Such retailing was evidently an activity which was

---

[38] Chester CRO, MB 6, ff.166v, 167v–168v, 169v–170v. Part of this list is printed in R.H. Morris, *Chester in the Plantagenet and Tudor Reigns* (Chester, n.d.), pp. 424–5.

[39] E.g. William Snede, Roger Hurlton, Ralph Birkenhead and Roger Burgess.

[40] Chester CRO, SB 3, f.64v.

[41] Chester CRO, SR 117/1.

accessible to many females, including those who were single or married to non-
citizens, whereas brewing on any significant scale was assuredly the prerogative
of the more well-to-do. Women were named in a fragmentary list of retailers
dating from the 1350s and half a century later, of the thirty ale-sellers who took
their measures to be sealed, all but one were female.[42] Among the women were
two daughters, seven wives, one widow, two apparently single women and
seventeen servants, all of them in the employ of prominent townsmen. Female
dominance of the retail trade apparently continued over the ensuing decades; in
May 1540 it was alleged that the number of women who kept alehouses and
taverns had given rise to slanderous reports of the city. 'Wantonnys, braules,
frays and other inconvenyents' frequently occurred, and the mayor ordered that
from the following month no woman aged between fourteen and forty was
henceforth to keep an alehouse.[43]

It seems clear that in the fifteenth century the participation of élite wives in
the ale trade extended to selling the household's production. One example is
provided by Margery Walsh, wife of a former lessee of the Dee mills and mother
of a man who several times held the mayoralty, who owned an ale-cellar in
Bridge Street in 1402.[44] In 1419, when Thomas Hope took over an important
tenement in Northgate Street, it was noted that it was his wife Agnes who was
to occupy the cellar.[45] Some years earlier, in 1393, the wife of the alderman
William Hawarden had actually been present in her husband's cellar when
trouble broke out. Metal bowls and containers filled with ale were knocked to
the ground and Margaret was among those who were physically assaulted.[46]

Much drink-related disturbance occurred in the city's undercrofts, and affrays
involving weapons not uncommonly broke out in the cellars beneath the homes
of leading citizens, marking these places out as rowdy establishments where men

---

[42] Chester CRO, SRE 3/1, 1d; MB 2, f.57. The list of *c.* 1408 contains some sixty names but only
thirty are legible.

[43] Chester CRO, AB 1, f.70. This order is printed in Morris, *Chester*, p. 425.

[44] Chester CRO, MB 2, f.4.

[45] *The Cheshire Sheaf*, 3rd series, XXXI (1936), no. 6848 (hereafter 3 *Sheaf*).

[46] Chester CRO, MB 1, f.15v.

gathered to drink and ultimately came to blows.[47] The close association of these ale-cellars with the owners perhaps helps to explain the absence of named drinking houses in fifteenth-century Chester. These establishments had multiplied in Westminster in the decades around 1400, an indication of the appearance of relatively smart hostelries with their own individual signs.[48] In a very modest and undoubtedly provincial way, Chester functioned as a mini-Westminster but named drinking houses did not line its streets, with the exception perhaps of 'Hell', which possibly served as a tavern selling wine rather than ale.[49] The absence of names may of course indicate the rudimentary nature of the city's drinking houses, many of which still lacked signs at the start of the sixteenth century.[50]

Semi-subterranean undercrofts were a familiar feature of many medieval towns and in Chester were to be found along all four main streets. Many survive, a number of them containing evidence of a staircase linking to the dwelling above; this would suggest that they were used by the occupier of the house. Other undercrofts, however, were held separately from the accommodation on the upper storeys.[51] Easy access from the upper levels may have been desirable in some respects, but if the premises were used as ale-cellars then their separation was not without merit. The more elaborate stone-vaulted undercrofts, of which five survive, perhaps served as taverns for the sale of wine.[52] Certainly the names of those associated with taverns are men known to have engaged in the wine trade, among them John de Overton who in 1425 leased two cellars at the corner of Bridge Street and Watergate Street.[53]

---

[47] E.g. Chester CRO, MB 1, f.14v; MB 3, ff.12v, 71v; SB 1, ff.42, 47.

[48] G. Rosser, *Medieval Westminster, 1200–1540* (Oxford, 1989), p. 122. Cellars in Winchester were used as taverns and had distinctive names: Keene, *Winchester*, I, pp. 166–7.

[49] For the undercroft in Bridge Street known as 'Helle', see 3 *Sheaf*, XXXVI (1941), no. 7921.

[50] Chester CRO, AB1, f.66v.

[51] *The Rows of Chester*, ed. A.N. Brown (forthcoming).

[52] Those which survive are at 12 Bridge Street, 28 Eastgate Street and 11, 21–3 and 37 Watergate Street.

[53] In 1393 John Coly owned a tavern in Bridge Street (Chester CRO, MB 1, f.14v); he was often recorded shipping and selling wine (e.g. ibid., SR 106/1; SR 110/1; SR 123/4d; *C. Recognizance Rolls . . . Chester*, p. 119). For John de Overton, see 3 *Sheaf*, LVI (1961), no.10,832.

The selling of ale in fifteenth-century Chester was not an élite monopoly. In November 1487 those summoned by the ward constables to bring their measures to be sealed included, in addition to the fifty-seven brewers, 101 other townspeople who sold ale retail.[54] Forty-six of these retailers were men, all of them of a lower economic status than the brewers, but similarly including husbands who appeared on behalf of their wives. That this was so is suggested by the two lists which survive for Northgate Street. One list named the wives of William Goldsmith and John Mascy, while the other named Goldsmith and Mascy themselves. In the second list *jur[atus]* was written beside these men's names, but not beside the names of other retailers, indicating that the two had taken the oath. More explicit evidence for a husband assuming responsibility for a wife's brewing activities is provided by the weaver Thomas Traves, who in January 1477 was presented for his wife's breaches of the assize of ale and who was himself amerced 40*d* as a result.[55]

Fifty-five of the retailers listed in November 1487 were female; twenty-seven of these women were described as wives and one was a widow. Female ale-sellers were commonly in the majority in lists dating from the closing decades of the century: fifty-four of the 104 who sold too dear or who used unsealed measures in 1484, ninety-three of the ninety-four who used false measures in 1497.[56] A list of August 1498 did not show the same female dominance; thirty-seven of the fifty-six retailers were men.[57] Among them, however, were nineteen whose wives had been named in 1497 and two whose servants had been cited. It would seem probable, therefore, that husbands and masters commonly assumed responsibility for offences committed by their wives or female servants.

Analysis of the 197 debts for ale recorded in the sheriffs' court rolls for the period 1350–1500 provides additional evidence of women's under-representation in official lists of retailers. In fifty-six cases the plaintiff was

---

[54] There are two lists for Northgate Street and the possibility of double recording exists.

[55] Chester CRO, SB 3, f.67.

[56] Chester CRO, SB 3, ff.91v–92v, 93–93v; SB 4, ff.94–94v. The sole male retailer in 1497 was Elis ap Tud, possibly a relatively poor man.

[57] Chester CRO, SB 4, ff.110v–111.

female, in sixteen cases a man and wife were named as joint plaintiffs, and in ten cases the plaintiff was male but it was noted that the wife had actually sold the ale. In at least twenty-three of the remaining 115 cases the plaintiffs were élite citizens who almost certainly initiated litigation to recover debts due for ale sold by the household's womenfolk.

It seems probable that only the wealthiest townswomen of late medieval Chester brewed on a substantial scale, and that the cellars beneath their homes provided the prime commercial outlets for the retail trade. Wives of middling status, with a small surplus of ale to sell on an occasional basis, possibly sold from the doorstep. Tapsters who traded regularly perhaps set aside a room for the purpose. In 1503 it was ordered that such 'ale-bowers', together with wine taverns and cellars, were to be closed at nine o'clock each evening.[58] These tapsters usually operated in a modest way, purchasing small quantities of ale as necessary from élite households, although the more ambitious could opt to trade as *femmes soles*, a status in law which allowed a wife some measure of independence from her husband.[59] In Chester it was only to retailers of bread and ale that this status was conceded, thus restricting any challenge to the economic power of the husband to the lowly trade of huckster.[60] Able to rent properties in their own right, some of these women are occasionally attested occupying cellars, although these premises were probably less salubrious than those beneath the aldermanic homes.[61]

A household's involvement in the ale trade could prove long-standing. Seven of the thirty-one women listed among the retailers in 1476–7 were still operating ten years later and at least one continued for another ten years beyond that.[62] Four family names appear to be common to the lists of 1476–7 and 1497.[63] Alice Buccy, wife of the tailor Thomas Buccy, brewed and sold ale

---

[58] Chester CRO, AB 1, f.66v.

[59] Barron, 'Golden Age', in *Reading Medieval Studies*, pp. 37–8, 39–40.

[60] Chester CRO, SR 349/3d; SR 352/1d; SR 419/1; SR 420/1d; SR 424/1.

[61] E.g. Chester CRO, SR 223/1; SR 272/1; SR 319/1.

[62] Elizabeth, wife of the cook John Hayward, was named in 1476–7 and in 1495.

[63] Margaret Bostock, Matilda Gile, and the wives of Hugh Hyne and of Nicholas Sherman were named in 1476–7; the wife of Charles Bostock, Elena Gile, Margery wife of Hugh Hyne and the wife of Henry Sherman were cited in 1497.

in Foregate Street from *c.* 1482–3 until 1497–8; from 1487 she operated as *femme sole*.[64] She was remembered by a leading citizen in his will in 1496 and perhaps obtained supplies of ale from him, although there is no specific evidence that this was indeed the case.[65] Ellen Buccy, married to the tailor Henry Buccy, may have been her sister-in-law; she sold bread and ale in Foregate Street from 1486 until 1502–3 and she too traded as *femme sole* from 1487.[66]

It is possible to glimpse – however dimly – the life cycle of other alewives. Alice Duy, for example, who first appeared in the city's records in 1427, was named in the following year as owing 2*s* for red cloth. In 1431 she was working, together with another Alice, as the servant of Alice Russell. She evidently learned her trade in this élite household and by 1436 she had branched out on her own and was now referred to as tapster. She pursued this calling throughout the 1440s and early 1450s, obtaining supplies of ale from various leading figures in the town. She never bought in any quantity and traded, for at least some of the time, from the cellar she rented from a prominent citizen. Apparently single all her life, she nevertheless managed to earn a livelihood – somewhat precariously perhaps, for she spent much of the time in debt – until 1456 when she disappeared from view, defaulting on a debt to one of Chester's aldermen.[67]

A generation later Agnes Filenes, another tapster, followed in Alice's footsteps. Possibly an immigrant (she had a relative called Patrick), she first came to the attention of the authorities in 1484, when she broke the assize of ale by selling too dear. She apparently spent the whole of her working life in Foregate Street, an area which throughout the fifteenth century saw a concentration of tapsters. Agnes married twice, her second husband – by June 1493 – being the citizen William Chamber. As a result she no longer had to pay for the privilege of retailing within the city and the next few years were probably the most prosperous of her career. Opting for the status of *femme sole*,

---

[64] Chester CRO, MB 6, f.166v; SR 351/1; SB 4, ff.75, 94.

[65] 3 *Sheaf*, XVII (1920), no.4105.

[66] Chester CRO, SR 351/7; SR 396/1; SR 414/1; SR 451/1; SB 4, ff.5, 27, 32; SB 5, f.7.

[67] For Alice Duy, see e.g. Chester CRO, SR 167/1d; SR 223/1d; SR 247/1d; SR 263/1; SR 272/1; SR 295/1d; SR 309/1d; MB 4, f.40v.

she is recorded baking cakes, selling beer and, somewhat unusually, wine. By 1496, however, her husband had vanished from the scene and her problems began. Shortly afterwards came the first accusation of brothel-keeping and over the next fifteen years she was often in debt, occasionally involved in brawls with other alewives and periodically charged with keeping a brothel, the last time in 1510, a quarter of a century after her first brush with the authorities.[68]

The surviving lists of brewers and retailers in Chester's sources indicate that the civic authorities monitored the price of ale and inspected the measures used. There is, however, no evidence for public aletasters and it is therefore possible that there was no official check on quality.[69] The assize of ale linked the price of ale to the price of grain, but although statutorily tied to the price of malt it seems that throughout the fifteenth century the accepted price of best ale was a penny a gallon and of second quality ale a halfpenny less; these prices remained the same in 1540.[70] In 1476–7 thirty-one brewsters refused to sell a gallon for a penny and in 1484 sixty-eight individuals were in trouble for selling at $2d$ and $2\frac{1}{2}d$ a gallon.[71] Prices for ale recorded in debt litigation in the sheriffs' court indicate that Chester's alewives commonly paid a penny a gallon for their supplies.[72] It would be harsh, therefore, to blame them excessively for selling at a higher price, or for seeking to eke out supplies by using false measures or by watering down their ale. The large number of retailers charged with such breaches of the assize would suggest that this may have been a legal fiction for a licence to trade.

Perhaps more worrying to the authorities were those anti-social activities – gambling, brawling, drunkenness and prostitution – which were widely believed to flourish in the alehouse environment. As the fifteenth century progressed, concern in Chester apparently intensified, although this may be an illusion,

---

[68] For Agnes Filenes, see e.g. Chester CRO, SB 3, f.92v; SB 4, ff.5, 9v, 52v, 75v; SB 5, f.84; SB 6, f.10; SR 372/1; SR 386/1; SR 389/1; SR 400/1; SR 411/1d.

[69] There is similarly no evidence for aletasters in Colchester (Britnell, *Colchester*, p. 89).

[70] For prices in the fifteenth century, see e.g. Chester CRO, SR 201/1; SR 223/1; SR 318/1d; SR 351/1d; SR 408/1; SR 425/1. For prices in 1540, see AB 1, f.73.

[71] Chester CRO, SB 3, ff.64v, 91v–92v.

[72] E.g. Chester CRO, SR 320/1; SR 351/1d; SR 420/1d.

resulting from a change in the nature of record-keeping and an increase in the number of surviving sources. Nevertheless, the evidence suggests a concerted drive against brothels from the 1460s, with poor immigrant females (Agnes Irish, Alice Scot and Marion of Man for example) commonly named.[73] Men too, prominent citizens among them, were charged with keeping disorderly houses. In 1463 William Rauson and Thomas Fernes, both of whom later served as sheriff, allegedly received prostitutes in their cellars. These cellars were probably used as alehouses; Rauson and Fernes, together with their wives, were numbered among those who sold ale contrary to the proclamation in 1469.[74] In 1473 five other leading townsmen, including two aldermen, were accused of receiving prostitutes in their homes and cellars.[75]

The names of known tapsters also appeared among the brothel-keepers; thus to the familiar sins of over-charging and under-serving was added that of immorality. Many of these offending alewives were married women and they therefore posed a serious threat to the patriarchal order of society, undermining its traditional values. Such behaviour scandalized the whole community. The ruling male élite brought charges and imposed fines but the respectable wives may also have joined in the chastisement of offenders. The attack which three of them made in 1494 on Alice Wright *alias* Alice Filpot, who had been charged with brothel-keeping, was surely not coincidental.[76]

In a recent article Judith Bennett has traced public antipathy towards alewives throughout the middle ages and beyond. She has suggested that the atmosphere of ridicule and opprobrium possibly discouraged women from working in the trade in the early sixteenth century, at precisely the time when men were assuming control of the rapidly expanding and lucrative beer-brewing industry.[77] The use of hops as a preservative enabled beer to be produced in

[73] Chester CRO, SB 2, ff.8, 25v, 40, 59, 85; SB 3, ff.19v, 20v, 37v, 39v, 64.

[74] Chester CRO, SB 2, ff.26v, 85v. In 1470 two monks from St Werburgh's were accused of entering Rauson's home and raping his servant (SB 2, f.87v).

[75] Chester CRO, SB 3, f.19v.

[76] Chester CRO, SB 4, f.31v.

[77] Bennett, 'Misogyny, Popular Culture and Women's Work', pp. 166–88.

larger quantities than had been possible with ale. Beer had been introduced into southern England by Flemings and Dutchmen in the early fifteenth century but its progress northwards was slow.[78] The first reference in the sources for Chester comes in 1477, when Gilbert Hiton 'beerman' paid the large sum of 3s 4d for permission to trade in the city.[79] Beer is mentioned five times in the 1480s and 1490s, in contexts which may hint at increasing male interest in a trade which ultimately developed into something of a male monopoly and from which women were effectively excluded.[80]

The scarcity of evidence for breaches of the assize of ale and for charges of brothel-keeping in earlier years makes it impossible to know whether the closing decades of the fifteenth century witnessed a deliberate policy in Chester of linking alewives with immoral behaviour. Alewives were certainly depicted in association with devils in the revels which celebrated the Midsummer Show, inaugurated in 1499, and in the Cooks' play in the city's Mystery Cycle, which is believed to have received its extant form in the early sixteenth century.[81] By this date, however, the Cooks' play was already of some antiquity. In 1448 a baker claimed that he was owed 2s 6d for playing the demon in the Bakers' pageant and in 1486 a weaver demanded 8d due to him for playing the demon

[78] P. Clark, *The English Alehouse: a Social History, 1200–1830* (London, 1983), p. 32.

[79] Chester CRO, SB 3, f.69.

[80] Chester CRO, SB 4, f.33; SR 367/1; SR 389/1; SR 403/1; SR 405/1. In 1493 there is mention of John Bruer *de Abbathia* (SR 403/1). The occupational byname is insecure evidence for occupation at this date of course but it may be significant that he was linked with the abbey precinct, an area associated with brewing in the early modern period. In 1637 Archbishop Laud wrote to the dean demanding that houses in the abbey court no longer be leased to brewers and maltsters; the noise, smoke and filth from the malthouse and brewhouse 'infinitlie' annoyed the bishop's house: *The Cheshire Sheaf*, 1st series, I (1878–9), no.14.

[81] For the Midsummer Watch and Show, see *The Annals of Chester*, one version of which is printed in G. Ormerod, *The History of the County Palatine and City of Chester*, 2nd edition, revised and enlarged by T. Helsby (3 vols. 1882), I, p. 234. For the scene portraying demons and an alewife in the cooks' play, see *The Chester Mystery Cycle: I, Text*, ed. R.M. Lumiansky and A.D. Mills (EETS, supplementary series, III, 1974), Play XVII, lines 277–336. For discussion of the date, see L.M. Clopper, 'The History and Development of the Chester Cycle', *Modern Philology*, LXXV (1978), pp. 219–46.

in the Cooks' play.[82] Whether these pageants already portrayed Satan and his companions welcoming an alewife to Hell remains uncertain; such a scene may have been a subsequent addition. If this were indeed the case, then it may have reflected a growing antipathy towards alewives in Chester in the early sixteenth century, an antipathy which ultimately led, in May 1540, to severe restrictions on female involvement in the ale trade.[83]

[82] Chester CRO, SR 262/1d; SR 356/1. In fifteenth-century Chester the trades of the cooks and bakers were closely related and the occupational terms were applied interchangeably to the same individual on occasion.

[83] Chester CRO, AB 1, f.70. Men and women who were discovered employing girls to sell ale were to be fined 40*d*. The practice evidently continued: on 10 March 1567 an alderman was 'bound in 40*s*. to kepe no kind of woman (after 20 March) except his wife or daughter, to retaile any sort of wyne, ale or bere in the tavarne under his new dwelling house', as too were fifteen other prominent citizens. On 15 December 1567 one city merchant was ordered to change his taverner within five days and to employ instead 'ether a young man or ells an olde woman . . . ' (Morris, *Chester*, p. 426).

9

GERONTOCOMIA, ON THE CARE OF THE AGED:
A FIFTEENTH-CENTURY ITALIAN GUIDE BY GABRIELE ZERBI (1445–1505)

Margaret Wade Labarge

It comes as something of a surprise to many medieval scholars that the Middle Ages not only had a more sensible approach to practical medicine than they have been given credit for, but also knew a good deal about old age. In fact, despite the popular papers, old age is not a modern invention, but has been with us for a very long time, and has been referred to in the medical literature since the time of Hippocrates and Galen. To my mind one of the most interesting, and surprising, facts that emerges from even the most cursory study of medieval medicine is the insistence of medieval physicians on their first duty being to keep their patients healthy, and to provide regimens to help to achieve this purpose. Holistic medicine is not a new idea.

Medieval physicians had earlier models to follow, for their medical writings and practices were inherited indirectly from the early Greeks, particular authority being given to the works of Galen, incontestably the most quoted and respected doctor for many centuries. Galen's medical writings were continuously pillaged by his successors in the Eastern Empire, and were then transmitted to Europe primarily through the works of the great Arab physicians of the ninth to the eleventh centuries. The major texts of such highly regarded doctors as Rhazes, Haly-Abbas and Avicenna included much of the classical medical knowledge, further amplified by their own practical observations. This body of material gradually became known to European doctors through the great translators of the late eleventh and twelfth centuries, who were active in Italy and Spain. Both Galen and the Arab physicians, especially Avicenna, provided models for the regimens of health which began to appear in Europe at the end of the twelfth century and continued to be a popular form during the later Middle Ages. The various authors borrowed from their predecessors and gradually added their own amplifications in matters where they had new ideas or practical experience. Plagiarism was not a medieval concern. In fact, the extensive citing or very often the appropriation of earlier authorities was considered proof of the reliability of the work and a proud boast. One reason for the popularity and ubiquity of the regimen texts may be found in the fact that the consultation of famous doctors in the Middle Ages was often done by correspondence, as when Alphonse of Poitiers sought aid for his eye trouble from a famous Jewish physician in Spain.[1]

Regimens were usually designed for a specific individual, or for a particular group with similar characteristics, but then might circulate generally. For example, in 1315 Peter Fagarola, a doctor from Valencia, sent a special regimen to his two sons studying at Toulouse. He gave them advice on food, sleep, proper clothing for the different seasons, and exercise; he recommended the control of the passions, and then added some cures for colds and coughs. Its style suggests that it was expected to be circulated among students.[2] In 1335 Guido de Vigevano, anatomist and physician at the French court, wrote a regimen for an older man planning to go to the Holy Land, as part of a larger treatise which included medical science. This was originally designed for King Philip VI, then forty-two and planning a crusade. Ten years later Guido updated his regimen, added Latin extracts from Galen and a third section on anatomy, primarily based on his own dissections. This was undoubtedly

---

[1] C.J. Webb, 'Roger Bacon on Alphonse of Poitiers', *Essays in History presented to Reginald Lane Poole*, ed. H.W.C. Davis (Oxford, 1927), pp. 290–2. France, Archives Nationales, *Layettes du Tresor des Chartes*, ed. A. Teulet and DeLaborde (4 vols. Paris, 1863–75), III, no. 4055.

[2] L. Thorndike, *University Records and Life in the Middle Ages* (New York, 1944), pp. 154–60.

intended more for doctors themselves, and less towards a more general public.[3] Sometimes the advice is unexpected, as in the early fifteenth-century regimen for a patient with rheumatism which recommended among other things the wearing of a scarlet furred doublet.[4]

Given the popularity of regimens, it is only surprising that it was the end of the fifteenth century before the first treatise appears specifically devoted to the general care of the elderly. It was published in highly urbanized Italy where the elderly had already become a substantial element of the population and was written by an eminent physician and professor of medicine at the respected University of Padua, Gabriele Zerbi (1445–1505). There had been two earlier medieval regimens dealing with the aged, but these were almost exclusively oriented towards medical care. Around 1239 the young Roger Bacon wrote a brief *Liber de Retardatione Accidentium Senectutis,* which placed its confidence in 'occult medicines'. These unfortunately were far removed from the more usual and less expensive herbal prescriptions. His work was not translated into English until 1683.[5] Around 1309 Arnold of Villanova, the famous Catalan doctor and philosopher who was also a professor at Montpellier, took over Bacon's little treatise for his own *De Conservando Juventute et Retardando Senectute,* which he dedicated to Robert the Wise, king of Naples. He made no acknowledgement of his wholesale borrowings, not even mentioning Bacon as an authority. Arnold provided only a few additions or modifications to the friar's work, but substituted his own prescriptions, with particular emphasis on the curative properties of variously spiced wines. Arnold's treatise was quite well known, soon translated into Italian, and in 1544 into English, but it was still emphatically a medical document.[6]

---

[3] G. Sarton, *Introduction to the History of Science* (3 vols. in 4, Baltimore, 1927–48) III, pt. 1, pp. 285–6.

[4] D. Jacquart, 'Le regard d'un medecin sur son temps: Jacques Despars (1380?–1458)', *Bibliothèque de l'École de Chartes,* CXXXVIII (1980), p. 54.

[5] Roger Bacon, *De Retardatione Accidentium Senectutis,* ed. A.G. Little and E. Withington (Oxford, 1928), p. xlii; Sarton, *History of Science,* II, pt. 2, p. 959.

[6] Arnold of Villanova, *The conservation of Youth and Defense of Age,* tr., Jonas Drummond 1544, ed. Charles L. Dana (Woodstock, VT, 1912). Sarton, *History of Science,* II, pt. 2, pp. 893–4.

In 1489 Gabriele Zerbi's *Gerontocomia, On the Care of the Aged* was published in Rome and illustrates how the Italian doctor was deeply influenced by both the medieval treatises on medicine and the newer currents of classical learning. The *Gerontocomia* was written in Latin, thus designed for the educated or the professional, and dedicated to Pope Innocent VIII.[7] The title was taken from the Greek, *gerontokomos*, used in the Justinian Code to describe the warden of a hospital or almshouse for the aged. The subtitle accurately describes the nature of the work, which indeed proposes useful information for the care of old men who were not necessarily sick. A very straightforward treatise, much of whose advice resonates with timeless common sense, it is unfortunately timebound in its total unwillingness to consider the care of aged women. Here Zerbi falls back on the authority of Aristotle (on whose *Metaphysics* he had already written a long treatise) and the Aristotelian dictum, generally accepted in the Middle Ages, on the imperfection of women. He borrows from Aristotle to justify his lack of interest in old women when he insists that the aged male is naturally nobler and stronger, since the female is merely a deformed male. Zerbi believed that a woman's only skill was her ability to raise chickens.[8]

Naturally his treatise exhibits many points of likeness with earlier regimens and accepts much of the medieval framework of belief. The doctrine of humours, which the Middle Ages had inherited from classical antiquity, was taken for granted along with the conviction that the four humours had the ability to condition people's temperaments and to affect their appearance, behaviour and susceptibility to disease. In addition, Zerbi like most medieval doctors felt it was wise to work with the astrologers. He remarks: 'These two masters, the physician and the astrologer, must in particular consult and provide for human nature' and he goes on to underline the effect of the signs of the zodiac on human life.[9] He was also concerned, as many medieval thinkers were, to recognize the proper balance required in health care by tailoring what were

---

[7] Gabriele Zerbi, *Gerontocomia: On the Care of the Aged*, tr., L.R. Lind, American Philosophical Society Memoirs, CLXXXII (Philadelphia, PA, 1988).

[8] Ibid., pp. 77, 157.

[9] Ibid., p. 35.

known as the 'non-naturals' – diet, exercise, rest, environmental conditions and psychological well-being – so as to provide the aged man with the optimum complexion possible.

Zerbi was a considerable scholar, conscious of the philosophical and literary currents of both classical and medieval thought, and he used them to complete his medical picture. His use of sources suggests that he was thoroughly aware of the competing portraits of old age in both classical and medieval times. Some classical authors like Plato, Cicero and Seneca had dealt positively with old age, but the opposing tradition of caricaturing aged men and women was much stronger in both classical and medieval literature, revelling in exaggerated descriptions of their physical infirmities and mental confusion. The Italian doctor quotes from both sides but has a generally positive approach to old age.

Before going on to analyse the *Gerontocomia*, it is useful to sketch briefly Zerbi's life, since he was an outstanding example of the élite of the Italian medical world of his time, providing the pattern of a successful career, yet ended by a dramatic death. He was born in Verona in 1445 of an old and aristocratic family. We do not know where or when he received his doctorate, but at the age of twenty-two he was already teaching medicine at Padua. From 1475 to 1483 he taught both medicine and logic at the University of Bologna (a remarkable honour for a non-citizen), and in 1478 was even allowed a leave of absence with pay to visit his ailing old mother in Verona. In 1483 Zerbi went to Rome where he gained favour at the papal court. His first book, *Quaestiones Metaphysicae*, a study in the medieval scholastic form of Aristotle's *Metaphysics* from the point of view of both theology and philosophy, was dedicated to Pope Sixtus IV. His second (the *Gerontocomia*) was still much influenced by Aristotle but dedicated to Sixtus's successor, Innocent VIII, a man of fifty-seven. Zerbi remained in Rome after his patron's death in 1492, but two years later he accepted the offer of a chair of theoretical medicine at the University of Padua, where he continued to teach until his death. By 1495, when he published the *De Cautelis Medicorum*, a pioneering study on the moral obligations of doctors, he already had a considerable reputation and the *De Cautelis*, like the *Gerontocomia*, broke new ground. In 1502 he completed another massive work, *Liber Anathomie Corporis*, on the structure of the body and its organs. In addition he had composed, probably in about 1486 while still in Rome, an unpublished treatise on the causes and cure of kidney and bladder stone for the benefit of a cardinal from Verona, Zerbi's birthplace.[10]

Such appointments and books suggest a solid if unspectacular career, but Zerbi had also gained a wider reputation, practised occasionally in Venice when the university was not in session, and was often sent for by the great. In May 1503, when Lorenzino de Medici had asked for the medical faculty at Padua to send him a doctor, Zerbi was one of the two suggested. In July of the same year the Signoria of Venice sent Zerbi and another doctor to Corfu to attend its captain-general there who was suffering from a flux, but the poor man died shortly after they arrived. An even more important patient was quite literally the cause of Zerbi's death. This was a most dramatic and tragic affair, mentioned in Marino Sanuto's *Diary* but told in gruesome detail in a book entitled *De Litteratorum Infelicitate*, published in Venice at the beginning of the seventeenth century. In October 1504 a galley came to Venice with a request to the signoria from Skander Pasha in Bosnia asking for a physician to cure his illness. Zerbi, accompanied by a young son, set out for Bosnia at the request of Andrea Gritti, then Venetian consul in Constantinople and later doge. Zerbi was successful in curing the pasha, who loaded him with gold and expensive gifts and assured his safe passage home. The doctor departed, having left a regimen with his patient, who almost immediately forgot the doctor's warnings and plunged into his previous excesses, from which he shortly died. His sons were infuriated with the wealth that Zerbi had been given and accused him of having poisoned their father. Having caught up with his cavalcade on the borders of Dalmatia, they seized the unsuspecting travellers, and convicted Zerbi of murder. With extraordinary brutality they proceeded at once to the execution of both the doctor and his young son, sawing them in two between two planks. By January 1505 the news of the murder had already become known in Venice.[11]

---

[10] Ibid., pp. 10–14: L.R. Lind, *Studies in Pre-Vesalian Anatomy*, American Philosophical Society Memoirs, CIV (Philadelphia, PA, 1975), pp. 141–6.

[11] Lind, *Studies*, pp. 145–6.

Perhaps Zerbi had some premonition, or was merely taking sensible precautions, for he had made his will in Venice, with two fellow doctors among his witnesses, at the apothecary and spice shop of the Golden Head, a few days before his departure for Bosnia. He named his wife and Piero of Mantua, godfather of his children, as his executors and provided specific bequests for a wide range of sisters, brothers and nieces, as well as his immediate family. It is interesting to note, in contrast to the purely masculine tone of the *Gerontocomia*, that he left his mother (aged at least eighty-eight at the time of his will) land and income for her remaining lifetime, and showed his confidence in his wife by entrusting her with the usufruct of all his property and the status of principal executrix. The remaining three sons were only to inherit their shares after their mother's death, while his daughters were left money to help provide their dowries, designed to be paid when they married.[12]

Zerbi's life, achievements and tragic death at the age of sixty provide an explanatory backdrop to his prescription for a suitable regimen for the aged, and testify to his concern for such care. Not all doctors were as conscientious, for Bernard de Gordon, who taught medicine at Montpellier at the end of the thirteenth century, could write disapprovingly: 'It is most shocking that physicians of our time do not care to know the regimen of health because they do not consider it lucrative'.[13] His treatise illustrates effectively the medieval practice of relying on earlier authorities, but even a quick reading of the *Gerontocomia* demonstrates how the author's knowledge not only went far beyond the usually quoted medical text but also included wide-ranging citations from both classical and medieval literature.[14] Besides such expected authorities as Galen, Pliny, Avicenna, Albucasis and Isaac Judaeus, the doctor frequently cited newly available materials and more contemporary figures. The Latin encyclopedist Celsus (first century AD) was rediscovered in the fifteenth century. His *De Medicina*, though very valuable and complete, was so large that it was

---

[12] Zerbi's will is printed in Lind, *Studies*, pp. 323–4.

[13] L. Demaitre, *Doctor Bernard de Gordon, Professor and Practitioner* (Toronto, 1980), p. 697.

[14] Lind, *Studies*, p. 148. Professor Lind's translation of the *Gerontocomia* is most helpful in its scrupulous identification of Zerbi's sources.

seldom copied and only became generally known in the fifteenth century. It is perhaps less surprising that Zerbi knew the work of Pietro d'Abano, professor of medicine and astrology at the University of Padua in the early fourteenth century. Pietro was one of the most learned of all medieval physicians and his major work, which attempted to harmonize the varying opinions of reputable physicians, was deservedly popular.

Quite apart from being knowledgeable in the purely medical sources, Zerbi was also conversant with a wide range of other learning. His familiarity with Aristotle results in some thirty direct quotations, while he also refers to such medieval thinkers as Boethius, Albertus Magnus and even Grosseteste. His knowledge of literature was wide and much influenced by the Renaissance emphasis on a wide range of classical authors, as well as the medieval favourites. He quotes, often extensively, Virgil, Ovid, Horace, Plautus, Cicero, Juvenal, Martial, Vitruvius, Jerome and his favourite poet, Maximinianus. In discussing etymologies, especially of the names of foodstuffs, Zerbi relies on Isidore of Seville, the great encyclopedist of the seventh century, a man copied by everybody in the Middle Ages. The Italian physician seems to have used his own wide-ranging interests to bolster his theory that old men 'delighted not only in conversation and riddles but in the pleasures of all kinds of knowledge'.[15]

The early chapters of the *Gerontocomia* are devoted to a certain amount of philosophical background on the definition, nature and signs of old age. Like most medieval and Renaissance men, Zerbi accepted a life pattern of several defined periods of age. The number might vary according to the whim of the author but Zerbi deals only with old age, and divides it into two very comprehensive periods. He states that the first, or early, period, which he calls *senectus*, begins anywhere from thirty to forty, and continues to fifty or sixty – rather premature we would feel. The doctor does admit that the early part of this period may well overlap with the age of maturity when men are at their peak of constancy, understanding and wisdom. Nevertheless, he argues, they are already on the slippery decline towards death. The final, decrepit period of old

---

[15] *Gerontocomia*, p. 268.

age, when physical and mental deterioration takes over, he calls *senis*, with all our modern sense of senility.[16] Having made his philosophical statements, with their unquestioned acceptance of the influence of the humours and astrology, Zerbi goes on to describe the more practical causes and marks of old age. It is amusing to note that the doctor shared the almost universal concern of early writers on old age about the inevitability of grey hair and wrinkles, as well as the probability of baldness, describing them as 'such disgraceful disfigurement'.[17] Nevertheless, despite old age's disadvantages and weaknesses, and the inevitability of death, this pioneer geriatrician felt that everything should be done to ensure what we now call 'quality of life' for the elderly until their death.

His non-medical concerns are particularly noticeable in his Chapter XIV on the requirements for a proper caretaker of the elderly, and his description of both his duties and those of this assistants. He felt it was necessary to have an experienced, well-educated man of middle age, who was frugal and careful of expenses and who could ensure the proper choice and functioning of his assistants, either male or female. Incidentally, Zerbi would now certainly be accused of racism, since he considered certain races totally unacceptable for such work, remarking that the English were immensely proud, the Swiss intolerably suspicious, the Illyrians foulmouthed, and the Hungarians hostile to Italians. He approved of Bretons and Germans and considered Lombards the most superior of the Italians.[18] Listed among the caretaker's supervisory duties was the very medieval requirement of examining each man's urine daily, as the best indicator of health or illness.[19]

Zerbi goes on to deal with the most suitable places and climates for a residence for the aged and emphasizes the importance of unpolluted air. It is not surprising that Italy was felt to be quite obviously the best of all lands. Within its boundaries Verona, Bergamo and Bologna were even better than the

[16] Ibid., p. 50.
[17] Ibid., p. 50.
[18] Ibid., p. 90.
[19] Ibid., p. 87.

other hill towns of northern Italy.[20] Practical matters are covered in considerable detail by chapters on the kind of house, suitable clothing and the right kind of bed.[21] Nevertheless, this description of standards is only theoretical, since there is no suggestion of how this perfect residence was to be financed.

Overall, Zerbi tried to make his treatise comprehensive, including a discussion of exercise and rest, bathing, sleep and wakefulness, and the problems of what he calls elimination and retention. This last heading covers a marvellous miscellany. The section on elimination dealt first with blood-letting, so often the medieval panacea. Zerbi, however, regarded it with great suspicion, considering it usually dangerous for the old, and preferably to be avoided. He is rather dubious about the wisdom of encouraging vomiting, and surprises us with his concern about the dangers of sneezing. Another piece of advice which is unexpected in this medieval context is the emphasis put on the need to clean the teeth and gums. An extraordinary recipe is even provided for a dentifrice made of burnt deer horn, sedge root and a spike of roses, combined with six times as much salt crystals. The resulting mixture, pounded and sifted, would provide an early variety of tooth powder.[22] His section on retention, on the other hand, includes drunkenness, which Zerbi tolerated if it was not too frequent or extreme. He was far more concerned about more characteristic problems of the elderly – constipation and, for men, difficulty of urination – but he relied on natural remedies to cure them. He recommended specific fruits, such as the fig and the prune as laxatives, with enemas as a last resort, and felt that vegetable diuretics, such as celery, herbs like basil, mint and dill, or the drinking of honey and water could help urinary difficulties.[23]

As is characteristic of almost all medieval regimens, the longest and by far the most detailed section deals with diet. This is not surprising, as all the medical authorities from Galen on laid great emphasis on the normative importance of

---

[20] Ibid., pp. 97–100.
[21] Ibid., pp. 100–9.
[22] Ibid., pp. 250–9.
[23] Ibid., pp. 260–2.

diet in maintaining good health. They quoted such authorities as Pliny, Isaac Judaeus, Isidore of Seville and Galen, and often included folk beliefs and remedies in their treatises. The *Gerontocomia* covers the whole gamut of food and drink in twenty rather brief chapters (XVIII–XXXVIII). There is a relatively compact discussion of all the possible varieties of edible meats, fish, eggs and dairy products, garden vegetables and legumes, aromatic herbs, condiments and preserves, bread, oil, salt, honey and sugar cane. Separate chapters are devoted to the use and types of wine, how to choose good water, or render polluted water potable.

The pattern of description of each item is very similar. Usually there is an etymology, often quoting Isidore of Seville; then a statement on which humour it suits, and the comments of varied authorities, especially Pliny. Sometimes there are suggestions about the best method of cooking or bits of folk knowledge. Rice, for example, is highly praised and its use as a cure for diarrhoea mentioned.[24] The poets are often quoted for or against certain substances, but the general tenor of this section is of careful observation and a firm belief in the need for a sensible and moderate diet to conserve good health.

Zerbi's two chapters on the emotional life of the elderly represent a consensus of medieval medical thought. Sex for the elderly was to be discouraged, if not forbidden completely. The doctor admits that this restraint is unlikely, for he says 'it is difficult for old men, as it is for those at other stages of life, to curb the use of sex', and suggests that autumn was the best time to indulge.[25] On the other hand, he was very positive about the emotional pleasure that could be given to old men by the presence of pleasant music and delightful fragrances, and by conversations whose subjects should be adjusted to individual interests, and he even suggested the use of certain colours which might aid their eyesight, as well as the avoidance of very bright light.[26] His own statement encouraging mild stimulation of the senses of the elderly is full of still applicable wisdom:

[24] Ibid., p. 215.
[25] Ibid., p. 274.
[26] Ibid., pp. 266–72.

Old men need the pleasure derived from stories which cause laughter and merriment and from suffumigations and pleasant odors. They should not abstain from any kind of hilarity by which the spirit of the old folks can find a relaxation from business affairs and in which it is good to indulge.[27]

Zerbi's final section is devoted to some current medicines, as well as considerable cosmetic advice for possible alleviations or even curses for the much dreaded signs of old age. He describes at length the methods which might help to remove wrinkles and delay grey hair and baldness. These include such unexpected suggestions as viper's flesh and potable gold along with various dyes and rinses of wildly varying ingredients. A recipe is given for the decoction of viper's flesh which, on the authority of Pliny and Avicenna, was good for a multitude of uses. Its broth was even reputed to drive away body lice.[28] On the purely medical side he lists proudly the electuaries prescribed by his predecessors. These were medicines made of several powdered ingredients – often exotic and expensive – mixed with honey, jam or syrup to facilitate their administration. One example, which is described as the 'electuary of the moderns', was to be made from a remarkably complex and varied collection of ingredients. Perhaps it merely demonstrates the frequent fondness of medieval doctors with exalted practices to rely heavily on the most costly treatments of their time, equating efficacy with expense. This 'marvellous electuary' included such items as precious stones, several spices, musk, ambergris, citron peel, scraped licorice, raisins, conserve of borage and bugloss, purified apple juice, rosewater and a pound of white sugar.[29] In the midst of such complexity, it is rather refreshing to find an ordinary infusion of rhubarb could be suggested as one possible tonic.[30]

Zerbi closed his work with a brief statement remarking that death in old age is natural and not to be lamented. Indeed, in one of his very few mentions of

[27] Ibid., p. 272.
[28] Ibid., pp. 290–1.
[29] Ibid., p. 303.
[30] Ibid., p. 287.

religion, he ends by stating the orthodox belief in eternal life, saying, 'By means of better deeds immortality with blessedness follows. This is the life which must alone be called life; I wish that some day, well deserving of it, we may attain it.'[31]

We do not know if Zerbi's work was influential, but the original edition is very rare and it does not seem to have been republished. However, his concern for suitable treatment of the aging was echoed by a fellow citizen of Padua, Luigi Cornaro, who in 1558 published a treatise entitled *Della Vita Sobria*. This was a popular essay on how to grow old gracefully and healthily by exercising great moderation in food and drink, and pursuing placid and simple pleasures. Cornaro certainly held many of the same principles as Zerbi, whom he may well have known by reputation if not in person, but he was a good exemplification of his own ideas, as he just missed the hundred-year span of life he had set as the attainable ideal. Cornaro's work certainly had wide and continuing circulation, for it was translated into English in the seventeenth century by the poet George Herbert and admired by Joseph Addison. In 1810 it even appeared in Philadelphia, and a later translation, entitled *The Art of Living Long*, was published in Milwaukee in 1903 and was included in a widely read cheap series known as the Little Blue Books.[32] Perhaps this is merely an early example of the unfair advantage of the popularizer over the professional, but Zerbi's work has at last been made generally available and his concerns and advice, even after five hundred years, can still be studied with profit.

[31] Ibid., p. 306.

[32] Luigi Cornaro, *The Art of Living Long* (with essays by Joseph Addison, Lord Bacon and Sir William Temple) (Milwaukee, 1903).

10

WHEN DID YOU LAST SEE YOUR GRANDFATHER?

Joel T. Rosenthal

Launce: Who begot thee?
Speed: Marry, the son of my grandfather.
W. Shakespeare, *Two Gentlemen of Verona*, Act III, Scene i, line 287.

'You could not with any confidence expect to see your grandchildren in the world we have lost.'
Peter Laslett: *The World We Have Lost* (1971), p. 103.

One of the characteristics of an articulated culture is the way in which it configures the inescapable rhythms and cycles of the celestial calendar and of the biological process so as to give definition and meaning to human activities conducted within a universe that might otherwise seem to be governed by disinterested and unpredictable forces. If we seek to decipher the life of medieval men and women as set against such larger patterns, we can think of the behaviour and activities of the people of fifteenth-century England as a series of case studies, now safely embedded within the context of our observations about society as a set of patterned responses designed to give life meaning and the living some modicum of reassurance. Though the framework within which we position the individual, the family and the institutions of the external world differs considerably from the one assumed in Lancastrian and Yorkist England, we strive – as students of that world – to pour the wine of their voiced and lived experience into the bottles of twentieth-century interpretation. And as trained and empathetic observers, we find that we not infrequently encounter themes in the symphony that are not only familiar, but that on many occasions still evoke a responsive chord of the world whence they emanate.

The rhythms imposed upon human activity by the exigencies of agrarian and pre-industrial life – from which few of the day were far removed – are too obvious to need elaboration. The day itself, the seasons of the year, and then the full cycle of the year all asserted an autonomy over individual volition, as they did over collective social and political behaviour. Their powerful grip, imposed from without, could not be ignored. We may argue that the week and the month were more arbitrary divisions to impose on human cycles of activity: social constructs rather than 'natural' phenomena. But they too were so deeply embedded in the rhythms and calculations of western thought, and from such an early time, that much of life was constructed to circle round them and to dance to their tunes.[1]

In addition to these prime movers of light and dark, heat and cold, we give heed to the beat of the ecclesiastical metronome, standing above and beyond localized human agency and adding to and dove-tailing with the legion of socio-cultural patternings. We can point to those repetitive cycles created by and expressed in the liturgy, those of the monastic day as spelled out in *The Rule of St Benedict*, those of the king's year with its festival-driven times for the accountings at the Exchequer and the crown wearings at court, those of leet courts and hundreds and sheriff's tourns, those of the labour services of the manor and the agricultural cycle, those of the festivals and fast days of the Church, and those of maypoles and ale-tastings and fairs and markets and ritualized spectacles of towns and villages. Whether we choose to see this predictable procession as moving across the stage of life with stately grace or, rather, as staggering and lurching towards its foreseeable *terminus*, we can stand as informed spectators of the endless and unfolding drama as it draws us along from year to year, from age to age.

---

[1] On time and the calendar, Jacques Le Goff, *Time, Work and Culture*, tr., A. Goldhammer (Chicago, 1980); for the week and general comments about how we mark divisions of the cycle, Eviatar Zerubavel, *Hidden Rhythms: Schedules and Calendars in Social Life* (Berkeley and Los Angeles, 1985).

Nor are the rhythms all impersonal and external ones. They meshed with the life cycle; biography and the tale of the generations became, in the long run, woven into those of the seasons and the years. Within each individual life the external calendars and rhythms of field and manor, alongside those of 'church and state' and town and village, were superimposed upon and blended into the weave that portrayed the days of our years: birth, youth, adulthood, courtship and marriage, parenthood and maturity, old age and the end. The sacramental *rites de passage* of the Church, along with birthdays and saints' days, held for each individual what the festivals of the Christian year held for the community: a cyclical explanation of life – or an explanation of cyclical life, if we prefer – set into a transcendental context and serving as a counter to the ephemeral and fleeting nature of lived experience and of the individualized versions of the human condition. The unique and specific found meaning against the backdrop of the common and the universal.

Life is lived in stages, most familiar in the simple model of youth, maturity, and old age. The medieval obsession with this issue, and the medieval fascination with the almost limitless number of stages into which the journey could be divided, has received considerable attention from modern scholars. An elaborate explication of the various theories and paradigms would take us into the learned if unconvincing byways of many disciplines.[2] Suffice it to say that if the most famous pronouncement on the matter is, 'And one man in his time plays many parts, His acts being seven ages,' from *As You Like It*, the view expressed in the play is but one position among many that were put forward. It is a particular window into a room cluttered with interpretations drawn from humoral theory, with morality tales about our worth or worthlessness as descendants of Adam and Eve, and with a stock of pretty indifferent medical advice. Medieval wisdom about age and ageing ranged from erudite and recondite scholasticism to the tritest of folk homilies:

---

[2] J.A. Burrow, *The Ages of Man: A Study in Medieval Writing and Thought* (Oxford, 1986); Mary Dove, *The Perfect Age of Men's Life* (Cambridge, 1986); Michael Goodich, *From Birth to Old Age: The Human Life Cycle in Medieval Thought, 1250–1350* (1989); Georges Minois, *History of Old Age from Antiquity to the Renaissance*, tr., Sarah H. Tenison (Chicago, 1989).

From the tyme that we were born
oure youthe passith from day to day,
And age encreesith moore & moore,
& so doith it now, the sothe to say.[3]

But for all the contemporary fascination with age and the stages of life, much of it reflected in the swelling currents of popular and vernacular literature, there were aspects of geriatric inquiry that rarely made the agenda. We find little focus on the concept or definition of generations; little on the tension or transition between age cohorts; not much on the stages of the family life cycle beyond the legal and economic concern for the transmission of real property; almost nothing on how long real people really lived.[4] Medieval thought ran more readily towards moral reflection than towards behavioural or domestic delineations. Neither demography as we study it, concerned as it is with the rate of milestones and events, nor the social history of the family, with its quantitative and interactional questions, were of any significant concern to the legions of poets and essayists, artists, preachers, astrologers, pharmacologists and medical theoreticians whose didactic and pastoral views governed the discourse of the day when it turned to questions of age and the life cycle.[5]

---

[3] Roger Bacon, *De Retardatione Accidentium Senectutis*, ed. A.G. Little and E. Withington (Oxford, 1928). There are also comments by Bacon on the weakening of all organisms in *Roger Bacon's Philosophy of Nature,* tr. and ed. David C. Lindberg (Oxford, 1983). The relevant part of the volume is the 'De Multiplicatione Specierum,' pp. 1–270.

[4] David Herlihy, 'The Generation in Medieval History', *Viator,* V (1974), pp. 347–66; Anthony Esler, *The Aspiring Mind of the Elizabethan Younger Generation* (Durham, N.C., 1966); Georges Duby, 'In North-Western France: The "Youth" in Twelfth Century Aristocratic Society', in *Lordship and Community in Medieval Europe,* ed. Frederic L. Cheyette (New York, 1968), pp. 198–209.

[5] We now have an accessible late medieval (or Renaissance) text on the issue: Gabriele Zerbi, *Gerontocomia, On the Care of the Aged,* tr., L.R. Lind, American Philosphical Society Memoirs, CLXXXII (1988) on which, see above ch. 9. For modern treatments, relying largely on late medieval vernacular literature, Alicia Nitecki, 'Figures of Old Age in Fourteenth Century Literature', in *Aging and the Aged in Medieval Europe,* ed. Michael M. Sheehan (Toronto, 1990), pp. 107–16; John Scattergood, 'Old Age, Love, and Friendship in Chaucer's "Envoy to Scogan"', *Nottingham Mediaeval Studies,* XXXV (1991), pp. 92–101; John M. Steadman, 'Old Age and "Contemptus Mundi" in the "Pardoner's Tale"', *Medium Aevum,* XXXIII, 2 (1964), pp. 121–30.

The rhythms of life and the passing of the years were realities that may well have forced themselves into consciousness, if not necessarily into the written record. The generations – be they long or short – and the children – be they none, few, or many – were very much the business of the day when it came time to consider beginnings and endings. The three-generation family, the living chain composed of grandparents, parents, and grandchildren was, beyond doubt, a more difficult trick for late medieval society to put together, with the woes of pre-modern medicine and pre-modern mortality, than it is for us. Peter Laslett's terse if thoughtful reflection on this issue, as quoted above, was not uttered without due deliberation.

As a model of patriarchal or family continuity, the idea of a living chain as the fruit of successful procreation that encompassed three generations in one embrace was undoubtedly an attractive one: a compelling goal, towards which all who played the mating game might aspire. There were impressive and familiar biblical parallels and analogues; who can forget the powerful image of the aged Jacob, blessing Joseph's children (albeit with some sort of dyslexic left-brain, right-brain confusion regarding birth order and birthright)?[6] When the ages of man and/or the stages of the life cycle were portrayed as consisting of three components – as was often the case in the illumination and iconography of high and late medieval Europe – the obvious parallels with the child, the adult, and the aged figure who was often the adult's own parent were apt to occur to even the dimmest of expositors.[7] Elegiac descriptions of deathbed scenes make much of the distinction between the dying hero who, at the end, was bereft of those who had eaten his bread and served at his right hand, and those fortunate champions now portrayed as surrounded by the vast progeny that had sprung from their loins: children and children's children, and to be found in some profusion. Compare the heroic last scene in the drama of

[6] Genesis, 48: 11–20. This is hardly the only instance in the Old Testament where the birth order and patriarchal pecking order are reversed.

[7] Samuel Chew, *Pilgrimage of Life* (New Haven, 1962); Elizabeth Sears, *The Ages of Man: Medieval Interpretations of the Life Cycle* (Princeton, 1986); E. Clive Rouse and Audley Baker, 'The Wall Paintings at Longthorpe Tower, near Peterborough, Northants', *Archaeologia*, XCVI (1955), pp. 1–57.

William the Marshal, the old patriarch and lineage-founder, with the pathetic and shameful passing of old Edward III.[8]

If we want to examine the question of the multi-generation family in a more systematic fashion, where can we go? How can we proceed? As is usually the case with medieval social and family history, the method whereby we analyse the data and records of our world is hardly a straightforward one. Difficult questions and laconic sources are a tough team to overcome. For fifteenth-century England (which is the 'long century' running from 1377 to 1509), we have several lines of inquiry about three-generation families and grandparent–grandchild links. Let us begin by looking at some samples from the voluminous body of inquisitions *post-mortem*. What do they tell us about the age of their heirs who were now coming into their inheritance, and then how confidently can we move – backwards and by inference – towards the probable or likely age of the recently-departed previous holder of the property? Finally, from there, how confidently may we move to the issue of grandparent–grandchild links or overlap? The inquisitions offer the largest body of demographic and quantitative material that has been preserved, and thanks to the valiant spirits who have calendared and published them for the Public Record Office and for the local record societies, we can make a quick and presumably representative dip into some of their testimony. Their accuracy and interpretation may be a bit problematic, but we should remember that they

---

[8] Deathbed scenes are a wonderful scenario for the theatre of solidarity or for its foil, that of desertion. For William the Marshal, see Sidney Painter, *William Marshal, Knight-Errant, Baron, and Regent of England* (Baltimore, 1933), pp. 276–9: the family house at Caversham could not hold the crowd that assembled, and even Henry III, among the relatives, barons, prelates, and the papal legate, had to cross the river and stay in Reading. But others of note were virtually unaccompanied. William Longman, *Life and Times of Edward the Third* (1869), II, p. 290: Alice Perrers stripped the rings from Edward's fingers and fled, and (as Longman quotes a contemporary account) 'Amongst a thousand there was only present at that time a certain priest.' Richard I refused to believe that Henry II was really dying, and he refused to come to Chinon at the very end: W.L. Warren, *Henry II* (1973), pp. 625–6. John was also pretty bereft of company: Kate Norgate, *John Lackland* (1902), pp. 283–5. That Richard II visited the dying John of Gaunt is 'inherently probable', though he was little compensation for the exiled Henry Bolingbroke: Anthony Goodman, *John of Gaunt: The Exercise of Princely Power in Fourteenth Century Europe* (1992), pp. 166–8.

generally passed the muster of the day – with its checks and balances of interested parties, of semi-informed neighbours, and of legal and economic filters – and we will use them here as we have them. A fuller discussion of their reliability can be found elsewhere.[9]

Table I

HEIRS OF MALE PROPERTY HOLDERS BY RELATIONSHIP AND BY AGE AT INHERITANCE: IPMs, VOLs. 17 & 18 (15 RICHARD II – 6 HENRY IV)

Age at succession

Relationship	0–10	11–20	21–9	30–9	40 & 40+	Totals
Sons	65	84	76	31	8	264
	25%	32%	29%	12%	3%	
Daughters	11	15	17	8	2	53
Nieces &						
Nephews	1	4	5	8	10	28
Totals	77	103	98	47	20	345
	22%	30%	28%	14%	6%	

If we look at the inquisitions presented in volumes XVII and XVIII of the Record Office's published series (covering, respectively, 15–23 Richard II and 1–4 Henry IV), we have a considerable body of material, permitting analysis and some speculation.[10] The tabular material indicates that for fathers succeeded by sons – which was the modal form of transmission or inheritance, occurring as it did in 264 of some 593 inquisitions – the son and heir was identified by the local jurors as being thirty years – usually stated as 'aged 30

---

[9] For a critical analysis, R.F. Hunnisett, 'The Reliability of Inquisitions as Historical Evidence', in *The Study of Medieval Records: Essays in Honour of Kathleen Major*, ed. D.A. Bullough and R.L. Storey (Oxford, 1971), pp. 206–35. Their value is defended, J.C. Russell, *British Medieval Population* (Albuquerque, NM, 1948); L.R. Poos, *A Rural Society after the Black Death: Essex, 1350–1525* (Cambridge, 1991).

[10] *CIPM*, XVII, XVIII.

years and more' – in 15 per cent of the instances of succession: 39 of 264 cases. For fathers who were succeeded by daughters the figures for older heirs reached 19 per cent: ten such daughters, of the fifty-three named as the heiress. Thus in about one instance in every six where the holder of the land was succeeded by a child of his body, at the time of his death the old man had clearly been old enough to have been a grandparent.

Though we now generally accept that the European Marriage Pattern – with the age for first marriage around the early to mid-twenties for women, in the mid-twenties or a little beyond for men – prevailed in post-plague/pre-modern England, it still seems likely that there had been sufficient years of parenthood for the third generation to have made its appearance, at least in many of these cases.[11] A lay man or woman named in an inquisition as heir and stated as being in his or her thirties was almost invariably married, and almost as surely had been married for somewhere between a half-decade and a decade. And since five to ten years of marriage more than sufficed to produce living children – in the absence of fertility problems and of infant mortality that had (so far) amounted to 100 per cent – we can posit the probable existence of unmentioned and undetected grandchildren in the forty-nine instances where the heir of the deceased is named as being aged thirty and more.

Beyond this simple numerical assertion, it is likely that the land-holding classes of the kingdom married their eldest children off at a younger age than did the population in general; we know this was the case for the peerage, and gentry studies – laconically and tersely supported by references in the inquisitions to daughters in their teens or early twenties *and* now married and even widowed – tend to run in this direction as well. So the probability of a living family chain embracing three generations at the death of the property

---

[11] J. Hajnal, 'European Marriage Pattern in Perspective', in *Population in History: Essays in Historical Demography*, ed. D.V. Glass and D.E.C. Eversley (1965), pp. 110–43; P.J.P. Goldberg, 'Marriage, Migration and Servanthood: The York Cause Paper Evidence', and R.M. Smith, 'Geographical Diversity in the Resort to Marriage in Late Medieval Europe: Work, Reputation and Unmarried Females in the Household Formation Systems of Northern and Southern Europe', in *Woman Is a Worthy Wight: Women in English Society, c. 1200–1500*, ed., P.J.P. Goldberg (Stroud, 1992), pp. 1–15, 16–69; P.J.P. Goldberg, *Women, Work, and Life Cycle in a Medieval Economy* (Oxford, 1992).

holder is a strong one in an appreciable number of instances, and it is reinforced by some tendency towards earlier-than-average age of marriage for the privileged universe that is the one generally under consideration in this essay.

When the heir of the deceased was identified as a nephew or a niece, or some combination or permutation thereof (as sisters' children, who would divide an inheritance), we find the chances of three-generation links to be even greater, though we are dealing now with unmentioned, albeit probable, great-nephews and great-nieces rather than with grandchildren. Since a nephew or niece represents the second generation, and since eighteen of twenty-eight heirs were identified as being aged thirty and more, this high percentage (64 per cent) of mature heirs offers further grist for our mill, a greater likelihood of children of children (though of a brother or sister). And because nephews and nieces were the offspring of a sibling younger than the deceased when they were descended from a brother, and likely to go in either direction when descended from a sister, the spread of years (and ages) on the day of death between the eldest and the youngest in the family might be even greater than when we are dealing with the model of eldest son's eldest son. This resort to a collateral path of descent enhanced the likelihood that more members of the third generation had had an opportunity to put in at least their first appearance.

In the inquisitions of men who had held property, some heirs whom we simply tallied above in the 'over thirties' category were actually named as being forty years or even more: eight sons, two daughters, ten nieces and nephews supposedly had reached this heady milestone. This subset of twenty heirs, of the 345 who fit into the several categories of descendants, is not of much significance in terms of its size (being but 6 per cent of the group). On the other hand, in a world where people spoke of the enfeebling grip of age while they were still in their thirties and forties, it is well worth a moment's attention.[12]

---

[12] As quoted, Sylvia L. Thrupp, The Merchant Class of Medieval London (Ann Arbor, 1948), p. 195. For Chaucer in this same vein, see 'Lenvoy de Chaucer a Scogan,' in The Works of Geoffrey Chaucer ed. F.N. Robinson (2nd ed., Boston, 1961), pp. 538–59.

Table II

HEIRS OF FEMALE PROPERTY HOLDERS BY RELATIONSHIP AND BY AGE
AT INHERITANCE: IPMs, VOLs. 17 & 18 (15 RICHARD II – 6 HENRY IV)

Relationship	Age of succession					
	0–10	11–20	21–9	30–9	40 & 40+	Totals
Sons	5	21	18	17	7	68
Daughters	1	1	8	8	4	22
Totals	6	22	26	25	11	90
	7%	24%	29%	28%	12%	100%

Widows, by definition, were women who had outlived their husbands; whether, given the original disparity between men's and women's ages at marriage, they actually had greater longevity and were older at the end than he had been is uncertain but likely. Whatever the case, the inquisitions for the widows present a pattern of more older heirs and heiresses being named by the jurors than had been the case for their dead husbands. Where 15 per cent of the fathers had had sons-as-heirs now named as being aged thirty and more, 35 per cent of the widows did. And where 19 per cent of the daughter-heiresses of their fathers were aged thirty and more, no less than 55 per cent of the daughters who inherited from their mothers had passed that barrier. Lastly, 12 per cent of these daughters, heirs of their widowed mothers, were named as being over forty.

So, to sum up at this point: if Laslett's pessimistic assertion about the chances of seeing one's grandchildren is still a good one, it should not deter us from noting that a family's aspirations of continuity and three-generation overlap were not necessarily all that far beyond reach, at least for groups of men and women where we know a fair proportion who survived to reach the age of twenty would go on to reach a life span of fifty or fifty-five (or sixty).[13] A woman

---

[13] For some assessments of longevity, though admittedly the material is from the upper classes: T.H. Hollingsworth, 'The Demography of the British Peerage', *Population Studies*, Supplement 18, 2; J.T. Rosenthal, 'Medieval Longevity and the Secular Peerage, 1350–1500', *Population Studies*, XXVII, 2 (1973), pp. 287–93.

(only knowable if she were a widow) who survived to a good age was perhaps more likely to be a grandparent, at the end, than her pre-deceased husband had been. Survival, not fertility – or perhaps we should say non-survival, as against infertility – was probably the main impediment in the construction of the three-generation chains we are looking for. Though we often have grim findings regarding replacement rates and infant mortality, when we follow the transmission of land through such a pathway it is quite conceivable that in chains which were forged and which held, a three-generation overlap at any particular time was far from unusual.[14]

Table III

THIRD GENERATION HEIRS BY RELATIONSHIP, AGE, AND BY SEX OF SUBJECT OF INQUISITION, IPMs VOLs. 17& 18 (15 RICHARD II – 6 HENRY IV)

Heir named in IPM	Age 0–10		11–20		21–9		30 & 30+		Totals
	Male	Fem.	Male	Fem.	Male	Fem.	Male	Fem.	
Grandchild	2	2	3	5	3	6	–	4	25
Great-niece or Great-nephew	3	1	1	1	1	–	5	1	13
Other	1	2	1	2	–	1	–	–	7
Totals	6+5=11		5+8=13		4+7=11		5+5=10		20+25=45

One further set of considerations based on the inquisitions *post-mortem* remains, and is perhaps the strongest and least speculative of the three. For twenty of the deceased male land holders, and for twenty-five of the women, the heir named was identified either as a grandchild or a great-niece or great-

[14] Sylvia L. Thrupp, 'The Problem of Replacement Rates in Late Medieval English Population', *EcHR*, 2nd series, XVIII (1965), pp. 101–19; Zvi Razi, *Life, Marriage, and Death in a Medieval Parish: Economic, Society, and Demography in Halesowen, 1270–1400* (Cambridge, 1981). For a recent exchange, E.D. Jones, 'Going Round in Circles: Some New Evidence for Population in the Later Middle Ages', *JMH*, XV (1989), pp. 329–45, and Mark Bailey, 'Blowing Up Bubbles: Some New Demographic Evidence for the Fifteenth Century?' ibid., pp. 347–58.

nephew, or (in a few instances) some other third-generation or third-generation-plus heir. This gives us some explicit and indisputable data, of the sort we have been searching for and conjuring up from the recalcitrant records about parents and children. Furthermore, the ages stated for the heirs in this final category show that, in at least some cases, the third-generation heir was well beyond the earliest stages of his or her own life cycle: of such heirs thirteen were named as being between ages eleven and twenty; eleven were between twenty-one and twenty-nine; ten were named as being thirty or more. While some scepticism at the far end of these claims is perhaps in order, we should nevertheless note that the forty-five heirs from the third generation who are explicitly identified in terms of such a relationship comprise 8 per cent of all the heirs named, in all the categories of relationship, in the inquisitions: sons and daughters, siblings, nieces and nephews, third-generation heirs, and an odd miscellany of cousins, aunts and uncles, etc. Since 8 per cent is roughly a one-in-twelve ratio, we are dealing, even at the outermost edges, with odds about three-generation overlapping that would seem attractive were we taking our chances on next year's Derby. The preference of a serious gambler for the odds on a horse as against the same likelihood of living to be a grandparent belongs, we suggest, to the history of *mentalité*, and as such is destined to remain beyond our simplistic exploration of such complex issues.

The aristocracy, no doubt, had their uses. Whatever justification and role they carved out in their own world, for us they have the distinction of being, for better or for worse, the lay group about whom, in their society, we can say the most. A look at fifteenth-century peerage families, whose genealogies are easily reconstructed from *The Complete Peerage*, gives an idea of the likelihood of over-lapping generations within a family, that is, of how frequently the first generation, in the person of the old peer, was still alive when the third generation made at least its first appearance, along with the duration of the overlap.[15] In addition to the grandfathers there is also a scattering of great-uncles, born later, as well as of the (younger)

[15] *GEC.*

grandmothers who were perhaps a good deal more familiar in terms of intimacy and interaction than the patriarchal grandfather had ever wished to be.

Counting peerage families is an uncertain exercise. However, by my tally some forty-eight aristocratic families could report at least one three-generation overlap in the years and generations between 1377 and 1509, whereas thirty-seven of the families that lasted long enough to be worth counting seem to have failed to reach this modest level of dynastic success at least once. Early marriages for eldest sons no doubt helped contribute to this high level of aristocratic family achievement. The peers thereby fare better in such a tally than would almost any group of lesser families, where the search for financial independence and the problems of establishing a neo-local residence had to be taken into account by the young husband and wife, factors working against early marriage and its accompanying quick start towards producing the children who would constitute the third-generation link.

A few case studies bring these points home and offer some straightforward (and probably typical) examples of the overlapping generations of the great families. John, Lord Berners, lived a long life (1407–74). His son and heir, Humphrey, predeceased him and died in 1471. However, Humphrey's eldest son, John, had been born in 1467: a seven-year overlap with his grandfather, and for the last three years of these seven John II had been the old man's heir. Did the family have a key to some secret fountain of continuity? Hardly: as we know from inquiries into family survival and longevity, demography – like the coin being tossed up over and over again in the probability demonstration – has no memory. Though John II lived into his mid-sixties he eventually died without any surviving legitimate male heirs. Survival in one generation alone did not make the grade for the next.

A number of studies have looked at the correlation between violent death, especially in the Wars of the Roses, and family survival rates. Yet is it interesting to note that some of the noble families that could boast of a series of grandfather–grandson links or overlaps were also (and simultaneously) families that suffered from a heavy toll on the battlefield or else by dint of political sentences and executions.[16] The whole string of the Lords Clifford certainly

shot through life at an accelerated pace, with a series of peers who died young
and from other than natural causes. Despite this bloody record, we see that
three of their patriarchs did cleverly contrive to be born before their
grandfathers had made their hasty exits from the stage. John Clifford
(1388–1422) overlapped by one year with Roger (1333–89), his grandfather;
Henry, 'The Shepherd Lord', (1452–1523) came a year before Thomas
departed (1414–55: killed on the Lancastrian side at the first battle of St
Albans); Henry, 12th Lord Clifford (c. 1515–70) was coeval with Henry, 10th
Lord Clifford, for about a decade. While only the last example offers anything
beyond the curiosity of mere survival in terms of an interval that might suffice
for some genuine grandfather–grandson interaction, the genealogical tenacity
and good fortune of these men was at least some sort of compensating factor for
their political stupidity and their well practised flair for being in the wrong
place at the wrong time.

The Percys, more famous than, and almost as ill-fated as, the Cliffords, had
five successive male heirs die unnatural deaths. However, they too had three
instances of grandfathers and grandchildren being on stage at the same time.
Henry Percy, 'Hotspur' (1364–1403) was aged four when his grandfather,
Henry, Lord Percy (1322–68) died. Hotspur's son, already an orphan for five
years (because of Hotspur's death at Shrewsbury), was already aged fifteen
when his own grandfather, Henry, earl of Northumberland (1341–1408) was
killed at Bramham Moor. And that son of Hotspur lived until 1455, when he
died at the first battle of St Albans, by which time his own son's eldest son was
already about six years old.

Many other instances of such three-generation overlap can be called from the
vasty deep of recorded aristocratic history. While the Lords Ogle never made
much splash in the waters of high politics, they too were able to survive. Ralph,
3rd Lord Ogle (1468–1513), was born when his father was alive (1440–86), his
grandfather but recently dead (Robert Ogle, c. 1425–65), and his great-

---

[16] K.B. McFarlane, *The Nobility of Later Medieval England* (Oxford, 1973), pp. 136–76; J.T.
Rosenthal, *Patriarchy and Families of Privilege in Fifteenth Century England* (Philadelphia, 1991),
pp. 102–36.

grandfather still hanging on (Robert Ogle, *c.* 1406–69). The Greys of Wilton are also worth mentioning. When Edmund, 9th Lord Grey (*c.* 1470–1519), was born his grandfather (Reginald Grey, 1421–94) had over twenty years yet to run. Edmund's elder sons, in turn, would have had at least five years shared with his old father, John Grey (d. 1499). The eldest son, George (1494–1514), died childless, and his younger brother Thomas (1497–1517) was next in line. Unlike his older brother, he probably had little memory of old John. Thomas likewise died without an heir of his body, and he was followed in succession by two more brothers; they, however and at long last, had been born after their grandfather's demise (Richard having been born in about 1505, William in 1509).

This is fairly bald material, only promising a rich tale could we mine it to better advantage, and hardly leading very far by itself. However, it does at least suffice to dispel any lingering views of a simple biological and demographic world of easy come, easy go. Nor are numbers the only criteria we can consider. Survival and longevity might be the *sine qua non* to open the door for other rewards, though we are not reluctant to accept that living long enough to share some years with a grandparent is no guarantee of much contact, let alone of a treasured memory-bank of reminiscence and tradition. However, mere survival, the bare fact of the overlapping of generations, is a mute prerequisite for that more intriguing world of intimacy and interaction which may have followed but whose tracks are invariably covered. When George Neville, 5th Lord Abergavenny (1469–1535), was born, his grandfather, Edward Neville (1404–76), had seven more years to live. George was the eldest of eight children; how many of his siblings came along in time to have at least some early memories of the old man? And was George socialized any differently, as the obvious heir and torchbearer? Hugh, 3rd Lord Burnell (*c.* 1347–1420) lost his son at Agincourt, but the son's three daughters had been born between 1391 and 1404. They had years and years in which to know their grandfather, though whether girls had much opportunity in this direction seems less likely, given the semi-segregated rearing of upper-class children, their removal to homes of other families, and the push towards early marriage.

We know of instances where the grandmothers survived and could have been the bridge between the generations, the bonding forces and the transmitters of family lore and tradition. In the full generation by which Cecily Neville outlived

Richard, duke of York (d. 1460), she presided over a great dowager household in which daughters, granddaughters, and countless nieces and great-nieces were to be found. We know, from her book of household ordinances, of the heavy piety and the meticulous ordering of board and expenditure that marked the great dowager household. That we hear nothing of a softer and more sentimental side does not necessarily mean that it did not exist.[17] The history of emotionality – of which family lore and nostalgia and the bonding of alternate generations is a rich chapter – lies mostly beyond our reach.

We can at least posit space within which personal interaction might have operated. Maurice Berkeley's grandson and successor, Thomas, was only three when the old man died in 1508. But Thomas was nine or ten when Maurice's widow, Isabel, died; we might see the years between the two deaths as the critical ones of character formation and of family bonding, especially as a boy of these years might still be at home, a member of the family's own household. Old Isabel's father, Philip Mead, had been thrice mayor of Bristol, and who knows with what treasure chest of tales of the Cannings, the Cabots, and the Merchant Adventurers she may have bored the youngster on the occasional rainy day in the West Country? Margaret Roos outlived her husband, Lord Botreaux, by twenty-two years. Perhaps Botreaux's granddaughters, who were also his heirs, were happy to maintain their ties to the old lady, even though she had remarried and gone on in life as a member of another family. Margaret's remarriage to Lord Burgh may have helped keep the Botreaux family afloat at the water-line of the aristocracy; their own resources had hardly been of any great magnitude. In addition Margaret Botreaux-Burgh had come into the world as a granddaughter of the earl of Warwick, and thence may have come both a touch of glamour and a wealth of anecdotes and apocryphal tales, not to mention some influential cousins and childhood connections.

If the data of the inquisitions *post-mortem* enabled us to surmise or deduce the

---

[17] For the household ordinances, *A Collection of Ordinances and Regulations for the Government of the Royal Household*, London Society of Antiquaries (1790); Kate Mertes, *The English Noble Household, 1250–1600* (Oxford, 1988); Jennifer C. Ward, *English Noblewomen in the Later Middle Ages* (1992); Rowena E. Archer, 'Rich Old Ladies: The Problem of Late Medieval Dowagers', in *Property and Politics: Essays in Later Medieval English History*, ed. A.J. Pollard (Gloucester, 1984), pp. 15–35.

pressure of the three-generation link from time to time, the genealogical material on the peerage reinforces the theme. Well over half the peerage families offer us at least one demonstrable three-generation link, between peer and his once-removed successor, at some point between the accession of Richard II and the death of Henry VII. More links and other links no doubt existed, and could we follow members of the families other than the peer himself, we might see some modest proliferation of the material. And if over half the families had at least one case to report, some had two or three, out of the five or six instances of succession in this interval: forty-eight families must mean several times that many cases of overlap. Admittedly, genealogical information is not intended to offer any insight into the quality of relationships. At best, it can provide a foundation without which such ties were literally impossible. I have tried to pinpoint a few cases where three-generation links are uncovered by the demographic and bare-bones material that has been preserved. We can at least lead these grandparents and their grandchildren to the water; beyond that they made their own decisions.

A third line of inquiry takes us into the world as revealed by wills and testaments. What do they offer in the search for bonds and identities that leaped over a generation – links that represented some slight victory, or at least some sort of successful holding action, against time and mortality? From a quantitative perspective the results of a search for bequests made directly by grandparents to their grandchildren are disppointing. One of the basic rules of using wills for social history is to accept that they tell us what they tell us; it is almost impossible to go much beyond the negative evidence of what a will does not say.[18]

Testators rarely give us very much regarding their grandchildren. A considerable number of wills have to be combed to find some reasonable number that include such explicit bequests. If we turn to R.R. Sharpe's edition

---

[18] Clive Burgess, 'Late Medieval Wills and Pious Convention: Testamentary Evidence Reconsidered', in *Profit, Piety, and The Professions in Later Medieval England*, ed. Michael A. Hicks (Gloucester, 1990), pp. 14–33.

of wills from the hustings court of the City of London we see how thin the ore lies: 561 wills cover the years 1399–1509.[19] Though there are some ambiguities regarding kinship terminology, and doubtless there are many bequests to unlabelled grandchildren – buried in the text as god-children or the ubiquitous *consanguines*, or simply picked up by name but without any specific tag – only sixteen wills make an explicit statement of a grandparent–grandchild path of transmission. A few others also refer to the three-generation family, but it was one that comprised the testator's parent (or other relative of the preceding generation) along with his or her children.

This is pretty thin stuff. Nor was it of the most generous sort in terms of substance on those few occasions when a grandparent–grandchild bequest did appear. The impression is that the grandchildren who still had living parents were not about to come in for much more than token or sentimental gift-giving; those of dead parents were, if affluence permitted, probably dealt with more seriously in some *inter vivos* fashion. John Payn left bequests to three daughters and to Joan, his servant; she is further identified as the daughter of John's deceased son, John Payn. The choice of language offers an insight into how an orphan girl might be called upon to justify her keep, even when, at the same time, she is acknowledged to be an integral part of the family. Joan's brother Thomas is also a beneficiary in the old man's will, and he is named as a beneficiary without any further status-identifying term. Perhaps a boy was not treated as cavalierly as a girl, though there are too many unknown variables to talk about the domestic and kin-based pecking order with much assurance.[20]

Sharpe may have been mining unusually thin material in his collection; whereas but 3 per cent of his wills had three-generation bequests, the figure rises to a heady 13 per cent when we look at the wills in Henry Chichele's *Register*.[21] We are back in the more familiar world of one-in-eight that we

[19] *Calendar of Wills proved and enrolled in the Court of Hustings, London, A.D. 1258–1688*, ed. R.R. Sharpe (2 vols. 1889–90).

[20] Ibid., pp. 558–9: the relevant passage is, 'To Johane his aforesaid servant, daughter of John his son, his tenement situated in Holy Rode parish in Southampton.' Joan's brother Thomas, 'son of the same John', was to receive the old man's lands and tenements in the city of Salisbury.

touched in some of our earlier probes into the inquisitions. Testators who made the pages of an archiepiscopal register were probably well up the socio-economic ladder, and perhaps greater resources are the key to the significant difference between the two collections of wills. In addition to the richer stream, mostly of unexceptional and modest bequests to grandchildren, a fair number of *Register* wills embrace the preceding generation, along with the succeeding: bequests to a wife, a sister, a daughter, and an aunt; to a wife, three children, a step-daughter, a brother and sister-in-law, and the latter's father; to a daughter, a bastard son, a nephew, an uncle, and a father-in-law. Clearly, our group of testators picked and chose with considerable personal freedom or idiosyncracy as they mulled over the question of which relatives, just as they picked and chose among their worldly goods when they passed on. Children were probably listed in birth order, more often than not. Can we use this as a reliable guide, regarding the number of grandchildren, when a will refers to three sons and one grandchild, she being the daughter of the middle boy? Her bequest, of 'a caldron, a pot, and a littell ponset', sounds like what one gives someone about to set up house. Was she going to use these household items now, or was the only grandchild a mere babe, now being allowed to lay a claim on the goods against the day when she would need them?[22]

Responsibility within the family tree could run in both directions from the testators: aged parents as well as just-emerging grandchildren. On the one hand we have the 200 marks left for Thomas Thurland's son's son, 'to be delyverd when he commys to xxj yeres of age', and the £20 for the grandson's cousin John Rochfort, 'son of Johanna, my doughter, late the wyff of Henry Rochfort'. On the other we have Elizabeth Swinburne, whose gifts to Mount Grace priory were on the condition that the nunnery accept both her mother and her daughter within its walls. And Thomas Markesfield remembered several children, including a widowed daughter, the daughter's son, son of Christopher Conyers ('late deide'), and – at the opposite end of a four-generation family – 'my moder Margaret',

[21] *The Register of Henry Chichele, Archbishop of Canterbury, 1414–1443*, ed. E.F. Jacob and H.C. Johnson, Canterbury and York Society (4 vols. Oxford, 1938–47), II.

[22] Ibid., II, pp. 451–3, 390–400.

now being set up with a bequest of 10 marks per annum for life.[23]

At the start I said we were embarking on a search for grandparents or grandchildren, that is, for the links between the alternating generations. By now I suggest that what we really should be searching for is a way to identify the not-inconsiderable number of such links that existed throughout society. As with so many other social phenomena, they may have been more common as well as more accessible to the historian's probing at the top of the social pyramid than farther down. From this perspective it would seem as though the three-generation family, and its blessing and opportunities, was yet another perquisite that came to some extent from being at the controls when the great chain was being wound up.

Different sources, and different kinds of sources, suggest that among those who survived to mature adulthood – whatever fraction of live births that number ultimately represented – a three-generation link was something in the nature of a one-in-ten bet, if not better, for a given surviving adult male or a middle-aged woman who would outlast him. Given that our sources were tilted heavily towards determining the direct string of male heirs, the other relatives who were able to help in constructing such (collateral) chains are apt to be lost, or to go unmentioned, in our quick examination. And if we think of grandmothers and great-aunts and elderly cousins – those with fewer formal responsibilities for pushing the generations forward – as being free for more nurturing, more inclined to transmit family lore and tradition, then the lost fragments of the whole story probably mean the loss of disproportionately more of cultural value, of much that pertains to socialization and the reinvention of tradition.[24]

In its crudest and least malleable sense, a three-generation link was an extra

---

[23] *Testamenta Eboracensia, III*, ed. J. Raine, Surtees Society, XLV (1865), pp. 185–6, 287–8; *Testamenta Eboracensia, IV,* ed. J. Raine, Surtees Society, LIII (1869), p. 208; *Somerset Medieval Wills, 1383–1500*, ed. F.W. Weaver, Somerset Record Society, XVI (1901), p. 58.

[24] Michael Young and Peter Willmott, *Family Life in East London* (Harmondsworth, 1962); Raymond Firth, Jane Hubert, and Anthony Forge, *Families and Their Relatives in a Middle-Class Section of London: An Anthropological Study* (1969); *The Invention of Tradition*, eds. Eric Hobsbawm and Terence Ranger (Cambridge, 1992).

guarantee or a next-resort hedge against the extinction of the family; the sooner we were to get on with the important business, the more likely we were to have long-range success. But there are further dimensions, a broader context against which to set the picture we have been working to sketch. A richer and more complex tale emerges on the odd occasions when we can follow this trail; our untangling of the tensions between Richard II and Henry Bolingbroke should take into account that they had both been on the early edge of manhood when their common grandfather, Edward III, died.

In the will of Margaret Paston we find bequests to some grandchildren. The estrangement between Margaret and her daughter Margery, after the latter's marriage to Richard Calle, strikes us today as a prime example of the difference between fifteenth-century family values and our more relaxed ones. In view of, or perhaps to lessen, this discrepancy, we are inclined to read reconciliation and forgiveness – at the end, if not before – into Margaret's testamentary bequests directed towards the Calles: 'I bequeth to John Calle, sone of Margery my doughter, xx*li*, when he cometh to the age of xxiiij yer, and if the seid John dye or he cometh to the seid age, than I wull that the seid xx*li* evenly be divided attwen William and Richard, sones of the seid Margery, whan they come to the age of xxiiij yer.'[25] Was a hand being extended to the grandchildren where it had hurt too much to extend it to their parents (if they were still alive)? We cannot answer these questions; there are gaps in both the genealogical and the affective record.

However, to end a discussion of the later Middle Ages on a note of sentimentality is self-indulgent. No matter how we see the mosaic of fifteenth-century society, there were innumerable bleak stretches, for both rich and poor, and who would wish to claim that living long enough to have grandchildren, *per se*, made life more rewarding than not having this particular fortune. At the beginning of this paper I referred to the rhythms and cycles of the universe, and to how the cloth of human existence and cultural definition was cut to accommodate and conform to the larger contours. The existence of the three-generation family would seem to have been some sort of prophylactic,

[25] *Paston L&P*, I, pp. 382–9.

some personal security blanket, against the starkness of the inevitable ending. And yet – perhaps to our surprise – it seems that there may well have been many more grandchildren, underfoot somewhere, than any voice of recording authority cared to include. And when we remember that this voice embraced innumerable grandparents, who in such sources as their wills certainly had their moment, had they been so inclined, we should pause for some reflection.

A popular bumper sticker displayed on autos in some parts of the United States proclaims, to the enlightenment of those who have just been overtaken on a high speed road, that 'Happiness is being a grandparent'. Alas, the historian of the medieval family is not so easily convinced; neither do we feel that we have the freedom to be so assertive about what we do not know and what they did not control. There is no calculus by means of which we can plot the curves and sums of fifteenth-century human experience and then assign a value system for equivalent life experiences, let alone for feelings. If Margaret Paston's will can be read as a document of reconciliation and re-bonding, perhaps we should set it against the laconic statement from an inquisition *post-mortem* of Richard II's reign. The jurors reported, in their effort to identify the next of kin, that 'Joan, daughter of Thomas his son, aged 2 years and more, is his heir, but whether she is still alive or not the jurors know not, because she has been taken out of the county.'[26] In this situation the grandchild who was needed in order to complete the three-generation chain was probably a lot closer to Abraham's bosom than she was to the bosom of the nurturing family that we hope to find in pre-industrial society.

---

[26] *CIPM*, XVII, p. 47.

INDEX

DATE DUE

			Printed in USA

HIGHSMITH #45230